Steven Raichlen's

HIGH-FLAVOR, LOW-FAT MEXICAN COOKING

Steven Raichlen's

HIGH-FLAVOR, LOW-FAT MEXICAN COOKING

Photography by Greg Schneider

Food Styling by Patty Forrestel

VIKING

VIKING
Published by the Penguin Group
Penguin Putnam Inc., 375 Hudson Street,
New York, New York 10014, U.S.A.
Penguin Books Ltd, 27 Wrights Lane, London W8 5TZ, England
Penguin Books Australia Ltd, Ringwood, Victoria, Australia
Penguin Books Canada Ltd, 10 Alcorn Avenue,
Toronto, Ontario, Canada M4V 3B2
Penguin Books (N. Z.) Ltd, 182–190 Wairau Road,
Auckland 10, New Zealand

Penguin Books Ltd, Registered Offices:
Harmondsworth, Middlesex, England

First published in 1997 by Viking Penguin,
a member of Penguin Putnam Inc.

1 3 5 7 9 10 8 6 4 2

LIBRARY OF CONGRESS CATALOGING-IN-PUBLICATION DATA
Raichlen, Steven.
[High-flavor, low-fat Mexican cooking]
Steven Raichlen's high-flavor, low-fat Mexican cooking /
photography by Greg Schneider ; food styling by Patty Forrestel.
p. cm.
ISBN 0-670-88388-3
1. Cookery, Mexican.   2. Low-fat diet recipes.   I. Title.
TX716.M4R33   1999
641.5′638—dc21   99-12872

This book is printed on acid-free paper.

Printed in the United States of America
Set in Goudy

To Barbara
con muchísimo amor

ACKNOWLEDGMENTS

The greatest pleasure in writing a book is thanking the people who helped make it possible.

At Viking:

Dawn Drzal, friend and editor extraordinaire
Barbara Grossman, publisher
Jariya Wanapun, editorial assistant
Doris Troy, copy editor
Kathryn Parise, designer
Alisa Wyatt, publicist

In the Kitchen and Studio:

Greg Schneider, for his enthusiasm and magnificent photographs
Patty Forrestel, for her lovely food styling
Elida Proenza, for her recipe testing and devotion
Roger Thrallkill, recipe tester and culinary hotshot
Donna Morton de Souza, for the nutritional analyses
Blanca Silva, for her editorial assistance
Boris Djokic, who kept the computers humming

In Mexico:

Lori Jones and Patricia Echenique, of the Mexican Tourism Board
Mercedes Amero, Burson-Marsteller, Mexico City
Ana Argaes, Yucatán Tourism Office
Federico Moreno-Nickerson and his staff, at the Four Seasons Hotel in Mexico City
Enrique and Susana Castillo Pesado, of La Valentina
Oscar Rodríguez, of La Valentina
Jesús Arroyo Bergeyre, of Arroyo Restaurantes
And the hundreds of street vendors, food hawkers, market cooks, and restaurateurs who opened their kitchens, hearts, and great store of culinary wisdom to me, and made writing this book a delectable adventure

In the United States:

Rick Bayless, the greatest practitioner of Mexican cuisine in the United States
Diana Kennedy, doyenne of Mexican cuisine
Josefina Howard, of Rosa Mexicano in New York
Zarela Martínez
Frank Romero, of the Gardens of Taxco in Los Angeles

Above all, a huge thanks to Barbara, my wife, partner, publicist, and best friend, for all her love, encouragement, support, and patience!

Coconut Grove, Florida
March 3, 1999

CONTENTS

INTRODUCTION

Can it really be nine years since I wrote the first *High-Flavor, Low-Fat* cookbook? Little did I realize that the book would be the beginning of a whole series (this is volume eight) and that its philosophy—using intense flavorings instead of fats to make food exciting and delicious—would become, not just for its author, but also for many of us in the United States, a way of life.

The first *High-Flavor, Low-Fat* cookbook grew out of an attempt to lower my cholesterol level after ten years of profligate dining as a restaurant critic. I'm pleased to say that it worked. But I've come to appreciate high-flavor, low-fat cooking not only for its health benefits, but also for its bold, clean, forthright taste.

Every revolution begets a counterrevolution, of course, and today we are experiencing a backlash. It's hard to pick up a newspaper or magazine without reading about the surging popularity of high-protein diets and steak houses. We guzzle martinis with the gusto we once reserved for mineral water. The anti-smoking crusade has gone up in clouds of cigar smoke.

Well, high-flavor, low-fat cooking is here to stay. However many steaks we eat or martinis we drink at the moment, most of us remain committed to healthy eating. Those of us who are in the baby boom generation become ever more mindful of the health benefits of a low-fat diet as we grow older. Gen-Xers, like my stepchildren, grew up on a low-fat diet and will follow it for the rest of their days. The truth is that high-flavor, low-fat cooking offers something for everyone.

Over the years, my books have explored many aspects of high-flavor, low-fat cooking; healthy vegetarian and Italian cooking; and high-flavor, low-fat appetizers, pasta, chicken, and desserts. So it's only natural that the eighth volume in the series should focus on what has become one of the favorite ethnic cuisines of the United States: Mexican.

If ever there was a cuisine in need of a heart-healthy makeover, it's Mexican. Many Mexican specialties are a nutritional nightmare. According to the Center for Science in the Public Interest, a typical serving of beef and cheese nachos, for example, contains as much fat as ten Dunkin' Donuts sugar-glazed doughnuts! A chile rellenos dinner can have as much saturated fat as twenty-seven slices of bacon!

Even such seemingly healthful side dishes as Mexican rice and refried beans can be nutritional minefields. A ¾-cup serving of Mexican rice and beans can gobble up two thirds of the USDA-recommended daily fat allowance and three fourths of the recommended limit for saturated fat.

The same is true for other popular Mexican dishes. A recent story in *Men's Health* magazine reports that two beef and cheese enchiladas contain some 650

Mexican ingredients

calories and 36 grams of fat. A typical quesadilla tips the scales at 500 calories and 34 grams of fat. A single appetizer-size tamale will set you back 300 calories and 16 grams of fat. (And who can eat just one?) As for chilaquiles (that wonderful tortilla, chili, cheese, and chorizo casserole), a single serving rings in at a whopping 540 calories and 41 grams of fat.

Fortunately, that's only part of the story. A great deal of Mexican cooking is really quite healthful. Think salsa, that explosively flavorful mix of tomatoes, onions, chilies, and cilantro served as a dip, seasoning, and table sauce. Think ceviche, uncooked seafood energetically seasoned with onion, tomato, aromatic herbs, and fresh lime juice. Think tikenxik, the annatto-spiced fish of the Yucatán that is remarkable for its bold flavors and lack of fat. Think carnitas, tiny bits of grilled meat served on warm tortillas with shredded cabbage and salsa in the north of Mexico—a paragon of healthy eating and a far cry from the fat-laden tacos served at Mexican restaurants north of the Rio Grande.

HOW TO MAKE MEXICAN COOKING MORE HEALTHY

Mexican food doesn't have to be unhealthy. Given the splendid raw materials—the gorgeous vegetables, the flavorful chilies and herbs, the freshly made tortillas, the incredible diversity of beans and grains—it should be one of the healthiest cuisines on the planet.

As with the other books in the *High-Flavor, Low-Fat* series, I've tried to take a three-pronged approach to make Mexican cooking in the United States more healthy.

First, I've tried to identify traditional Mexican dishes that are naturally low in fat. Some will be very familiar to you: salsa, for example, ceviche, tortillas, sopa de lima (Yucatán lime soup), and a host of Mexican salads. Other dishes—regional specialties like Veracruz-style snapper and Yucatán poc chuk (grilled pork)—fit easily within the nutritional guidelines set by health experts in the United States.

Next, I've created a few low-fat dishes that are

Mexican in inspiration and flavor, although they may never actually have been served south of the border. On page 155, for example, you'll find a recipe for fruit flautas (flutes), slender tubes of "bake-fried" tortillas topped with a fruit salsa enlivened with mint. The dish is certainly Mexican in spirit, but the recipe is my own invention.

Finally, I've tried to rework traditional Mexican dishes with unacceptably high fat levels, using the high-flavor, low-fat cooking techniques I've developed over the years, such as high-heat roasting and bake-frying. By bake-frying empanadas, for example, I slash the fat by 80 percent. Another good way to trim the fat is to use some of the new low- and no-fat dairy products (but only when you don't sacrifice taste). When making enchiladas, for example, I soften tortillas in simmering broth instead of oil and use no-fat sour cream instead of regular sour cream. The fat savings are enormous.

Let's look at a few of the other techniques—both traditional and contemporary—used to slash the fat in Mexican cooking.

TECHNIQUES AND INGREDIENTS FOR HIGH-FLAVOR, LOW-FAT MEXICAN COOKING

You may be surprised to learn that one of the most useful techniques in healthy Mexican cooking is as widespread as tortillas and as old as Mexican civilization itself: roasting vegetables. It's done over campfires and hearths in the Mexican countryside, and on stoves in wealthy homes and in fancy restaurants in the major cities.

Throughout this book, you'll be asked to heat a comal (a Mexican griddle) or a dry cast-iron skillet over a medium-high flame and roast vegetables until the skins are darkened and blistered. This roasting heightens the natural flavors of tomatoes, onions, garlic, and chilies, and adds an intriguing charred smoky taste all its own.

Talk about the quintessential high-flavor, low-fat

cooking method! So flavorful is roasting vegetables in a comal that I often use this venerable technique for dishes not in the Mexican repertoire.

Vegetables aren't the only foods whose flavor can be intensified by roasting. Chilies are often toasted on the comal, then soaked in water or crumbled. Pepitas (pumpkin seeds), sesame seeds, almonds, and walnuts are toasted on a comal to heighten their flavor and impart smoky overtones. (There's another advantage here: Thanks to the increased flavor, you need less of these oil-rich foods.) Tortillas are traditionally cooked on the comal, which brings out the natural sweetness of the corn.

Another Mexican technique is grinding vegetables (sometimes raw, sometimes roasted or boiled) to make a flavorful base for sauces and moles. The traditional device for grinding is a molcajete and tejolote, a lava stone mortar and pestle. (On page 2, you'll find a guacamole prepared in this ancient utensil.) These days, most Mexicans are apt to do their grinding in a blender. This is one instance when low tech surpasses high tech: A blender generally works better than a food processor for grinding.

Of course, some of the techniques I recommend in this book would be bewildering to a traditional Mexican cook. Consider bake-frying. Throughout, you'll be instructed to lightly brush tortillas with oil or lard, then bake them in the oven. What results is a crackling crisp crunch—without the fat associated with deep-frying. Fritters and turnovers, stuffed chilies, and crusts can be bake-fried instead of deep-fried. Of course, you lose some of the richness when you decrease the fat, so you'll need to make up for it by using extra seasonings or salsas.

Please note that this book, like the others in this series, is low fat, not no fat. I believe that a little fat—used judiciously—can go a long way in boosting flavor. This brings us to the next strategy for high-flavor, low-fat Mexican cooking: a technique I call the surface application of fats.

The theory is simple enough: You brush the fat over the surface of the food, so it's the first thing you taste when you take a bite. This gives your taste buds the impression that fat will be found throughout the dish, when, in fact, the overall fat content may be quite modest. This technique works especially well with tortilla dishes, where the brushing of fat also helps crisp the exterior. What may surprise you in a low-fat book is that the fat I often call for is lard.

Lard (rendered pork fat) isn't the most fashionable ingredient in the United States these days, but it's much beloved and widely used in Mexico. Lard has a rich, meaty, almost smoky flavor that gives many Mexican dishes, from tostadas to refried beans, their character—especially if you use freshly rendered lard, the kind you would buy at a neighborhood carniceria (meat market) or grocery story.

Now here's another surprise. Lard is actually a healthier fat than is butter. Lard contains only half the cholesterol and one third the saturated fat of butter. One tablespoon of lard actually contains less overall fat than an equal amount of olive oil. (That's because lard contains more water.) If you can overcome your prejudice against this fat, your Mexican food will not only taste more authentic, but will be healthier, too. As some of us may not be able to make this leap of faith, know that olive oil or canola oil will give you delectable results as well.

Another ingredient I use extensively in high-flavor, low-fat Mexican cooking is broth. Chicken and vegetable broth can be added to soups, stews, and bean dishes in place of cream and/or lard or butter. You can also soften tortillas in simmering broth instead of pan-frying them in fat, as would be done in traditional Mexican recipes. On pages 178–180 you'll find recipes for making chicken, fish, and vegetable broth from scratch. Take the time to do so (the broth can be frozen in convenient 1- and 2-cup containers): Your food will taste much better.

Mexicans love dairy products, especially tangy cheeses, like queso fresco, and a rich, sourish, cultured cream similar to French crème fraîche. (Most Mexican restaurants in the United States substitute sour cream for crème fraîche.) Because Mexican cheeses are so flavorful, a tablespoon or two grated is usually enough to give a dish the proper zing—without tipping the scales in fat grams.

As for sour cream, the no-fat sour creams available

in our supermarkets are among the most successful fat-free dairy products ever invented, boasting great flavor and rich mouthfeel without the traditional fat. I call for them widely in this book, as well as two other non-Mexican dairy products: evaporated skim milk and sweetened condensed skim milk.

This brings us to another low-fat ingredient that the average Mexican probably wouldn't be familiar with: egg substitute. Actually, the name "egg substitute" is a misnomer, as this product is made almost exclusively with egg whites. Because virtually all the fat resides in the yolk, egg substitutes are great for jelling flans and other desserts and making scrambled egg dishes without adding extra fat. As egg substitutes tend to lack the richness of whole eggs, however, I generally add sautéed vegetables, spices, or citrus zest to bolster the taste.

One final note about the recipes in this book. Like French cuisine in particular (and all of the world's great cuisines in general), Mexican cooking is a cuisine of sauces. Throughout this book, you'll be asked to add a cup of salsa verde here, of salsa ranchera there, some mole verde or some mole poblano. When I make these salsas, I often prepare a double or triple batch, so I'll always have some in the refrigerator.

The same holds true for refried beans, cooked shredded chicken, and rajas (roasted, peeled strips of poblano chilies). Try to keep some extra of these preparations on hand so you can make tostadas, enchiladas, and many other dishes without a lot of advance preparation.

There are, of course, commercial versions of salsas, refries, and roasted chilies, and while I don't call for them in this book, they can certainly make your life easier. In any cooking, there's always a trade-off between authenticity and convenience. I want you to make these recipes, so draw the line where you feel comfortable. I consider myself a purist, but I'm not above using canned roasted chilies and refried beans in a pinch. However, I always make salsas from scratch.

So there you have it: high-flavor, low-fat Mexican cooking. No, it's not an oxymoron! I've tried to include something for everyone in this book: classics of haute Mexican cuisine, like chiles en nogada and mole poblano; regional specialties, such as poc chuk and huevos motulenos from the Yucatán; and Tex-Mex favorites like nachos and tacos.

I've spent much of the last year exploring the vibrant flavors of Mexico (the oldest and most complex cuisine in the hemisphere, I might add). I hope you have as much fun cooking the recipes as I had researching them.

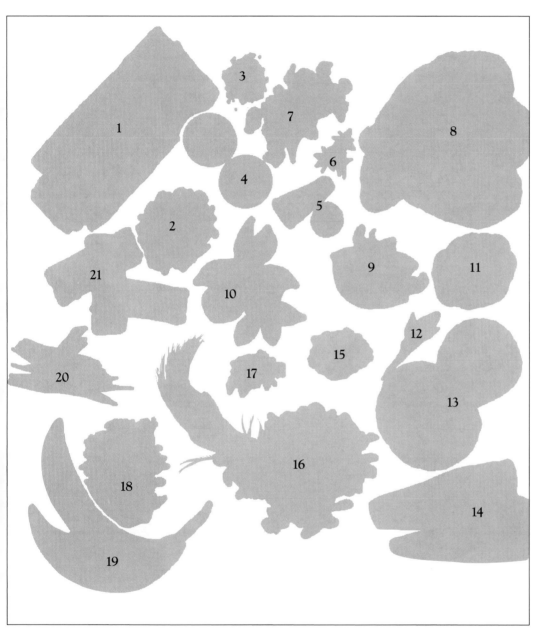

Mexican Ingredients
(*photo page x*)

1. Banana leaves
2. Pumpkin seeds
3. Annato seeds
4. Sour orange
5. Piloncillo
6. Star anise
7. Jamaica flower
8. Nopales (cactus paddles)
9. Avocado leaves
10. Tomatillos
11. Amaranth
12. Epazote
13. Jícama
14. Cornhusks
15. Aniseed
16. Cilantro
17. Queso fresco
18. Masa harina
19. Plantain
20. Cinnamon sticks
21. Mexican chocolate

COLD APPETIZERS

CHIPS WITHOUT HIPS

Tortilla chips are a staple on both sides of the Rio Grande. Tradition calls for them to be deep-fried, a tasty but fat-laden snack. Baking produces an equally crisp chip that won't add inches to your waistline. For a colorful presentation, use both yellow and blue corn tortillas—the latter a specialty of the American Southwest. Blue corn tortillas are available at most supermarkets; if you can't find them, just use yellow tortillas. Serve with any of the salsas on pages 21–31.

PREPARATION TIME: 5 MINUTES   COOKING TIME: 10 MINUTES

4 yellow corn tortillas

1. Preheat the oven to 350°F. Cut each tortilla into six wedges. Arrange the wedges in a single layer on nonstick baking sheets.
2. Bake the chips until they are lightly browned

4 blue corn tortillas

and crisp, 10 to 15 minutes. Don't let them burn. Transfer the chips to a rack to cool.

Makes 48 chips, enough to serve 6 to 8

6 CALORIES PER SERVING (6 CHIPS PER SERVING); 0.2 G PROTEIN; 0.1 G FAT; 0 G SATURATED FAT; 1 G CARBOHYDRATE; 6 MG SODIUM; 0 MG CHOLESTEROL

Chips Without Hips and Guacamole en Molcajete

GUACAMOLE EN MOLCAJETE
(MADE IN A LAVA STONE MORTAR WITH PESTLE)

The creamy avocado dip known as guacamole is a staple at Mexican restaurants everywhere. But no one prepares it with quite the theatrics of a New York City restaurant called Rosa Mexicana. The waiter wheels over a cart with bowls of crimson diced tomatoes, pearly white chopped onion, dark green cilantro and chopped serrano chilies, and a giant molcajete, a black lava stone mortar, and tejolote, the pestle. He pounds half the flavorings (onions, chilies, and cilantro) to a fragrant paste in the molcajete, then adds the avocado, tomatoes, and remaining seasonings in large pieces, so you get pungent pointillistic blasts of flavor. The result is one of the most explosively flavorful guacamoles ever to meet a tortilla chip. If you're inclined to such drama at home, you can buy a molcajete and tejolote at a Mexican market or specialty cookware shop (see Mail-Order Sources). If not, follow the instructions for making guacamole in your food processor.

By the way, you might be surprised to find a guacamole recipe in a low-fat cookbook: After all, avocados are very high in fat (as much as 15 g per half avocado serving). The oils in avocados are monounsaturated fats, however, which have actually been shown to lower levels of LDL (the "bad" cholesterol) and raise levels of HDL (the "good" cholesterol). Besides, by increasing the proportion of tomato and other flavorings to avocado, we reduce the overall fat to acceptable levels. Note: Keep the avocado seeds in the guacamole until serving; they help prevent browning.

PREPARATION TIME: 10 MINUTES

1 clove garlic, chopped
½ medium white onion, finely chopped
3 to 6 serrano chilies, finely chopped (for milder guacamole, seed the chilies before chopping)
½ cup coarsely chopped fresh cilantro
2 ripe avocados, pitted, peeled, and diced (see page 3)

2 red ripe tomatoes, seeded and diced
2 tablespoons fresh lime juice, or to taste
1 teaspoon salt, or to taste
½ teaspoon freshly ground black pepper

MOLCAJETE METHOD

1. Place the garlic and half the onion, chilies, and cilantro in a molcajete and mash to a smooth paste with the pestle.

2. Using a pestle or a wooden spoon, stir in the avocados, tomatoes, lime juice, salt, pepper, and remaining onion, chilies, and cilantro. Stir just to mix; the idea is to create a chunky dip. Correct the seasoning, adding lime juice or salt to taste. Serve with the Chips Without Hips on page 1.

MACHINE METHOD

1. Place the garlic and half the onion, chilies, and cilantro in a mini-chopper or food processor and purée to a smooth paste.

2. Add the avocados, tomatoes, lime juice, salt, pepper, and remaining onion, chilies, and cilantro and process just to mix, running the machine in short bursts. Correct the seasoning, adding lime juice or salt to taste.   *Makes 3½ cups, enough to serve 8*

89 CALORIES PER SERVING; 1 G PROTEIN; 8 G FAT; 1 G SATURATED FAT;
6 G CARBOHYDRATE; 10 MG SODIUM; 0 MG CHOLESTEROL

HOW TO SEED AND DICE AN AVOCADO

To seed the avocado: Cut it in half lengthwise to the pit. (Move the knife in a circular motion.) Now twist the halves in opposite directions: The avocado will separate into two halves, with the seed in one half. With a flick of the wrist, sink the knife into the avocado seed. Twist the seed and pop it out of the avocado.

To dice the avocado: Using the tip of a paring knife, cut a crosshatch in the flesh of each avocado half, to but not through the skin. With a spoon, scoop the avocado out of the skin—it will break into a neat dice.

CHICKPEA DIP WITH CHIPOTLE CHILIES

I like to think of this dip as hummus from south of the border. Hummus (Middle Eastern chickpea dip) is, indeed,
enjoyed in Mexico—particularly among the descendants of Lebanese immigrants in the Yucatán and Mexico City.
Serve this dip with toasted or grilled pita bread or tortilla chips (see Chips Without Hips, page 1). I've made the oil optional:
The dip will be a little smoother and more flavorful with it, but it's perfectly delicious without it, too.

PREPARATION TIME: 5 MINUTES

2 cups cooked chickpeas
1 to 3 canned chipotle peppers, minced, plus up to
    1 tablespoon juice from the can
3 tablespoons fresh lime juice
1 clove garlic, minced
2 scallions, minced
3 tablespoons minced fresh cilantro, plus a few
    sprigs for garnish

¼ to ½ cup chickpea cooking liquid or chicken or
    vegetable stock (or as needed)
½ teaspoon ground cumin
1 tablespoon extra-virgin olive oil, plus 1
    tablespoon for drizzling over the dip (optional)
Salt (optional)

1. Purée all the ingredients (except the optional oil and salt and the garnish) in the processor, adding enough chickpea cooking liquid or stock to obtain a soft purée. Correct the seasoning, adding salt or lime juice to taste. The dip should be highly seasoned.

2. Transfer the dip to a serving bowl. Drizzle the top with the remaining 1 tablespoon of oil, if using, and garnish with the sprigs of cilantro.

Serves 8

60 CALORIES PER SERVING; 4 G PROTEIN; 0 G FAT; 0 G SATURATED FAT;
11 G CARBOHYDRATE; 33 MG SODIUM; 0 MG CHOLESTEROL

CHILI-MANGO "POPSICLES"
(MANGO CON CHILE)

This popular Mexican street snack was my first introduction to mango, and when I took a bite, a quarter of a century ago, I didn't know whether to grin with pleasure or to grimace from the sting of the chili powder. The notion of seasoning fruit with chili pepper, salt, and lime juice may seem odd to someone from the United States, but you'll be amazed how these savory seasonings sharpen the flavor of the fruit. I call this preparation a "Popsicle" because it's served on a stick. Mexicans prepare both green and ripe mangoes this way: The green are enjoyed for their mouth-puckering tartness, the ripe for their succulence and sweetness. Note: If you have sensitive skin, wear rubber or plastic gloves when working with mango. Some people have an allergic reaction to the sap.

PREPARATION TIME: 10 MINUTES

4 medium mangoes
4 thick wooden skewers, Popsicle sticks, or
  chopsticks

2 limes, cut into wedges
Coarse sea salt
Hot chili powder

1. Peel the mangoes. Stick a skewer through the bottom of each mango to impale it like a Popsicle.

2. Hold a mango upright. Using a sharp paring knife, make a series of downward cuts in the sides of the mango, spacing them about ½ inch apart. Gently twist the knife blade with each cut to open the slits, turning the fruit as you work. The idea is to cut the mango so that it looks like a heliconia or other vertically petaled flower.

3. Squeeze fresh lime juice over each mango, working over a bowl to catch any drips. Generously sprinkle each mango with the salt and the chili powder. Serve at once, with extra lime wedges for squeezing. Mango Popsicles can be messy to eat, so be sure to provide plenty of napkins.   *Serves 4*

152 CALORIES PER SERVING; 2 G PROTEIN; 1 G FAT; 0 G SATURATED FAT;
39 G CARBOHYDRATE; 16 MG SODIUM; 0 MG CHOLESTEROL

MEXICAN BAR SNACKS
(BOTANAS)

"Botanas" refers to a broad range of hors d'oeuvres served at a bar or with drinks at a restaurant. (Another word for botana is bocadito, meaning "little mouthful.") Order a beer or a shot of tequila and tiny plates of these simple snacks will appear on your table—usually with no extra charge to the customer. A simple botana might be chili- and garlic-spiced peanuts. A more elaborate spread could include chilied fruit, spiced cucumbers, stewed pumpkin, pickled vegetables, ceviche—the selection is almost endless. Here are some of the botanas served at a charming open-air seafood restaurant called Le Saint Bonnet in the town of Progreso on the Gulf of Mexico in the Yucatán.

CHILIED PINEAPPLE

Here in the United States, we don't usually season fruit with chili powder, but Mexicans (and, for that matter, Indians and Southeast Asians) love the way chilies and salt bring out the succulence and sweetness of fruit. For the best results, use a golden pineapple—available at gourmet shops and most supermarkets.

PREPARATION TIME: 5 MINUTES

1 pineapple, peeled, cored, and cut into 1-inch
  pieces (4 to 6 cups)
2 tablespoons fresh lime juice

1 tablespoon hot chili powder, or to taste
Coarse sea salt or kosher salt

Place the pineapple in a bowl and toss with the lime juice. Sprinkle with the chili powder and salt and serve at once, with toothpicks for skewering.

Serves 8 to 12

33 CALORIES PER SERVING (BASED ON 8 SERVINGS); 0.4 G PROTEIN; 0.4 G FAT; 0 G SATURATED FAT;
1 G CARBOHYDRATE; 10 MG SODIUM; 0 MG CHOLESTEROL

SPICED CUCUMBER

There's nothing more refreshing on a hot day than cool cucumber—especially when it's seasoned with fresh lime juice and cilantro.

PREPARATION TIME: 10 MINUTES

1 European-style cucumber
2 tablespoons fresh lime juice, or as needed
½ cup coarsely chopped fresh cilantro

¼ white onion, finely chopped
Salt and freshly ground black pepper

1. Peel the cucumber and cut it lengthwise into quarters, then widthwise into 1-inch chunks.
2. Place the cucumber in an attractive serving bowl and stir in the lime juice, cilantro, onion, salt, and pepper. Correct the seasoning, adding salt and lime juice to taste. Serve with toothpicks for skewering.

Serves 4 to 6

8 CALORIES PER SERVING (BASED ON 4 SERVINGS); 0.3 G PROTEIN; 0.1 G FAT; 0 G SATURATED FAT;
2 G CARBOHYDRATE; 2 MG SODIUM; 0 MG CHOLESTEROL

STEWED PUMPKIN BOTANA

You might not think of pumpkin as a bar snack, but this one—stewed with onions and garlic and topped with grated queso fresco—is as delectable as it is unexpected. If fresh pumpkin isn't available, use butternut squash.

PREPARATION TIME: 10 MINUTES   COOKING TIME: 10 MINUTES

1 pound peeled pumpkin, cut into 1-inch dice
1 small onion, thinly sliced
2 cloves garlic, thinly sliced
1 tomato, peeled, seeded, and diced

2 sprigs cilantro
Salt and freshly ground black pepper
2 tablespoons finely grated queso fresco or feta
  cheese

1. Place the pumpkin, onion, garlic, tomato, cilantro, salt, and pepper in a saucepan. Add water to cover and bring to a boil. Reduce the heat to medium and simmer the vegetables until the pumpkin is just tender and most of the water has evaporated, about 10 minutes, stirring occasionally. (If the water evaporates before the pumpkin is tender, add a little more.) Correct the seasoning, adding salt and pepper to taste.

2. Transfer the pumpkin mixture to a serving bowl and let cool to room temperature. Sprinkle the cheese over the pumpkin and serve at once. Serve with toothpicks for skewering.   *Serves 4 to 6*

72 CALORIES PER SERVING (BASED ON 4 SERVINGS); 3 G PROTEIN; 2 G FAT; 0.1 G SATURATED FAT;
11 G CARBOHYDRATE; 49 MG SODIUM; 7 MG CHOLESTEROL

CHIPS WITH REFRIES

Most of us think of frijoles refritos (refried beans) as a burrito filling or side dish. But sprinkled with a little queso fresco, refries make an excellent dip for tortilla chips. Note: If you're in a hurry, you could use a good commercial brand of fat-free refried beans.

PREPARATION TIME: 5 MINUTES (PLUS THE TIME IT TAKES TO MAKE THE REFRIES AND CHIPS)

½ batch refried beans, cooled to room temperature
  (page 138)
2 tablespoons crumbled or finely grated queso
  fresco or feta cheese

Chips Without Hips (made with 6 tortillas—
  page 1)

Mound the beans in a bowl or platter and sprinkle with queso fresco. Arrange the chips around the beans or in a bowl on the side and serve at once. (Use chips for scooping up the beans.)   *Serves 6*

142 CALORIES PER SERVING; 6 G PROTEIN; 3 G FAT; 0.3 G SATURATED FAT;
23 G CARBOHYDRATE; 277 MG SODIUM; 5 MG CHOLESTEROL

GROUPER CEVICHE

No botana spread would be complete without some sort of ceviche. This one features grouper marinated in sour orange juice—a local citrus fruit that has the tartness of lime with the fruity overtones of fresh orange and grapefruit. If you live in an area with a large Hispanic community, you may be able to find fresh sour oranges. Otherwise, use lime juice flavored with a little fresh orange juice and grapefruit juice.

PREPARATION TIME: 10 MINUTES (PLUS 20 MINUTES FOR MARINATING)

1 pound fresh grouper fillets or other impeccably fresh fish
½ medium white onion, finely chopped
1 cup fresh sour orange juice, or ¾ cup fresh lime juice, plus 2 tablespoons each fresh orange juice and grapefruit juice

1 tomato, peeled, seeded, and diced
1 or 2 serrano chilies, thinly sliced
¼ cup chopped fresh cilantro
Salt

1. Cut the fish fillets lengthwise into 1-inch strips. Cut each strip widthwise on the diagonal into ⅛-inch slices. (The idea is to obtain pieces that are about 1 inch square and ⅛ inch thick.) Transfer the fish and onion to a mixing bowl and stir in the sour orange juice. Marinate for 15 minutes.

2. Stir in the tomato, chili, cilantro, and salt to taste; the ceviche should be highly seasoned. Marinate for 5 minutes, then transfer to an attractive bowl for serving. Serve with little plates and forks.

Serves 4

153 CALORIES PER SERVING; 23 G PROTEIN; 1 G FAT; 0.3 G SATURATED FAT;
11 G CARBOHYDRATE; 65 MG SODIUM; 41 MG CHOLESTEROL

SHRIMP CEVICHE MINI-TOSTADAS

Here's a ceviche for people who don't think they can eat uncooked seafood. If you can find them, buy true baby shrimp (the kind that are so small that a dozen will fit in a tablespoon). Otherwise, you'll need to cut large cooked shrimp into ½-inch dice. I've called for the ceviche to be served on tortilla chips, canapé-style. But you can certainly present it, shrimp cocktail–style, in a martini glass. However you serve it, the vibrant flavors of fresh lime juice, cilantro, and serrano chilies will get your meal off to an electrifying start.

PREPARATION TIME: 15 MINUTES   COOKING TIME: 10 MINUTES

6 corn tortillas
1 tablespoon melted lard or olive oil (optional)

FOR THE SHRIMP CEVICHE:
1 cup cooked baby shrimp or diced large shrimp
½ medium white onion, finely chopped
1 ripe red tomato, peeled, seeded, and diced

½ ripe avocado, peeled and finely diced
1 or 2 serrano chilies, finely chopped (for a milder ceviche, seed the chilies)
¼ cup chopped fresh cilantro, plus 36 sprigs fresh cilantro for garnish
¼ cup fresh lime juice
Salt and freshly ground black pepper

1. Preheat the oven to 350°F. Brush the tortillas on both sides with the optional lard or olive oil. Cut each tortilla into six wedges and arrange them in a single layer on a baking sheet. Bake the tortillas until they are lightly browned, 8 to 10 minutes. Transfer to a cake rack to cool: They'll crisp as they cool.

2. Meanwhile, prepare the ceviche. Place the shrimp, onion, tomato, avocado, chili, chopped cilantro, and lime juice in a bowl and toss to mix. Add salt and pepper to taste.

3. At the moment of serving, arrange the tortilla chips on a platter. Top each with a spoonful of ceviche and a sprig of cilantro and serve at once.

Makes 36 pieces, enough to serve 6 as an appetizer

176 CALORIES PER SERVING (BASED ON 4 SERVINGS); 10 G PROTEIN; 5 G FAT; 1 G SATURATED FAT;
24 G CARBOHYDRATE; 142 MG SODIUM; 63 MG CHOLESTEROL

STUFFED JALAPEÑO PEPPERS

Stuffed jalapeño peppers have become common currency at Tex-Mex restaurants in the United States (where they go by fanciful names such as poppers and armadillo eggs). Mexicans also enjoy stuffed jalapeño peppers—often without the oil-sodden, deep-fried crust so popular north of the border. Below are a few of the stuffings I discovered on my heart-healthy tour of Mexico. Note: I like the lip-stinging fire of simple roasted jalapeños. You can tame the heat somewhat by soaking the peppers in 2 cups of water sweetened with 2 tablespoons of sugar for about 1 hour. Rinse and dry the chilies before stuffing.

JALAPEÑO PEPPERS STUFFED WITH SARDINES

Sardines may not sound like the stuff of elegance, but these chilled stuffed jalapeños are as delectably different as they are refreshing. To slash the fat, use water-packed sardines. Note: For an interesting if not strictly traditional filling, substitute 3 ounces of smoked trout or whitefish for half the sardines.

PREPARATION TIME: 15 MINUTES   COOKING TIME: 8 MINUTES

24 large green jalapeño peppers
2 cans (3.7 ounces each) water-packed sardines
⅓ cup minced white onion

⅓ cup minced cilantro
Plenty of freshly ground black pepper and salt

1. Flame-roast the chilies until the skin is charred on all sides. To do this over a gas burner on the stove, place a wire rack on the burner. Arrange the jalapeños on top and cook over high heat until they are charred on all sides, turning with tongs. If you are using an electric burner, preheat it to medium-high and lay the chilies directly on the burner. Alternatively, you can char the chilies under a preheated broiler or on a hot barbecue grill. This will take 6 to 8 minutes in all.

2. Transfer the chilies to a paper bag or bowl to cool (if using a bowl, cover with plastic wrap). When cool, scrape off the burnt skin with a paring knife. (Don't worry about removing every last bit of skin.)

3. Cut the top (the stem end) three fourths of the way off each chili. (Leave it attached at the bottom.) Fold back the top and, with a slender paring knife, remove the seeds and veins.

4. Drain the sardines well, scrape off the skin, and blot dry. Transfer the sardines to a mixing bowl and mash with a fork. Stir in the onion, cilantro, and pepper and salt to taste. Using a small spoon, stuff the sardine mixture into the chilies. Replace the caps.

I like to serve the stuffed chilies on plates lined with thinly sliced tomatoes. You can also pass them around on a platter as finger food.

Serves 6 to 8

73 CALORIES PER SERVING (BASED ON 6 SERVINGS); 9 G PROTEIN; 1 G FAT; 0.2 G SATURATED FAT;
7 G CARBOHYDRATE; 39 MG SODIUM; 50 MG CHOLESTEROL

Jalapeños Stuffed with Picadillo

*Picadillo lends these stuffed chilies both sweet and salty accents—the sweetness is provided by
the raisins and almonds; the saltiness comes from the capers and olives.*

PREPARATION TIME: 10 MINUTES (PLUS THE TIME IT TAKES TO MAKE THE PICADILLO)
COOKING TIME: 8 MINUTES

24 large green jalapeño peppers

1. Roast, peel, and seed the peppers, as described in the recipe above.
2. Prepare the picadillo and stuff each pepper with a spoonful. You may have some filling left over. Reward yourself with a little snack.

Fruit and Nut Picadillo (see page 144)

3. The stuffed peppers can be served at room temperature or hot. (To serve hot, heat the peppers on a nonstick baking sheet in a 400-degree oven for 10 to 15 minutes.)
Serves 6 to 8

109 CALORIES PER SERVING (BASED ON 6 SERVINGS); 9 G PROTEIN; 3 G FAT; 1 G SATURATED FAT;
13 G CARBOHYDRATE; 28 MG SODIUM; 15 MG CHOLESTEROL

HOT APPETIZERS

A NEW NACHO
(PREPARED IN THE STYLE OF A TOSTADA)

Nachos aren't exactly what you'd call paragons of a heart-healthy diet—at least not the Tex-Mex version served at bars and casual eateries across the United States. Here's a nontraditional nacho prepared like a tostada (a Mexican open-faced sandwich) that's loaded with flavor, not fat. The recipe can be doubled or tripled as desired.

12 corn tortillas
1 cup no-fat sour cream
2 tablespoons minced cilantro, plus 36 whole
   cilantro leaves
½ teaspoon ground cumin
½ teaspoon ground coriander
Salt and freshly ground black pepper

1 ripe tomato, seeded and cut into ¼-inch dice
6 pitted black olives, thinly sliced
6 drained pickled jalapeño peppers, thinly sliced
4 scallions, trimmed and thinly sliced
½ cup (1½ to 2 ounces) coarsely grated sharp
   cheddar cheese (preferably an orange cheese)

1. Preheat the oven to 350°F. Arrange the tortillas on baking sheets and bake until they just begin to brown, about 10 minutes. Remove from the oven and let cool; the tortillas will crisp as they cool.

2. Meanwhile, in a mixing bowl whisk together the sour cream, minced cilantro, cumin, coriander, salt, and pepper. The mixture should be highly seasoned.

3. Just before serving, preheat the broiler. Spread each tortilla with a spoonful of the sour cream mixture. Sprinkle the diced tomato, olive and jalapeño slices, scallions, cilantro leaves, and grated cheese on top. Broil the nachos until the cheese melts and the topping is hot, about 2 minutes. Transfer to a platter and serve at once.

Makes 12 nachos, enough to serve 6

81 CALORIES PER NACHO; 4 G PROTEIN; 3 G FAT; 1 G SATURATED FAT;
4 G CARBOHYDRATE; 141 MG SODIUM; 5 MG CHOLESTEROL

A New Nacho

BLACK BEAN MINI-TOSTADAS WITH QUESO AÑEJO

These crisp mouthfuls are simplicity itself, yet the striking flavors of avocado leaf–scented refried black beans (smoky, with a touch of anise flavor) and salty queso añejo (aged cheese) are downright symphonic. Queso añejo is a salty, sourish, tangy white cheese available at Mexican markets. (Feta cheese makes the best substitute.) Note: If you're in a hurry, use a good commercial brand of fat-free refried beans. If epazote is unavailable, substitute sprigs of cilantro, although the flavor won't be quite the same. Also, you could make four large tostadas by omitting cutting the tortillas in step 1.

PREPARATION TIME: 10 MINUTES (PLUS THE TIME IT TAKES TO MAKE THE BEANS)
COOKING TIME: 10 MINUTES

4 corn tortillas
1 tablespoon melted lard or olive oil (optional)
1 cup refried black beans with avocado leaves
  (page 139)

¼ cup crumbled queso anejo
24 sprigs epazote

1. Preheat the oven to 350°F. Brush the tortillas on both sides with lard or olive oil (if using). Cut each tortilla into six wedges and arrange them in a single layer on a baking sheet. Bake the tortillas until they're lightly browned, 8 to 10 minutes. Transfer to a cake rack to cool; they'll crisp as they cool.

2. Just before serving, warm the black beans. Place a spoonful of the beans on each tortilla chip. Top with a sprinkle of cheese and a sprig of epazote. Serve at once.
Makes 24 pieces, enough to serve 4 to 6 as an appetizer

158 CALORIES PER SERVING (BASED ON 4 SERVINGS); 7 G PROTEIN; 6 G FAT; 0.2 G SATURATED FAT;
20 G CARBOHYDRATE; 294 MG SODIUM; 14 MG CHOLESTEROL

SHRIMP TAQUITOS COOKED IN THE STYLE OF ESCAMOTES

One of the most delectable—and disconcerting—delicacies that await a non-Mexican visitor at a fine restaurant in Mexico City is an appetizer composed of three pre-Columbian foods that are staging a rousing comeback these days: deep-fried escamotes (ant eggs), chapolinas (baby crickets), and gusanos (agave cactus worms). All three have a delicate flavor, the escamotes and gusanos being more fatty and buttery (a little like cracklings), the chapolinas somewhat shellfishy (like soft-shell crab legs or fried shrimp). But what Mexicans really prize in these ancient foods, I suspect, is their softly crunchy texture (think chicharrones and caviar) and their superb ability to absorb other flavors. The idea of eating bugs probably sounds revolting to most of us, but Mexicans devour them with gusto. This recipe comes from the Four Seasons Hotel in Mexico City, where the pre-Columbian treats are served on a magnificent earthenware platter at a price reminiscent of caviar. The following version calls for shrimp, which is more readily available (and certainly more socially acceptable) than insects, and while the flavor is decidedly different, you'll get an idea of just how much fun this dish is to eat. Besides, think of what a great story you'll have to tell when you serve it.

PREPARATION TIME: 15 MINUTES   COOKING TIME: 10 MINUTES

1 pound fresh shrimp
1 tablespoon olive oil
½ white onion, finely chopped
1 clove garlic, finely chopped
1 serrano chili, finely chopped (for a milder dish, seed the chili)
1 to 2 teaspoons pure chili powder
Salt and freshly ground black pepper

TO SERVE:
½ white onion, finely diced (about ¾ cup)
¾ cup finely chopped cilantro
8 small corn tortillas (preferably freshly made; page 61)
1 batch roasted salsa verde (page 26)

1. To prepare the shrimp, peel and devein them, then cut each into ¼-inch dice. Heat the olive oil in a nonstick skillet. Add the onion, garlic, and chili and cook over medium heat until golden brown, about 4 minutes, stirring often. Stir in the shrimp and chili powder. Sauté until the shrimp are firm and pink, 2 to 3 minutes, stirring well. Correct the seasoning, adding salt or chili powder; the shrimp should be highly seasoned. Transfer the shrimp to a serving bowl and keep warm.

2. Combine the onion and cilantro in another serving bowl and toss to mix. Heat the tortillas in a 350-degree oven until they are warm, soft, and pliable (3 to 5 minutes), or warm them on a comal or griddle. (If you are serving fresh tortillas, they may still be warm.) Place the tortillas in a cloth-lined basket and wrap to keep warm. Place the salsa verde in an attractive bowl.

3. To assemble, have each diner place a spoonful of the shrimp, the onion mixture, and salsa verde in the center of a tortilla and then fold it in half. To eat? Just pop it into your mouth. The appropriate beverage? The sangrita with tequila chaser on page 165 would make a great start.

Makes 8 pieces, enough to serve 4 as an appetizer

334 CALORIES PER SERVING; 29 G PROTEIN; 8 G FAT; 1 G SATURATED FAT; 39 G CARBOHYDRATE; 183 MG SODIUM; 172 MG CHOLESTEROL

QUESADILLAS WITH CHILIES AND CHEESE

When I was growing up, few of us in the United States had ever heard of quesadillas. Today, you can hardly dine anywhere without encountering these Mexican grilled-cheese "sandwiches," made with flour tortillas instead of bread. This recipe plays the richness of cheese against the smoky piquancy of freshly roasted poblano chilies. For milder quesadillas, use canned green chilies.

PREPARATION TIME: 20 MINUTES (INCLUDING THE TIME FOR ROASTING THE CHILIES)
COOKING TIME: 5 MINUTES

2 large poblano chilies or 1 (4-ounce) can roasted green chilies
8 (8-inch) fat-free flour tortillas
¾ cup no-fat sour cream

½ cup grated jack or sharp white cheddar cheese (2 ounces)
Salt and freshly ground black pepper

1. Flame-char the chilies as described on page 177. Transfer the chilies to a sealed paper bag or a bowl covered with plastic wrap to cool.

2. Scrape off most of the burned skin. Cut open each chili, remove the veins and seeds, and cut the chili into long thin strips. (Skip this step if you're using canned chilies.)

3. Lay four tortillas on a work surface. Spread each with a little sour cream. Arrange the chili strips and cheese on top. Spread the remaining sour cream on the remaining tortillas and place them, cream side down, on top to make a sort of sandwich.

4. Preheat a comal, griddle, or large dry frying pan over medium-high heat. Cook the quesadillas until the tortillas are lightly browned and the cheese inside is melted, 1 to 2 minutes per side. Cut each quesadilla into eight wedges and serve at once.

Serves 4

282 CALORIES PER SERVING; 16 G PROTEIN; 9 G FAT; 5 G SATURATED FAT;
41 G CARBOHYDRATE; 750 MG SODIUM; 25 MG CHOLESTEROL

POTATO AND CHORIZO QUESADILLAS

The first thing I do whenever I get to a new city is walk to where the sidewalk food vendors are. You can learn a lot about a place by its street food, and nowhere is this truer than in Mexico City. I'd never seen a potato quesadilla before, and this one—flavored with fried onion and fried in chorizo fat—was love at first bite. To decrease the amount of fat, I use a little chorizo to flavor the potatoes and I dry-fry the tortillas on a comal or griddle. The result is quesadillas bursting with the earthy flavors of chorizo and potato, with merely a fraction of the fat.

PREPARATION TIME: 10 MINUTES   COOKING TIME: 15 MINUTES

1 baking potato (about 14 ounces), peeled and cut into 1-inch pieces
Salt
1 tablespoon canola oil
½ to 1 ounce chorizo sausage, finely chopped
½ medium white onion, thinly sliced

¼ cup chicken broth or skim milk, or as needed
½ cup coarsely grated sharp white cheddar or Muenster cheese
Freshly ground black pepper
8 (8-inch) flour tortillas

1. Place the potato in a saucepan with cold salted water to cover. Bring to a boil, reduce the heat, and simmer until the potato is soft, about 10 minutes. Drain the potato in a colander, then return it to the pan and cook over medium heat for 1 minute to evaporate the excess liquid.

2. Meanwhile, heat the oil in a small frying pan. Add the chorizo and onion and cook over medium heat until the onion is golden brown, about 5 minutes. Stir this mixture into the potatoes and mash with a potato masher or pestle. Add enough chicken broth or milk to obtain a soft but thick purée. Stir in the cheese and salt and pepper to taste.

3. Arrange four tortillas flat on a work surface. Evenly spread the mashed potatoes on top. Arrange the remaining tortillas on top to make a sort of sandwich, pressing hard to adhere the two halves.

4. Preheat a comal, griddle, or large dry frying pan over medium-high heat. Cook the quesadillas until the tortillas are lightly browned and the filling is heated, 1 to 2 minutes per side. Cut each quesadilla into eight wedges and serve at once.

Makes 32 pieces, enough to serve 8 as an appetizer or snack, 4 as a light main course

329 CALORIES PER SERVING (BASED ON 8 SERVINGS); 9 G PROTEIN; 11 G FAT; 2 G SATURATED FAT; 50 G CARBOHYDRATE; 429 MG SODIUM; 6 MG CHOLESTEROL

CRAB QUESADILLAS

Quesadillas go uptown in this recipe, flavored with tomatoes, corn, and fresh crab. There are several options for crab: backfin lump meat from the blue crab (my favorite), delicate shreds of Maine crab, Dungeness crab, or even king crab. You can also make a quesadilla from minced cooked or smoked shrimp or from baby shrimp.

PREPARATION TIME: 10 MINUTES   COOKING TIME: 5 MINUTES

½ pound crabmeat (about 8 ounces)
½ cup no-fat sour cream
½ cup grated Muenster or white cheddar cheese (about 2 ounces)
3 scallions, finely chopped
½ cup cooked corn kernels

1 small tomato, seeded and diced
3 tablespoons coarsely chopped fresh cilantro leaves
½ teaspoon ground cumin
Salt and freshly ground black pepper
8 (8-inch) fat-free flour tortillas

1. Preheat the grill or broiler to medium-high. Pick through the crabmeat, removing any bits of shell. Place the sour cream in a mixing bowl and stir in the crabmeat, cheese, scallions, corn, tomato, cilantro, and cumin. Correct the seasoning, adding salt or pepper to taste.

2. Lay four tortillas on a work surface. Spread the crab mixture evenly over each of them, using a spatula or the back of a spoon. Place the remaining tortillas on top to make a sort of sandwich.

3. Grill or broil the quesadillas until the tortillas are lightly browned and the filling is heated through, 1 to 2 minutes per side. Alternatively, you can cook the quesadillas in a comal, griddle, or dry skillet over high heat until the tortillas brown and blister, 1 to 2 minutes per side. (The sour cream mixture holds the halves together.) Cut each into eight wedges and serve at once.

Serves 4 as an appetizer or snack

297 CALORIES PER SERVING; 21 G PROTEIN; 6 G FAT; 3 G SATURATED FAT; 46 G CARBOHYDRATE; 1,160 MG SODIUM; 72 MG CHOLESTEROL

BAKE-FRIED EMPANADAS

At first glance, few dishes would seem a less likely candidate for a heart-healthy makeover than the lard-laden, deep-fried Mexican meat turnovers known as empanadas. But a Mexican cookbook just wouldn't be complete without this tasty snack. A few years ago, I got the idea of using Chinese wonton wrappers instead of fatty dough for wrapping the filling and then baking the empanadas in the oven instead of deep-frying them. The fat savings were enormous and—even better—my low-fat empanadas could be prepared in a matter of minutes. Wonton wrappers (or their cousins, egg-roll wrappers) can be found in the produce section of most supermarkets.

PREPARATION TIME: 10 MINUTES (PLUS THE TIME IT TAKES TO MAKE THE PICADILLO)
COOKING TIME: 10 MINUTES

36 (3-inch) wonton wrappers or round Chinese dumpling wrappers (or egg-roll wrappers cut into 3-inch squares)
1 egg white, lightly beaten

1 batch Fruit and Nut Picadillo (page 144) or Mexican-Style Picadillo (page 123)
Spray oil
1 tablespoon sesame seeds

1. Preheat the oven to 400°F. Arrange a few wonton wrappers on a work surface. Very lightly brush the outside edge (¼ inch in from the edge) of each wrapper with egg white. (The egg white acts as glue.) Place a heaping teaspoon of picadillo in the center and fold the wrapper in half to make a half-moon-shaped turnover (or a triangular turnover if you are using square wrappers). Crimp the edges with a fork. Place the finished empanadas on a cake rack while you make the remainder.

2. Arrange the empanadas on a no-stick baking sheet you've sprayed generously with oil. Spray the tops of the empanadas with oil and sprinkle with the sesame seeds. Bake the empanadas until they are crisp and golden brown, 6 to 10 minutes, turning once with a spatula.

Makes 36 empanadas, enough to serve 6 to 9

43 CALORIES PER EMPANADA; 3 G PROTEIN; 1 G FAT; 0.2 G SATURATED FAT;
6 G CARBOHYDRATE; 53 MG SODIUM; 4 MG CHOLESTEROL

SALSAS

BASIC MEXICAN SALSA
(SALSA MEXICANA)

Here's the basic Mexican salsa, whose colors—the bright red of tomatoes, the white of the onion, and the green of the chilies and cilantro—echo those of Mexico's flag. Depending on where you are in Mexico, the salsa will be known as salsa mexicana, salsa cruda (raw salsa), salsa fresca, or even pico de gallo (rooster's beak). Salsa mexicana is the world's easiest dish to make, but unless you use juicy, red, vine-ripened tomatoes—the kind that go splat when you drop them—you won't get the full effect. With the salsa, serve the Chips Without Hips on page 1.

PREPARATION TIME: 10 MINUTES

2 ripe, red tomatoes, finely chopped
2 to 6 serrano or jalapeño chilies, finely chopped, with seeds (for a milder salsa, seed the chilies)
½ medium white onion, finely chopped

1 clove garlic, minced
⅓ cup finely chopped fresh cilantro
2 tablespoons fresh lime juice, or to taste
½ teaspoon salt, or to taste

In a mixing bowl combine the tomatoes, chilies, onion, garlic, cilantro, lime juice, and salt and toss gently. Correct the seasoning, adding lime juice or salt to taste.   *Makes 2 cups, enough to serve 6 to 8*

20 CALORIES PER SERVING (BASED ON 6 SERVINGS); 1 G PROTEIN; 0 G FAT; 0 G SATURATED FAT;
5 G CARBOHYDRATE; 5 MG SODIUM; 0 MG CHOLESTEROL

Clockwise from top: Basic Mexican Salsa, Salsa Chipotle, Cooked Salsa Verde

COUNTRY-STYLE COOKED TOMATO SAUCE
(SALSA RANCHERA)

This is one of the most basic of all Mexican salsas, an essential component in Huevos Rancheros (page 55)
and a good overall pick-me-up whenever you need a sauce that's packed with flavor and low in fat.

PREPARATION TIME: 10 MINUTES   COOKING TIME: 10 MINUTES

1½ tablespoons lard or olive oil
1 large white onion, finely chopped
4 cloves garlic, thinly sliced
2 to 6 serrano chilies, thinly sliced (for a milder
  salsa, seed the chilies)
4 medium ripe red tomatoes (about 1½ pounds),

peeled and coarsely chopped in the food
  processor (with juices)
¼ cup chopped fresh cilantro
2 tablespoons fresh lime juice, or to taste
Salt and freshly ground black pepper

1. Heat the lard in a nonstick frying pan. Add the onion and cook over medium heat until it is soft but not brown, 4 minutes. Add the garlic and chilies halfway through.

2. Increase the heat to high and add the tomatoes. Cook until most of the tomato liquid has evaporated,

3 to 5 minutes. Stir in the cilantro, lime juice, and salt and pepper to taste. Cook for 1 minute. Correct the seasoning, adding salt or lime juice as needed; the salsa should be highly seasoned. *Note:* Salsa Ranchera is generally served hot.

Makes 3 cups, enough to serve 6

63 CALORIES PER SERVING; 1 G PROTEIN; 4 G FAT; 1 G SATURATED FAT;
7 G CARBOHYDRATE; 9 MG SODIUM; 0 MG CHOLESTEROL

COOKED TOMATO SALSA
(SALSA DE TOMATE COCIDO)

This mild, simple salsa, brimming with rich tomato flavors and virtually without heat, is what an Italian grandmother would make—if she had grown up in Mexico City. Serve it with tacos, burritos, chiles rellenos, even over pasta—in any dish that calls for lots of salsa flavor, but not too much heat.

PREPARATION TIME: 10 MINUTES   COOKING TIME: 10 MINUTES

1¾ pounds fresh plum tomatoes (7 or 8 tomatoes)
    or 1 (28-ounce) can plum tomatoes, with juices
½ medium white onion, cut in half again
2 to 4 serrano chilies
2 cloves garlic

1½ tablespoons lard or canola oil
4 sprigs cilantro
1 teaspoon dried oregano (preferably Mexican)
1 (2-inch) piece cinnamon
Salt and freshly ground black pepper

1. Heat a comal or cast-iron skillet over medium-high heat. Roast the tomatoes in the pan until they are nicely browned on all sides, 8 to 10 minutes. Roast the onion wedges, chilies, and garlic the same way: 8 minutes for the onion; 4 minutes for the chilies and garlic. Transfer to a plate and let cool. Seed the chilies. (For a spicier salsa, leave in the seeds.)

2. Scrape most of the burnt bits off the vegetables and purée in a blender.

3. Heat the lard or oil in a deep saucepan. Add the vegetable purée, cilantro, oregano, and cinnamon. Fry the sauce until it is thick and richly flavored, about 5 minutes, stirring with a wooden spoon. Discard the cinnamon stick. Correct the seasoning, adding salt and pepper to taste.

Makes 3 cups, enough to serve 6 to 8

68 CALORIES PER SERVING (BASED ON 6 SERVINGS); 1 G PROTEIN; 4 G FAT; 0.3 G SATURATED FAT; 9 G CARBOHYDRATE; 13 MG SODIUM; 0 MG CHOLESTEROL

Flame-Charred Tomato Salsa in the Style of Northern Mexico

I first tasted this smoky, flame-charred tomato salsa in the state of Chihuahua in northern Mexico. I loved the way its gutsy flavor and brash bite electrified whatever I was eating. The salsa owes its firepower to a long, slender, bright red, dried pepper called chile de árbol. The intense smoke flavor comes from grilling the tomatoes and onion over mesquite. If you have access to mesquite logs or chunks for building your fire, you can make your salsa the way Mexicans do. If not, a handful of mesquite chips tossed on the coals of your grill will provide the requisite smoke flavor. (This is the solution I opt for here.) This salsa is great on a tortilla chip, and its robust flavor is sure to impress.

PREPARATION TIME: 10 MINUTES, PLUS 30 MINUTES FOR SOAKING THE CHILIES AND WOOD CHIPS
COOKING TIME: 10 MINUTES

3 to 6 chiles de árbol
2 large ripe tomatoes
½ medium onion, cut in half lengthwise (leave the root end intact)
1 clove garlic

3 tablespoons chopped fresh cilantro
2 tablespoons fresh lime juice, or to taste
Salt and freshly ground black pepper
1 cup mesquite chips

1. Soak the chilies in a bowl of warm water until they are pliable, about 30 minutes. Soak the mesquite chips the same way in a separate bowl. Build a brisk fire in your grill.

2. Drain the mesquite chips and toss them on the coals. Grill the tomatoes until the skins are charred on all sides, 6 to 8 minutes. Char the onion pieces the same way. Transfer to a plate and let cool. Scrape off any really burnt parts, but be sure to leave some flame-charred skin intact for color and flavor.

3. Drain the chilies. If a milder salsa is desired, tear them open and remove the seeds. (I don't.) Place the chilies, tomatoes, onion, garlic, and cilantro in a blender and purée to a coarse paste. Add the lime juice and the salt and pepper to taste; the salsa should be highly seasoned.

Makes about 2 cups, enough to serve 6 to 8

18 CALORIES PER SERVING (BASED ON 6 SERVINGS); 1 G PROTEIN; 0 G FAT; 0 G SATURATED FAT;
4 G CARBOHYDRATE; 10 MG SODIUM; 0 MG CHOLESTEROL

COOKED SALSA VERDE
(GREEN SALSA OF TOMATILLOS)

This piquant green sauce is one of Mexico's principal salsas. Sometimes it's served by itself (with chips, that is); more often, though, it's used as a flavoring for egg dishes, seafood, poultry, and all manner of tortilla dishes (especially enchiladas). Salsa verde owes its distinctive tart, fruity flavor to its main ingredient: tomatillos. A member of the gooseberry family (it's a fruit, not a vegetable), the tomatillo looks like a small green tomato encased in a tan, papery husk. The flavor lies somewhere between that of a green tomato and that of a very tart apple. There is no substitute: Fortunately, fresh tomatillos can be found at Mexican markets, natural foods stores, and most supermarkets. Canned tomatillos are widely available as well. When you husk a tomatillo, the fruit itself will feel sticky—this is perfectly normal. Simply rinse the fruit under running water before you use it.

PREPARATION TIME: 5 MINUTES   COOKING TIME: 15 MINUTES

1 pound fresh tomatillos, husked
2 to 4 serrano or jalapeño chilies, stemmed (for a milder salsa verde, seed the chilies)
1 small onion, coarsely chopped
2 cloves garlic, minced

¼ cup chopped fresh cilantro
1 tablespoon olive oil or lard
½ teaspoon sugar, or to taste
Salt and freshly ground black pepper
1 cup chicken or vegetable broth, or as needed

1. Cook the tomatillos and chilies in 1 quart of simmering water in a saucepan over medium heat until just tender, 4 to 6 minutes. With a slotted spoon, transfer the tomatillos and chilies to a food processor or blender. Add the onion, garlic, and cilantro and purée until smooth.

2. Heat the oil in a deep, nonstick frying pan. Add the tomatillo mixture, sugar, salt, and pepper and fry over medium-high heat, stirring steadily with a wooden spoon, for 3 to 5 minutes, or until the mixture darkens slightly and is very aromatic. (Be careful: The salsa will spatter.)

3. Stir in the stock and simmer until the salsa is richly flavored and thick but pourable, 5 to 10 minutes. If it becomes too thick, add a little more stock. Correct the seasoning, adding salt or sugar to taste.

When using canned tomatillos (you'll need 1 can), there is no need to cook them. Simply drain well. In this case, skip boiling the chilies, too.

Makes about 3 cups, enough to serve 6

62 CALORIES PER SERVING; 2 G PROTEIN; 3 G FAT; 0 G SATURATED FAT;
8 G CARBOHYDRATE; 58 MG SODIUM; 0 MG CHOLESTEROL

FRESH SALSA VERDE
(SALSA VERDE CRUDA)

This salsa verde contains the same ingredients as the preceding recipe, but the flavor is quite different, because the vegetables are roasted in a comal, without frying the finished salsa. Use this one when a more robust tomatillo flavor is desired.

PREPARATION TIME: 5 MINUTES   COOKING TIME: 12 MINUTES

1 pound fresh tomatillos, husked
½ medium white onion, cut in half again
2 cloves garlic
3 to 5 serrano or jalapeño chilies (for a milder salsa verde, seed the chilies)

¼ cup chopped fresh cilantro
½ teaspoon sugar, or as needed
Salt and freshly ground black pepper
½ to 1 cup chicken or vegetable stock or water

1. Heat a comal or skillet over medium-high heat. Roast the tomatillos until they are lightly browned on all sides, turning with tongs, 6 to 8 minutes. (For additional instructions on roasting vegetables, see page 175.) Transfer to a plate to cool. Add the onion, garlic, and chilies to the pan and roast until they are lightly browned: 8 to 10 minutes for the onion; 4 to 6 minutes for the chilies and garlic.

2. Place the roasted vegetables in a food processor with the cilantro, sugar, salt, and pepper and purée to a coarse paste. Add stock or water as needed to obtain a pourable sauce. Correct the seasoning, adding salt or sugar to taste.

Makes 2 cups, enough to serve 4 to 6

5 CALORIES PER SERVING (BASED ON 4 SERVINGS); 0 G PROTEIN; 0 G FAT; 0 G SATURATED FAT; 1 G CARBOHYDRATE; 2 MG SODIUM; 0 MG CHOLESTEROL

SMOKED CHILI SALSA WITH TOMATOES AND TOMATILLOS (SALSA CHIPOTLE)

Here's a handsome salsa that's brimming with smoke and fire. The heat comes from chipotle chilies (smoked jalapeños) and the smoke flavor is reinforced by charring the vegetables in a comal or under the broiler. Serve this salsa with the Chips Without Hips on page 1. I guarantee your guests will sit up (or bolt upright) and take notice.

PREPARATION TIME: 5 MINUTES   COOKING TIME: 10 MINUTES

5 tomatillos (about 6 ounces), husked
4 plum tomatoes (about 10 ounces)
5 cloves garlic
1 (3-inch) piece white onion
3 to 5 canned chipotle chilies, with 1 to 2
   tablespoons juice from the can

2 tablespoons chopped fresh cilantro
½ teaspoon salt, or to taste
¼ teaspoon sugar, or to taste

1. Heat a comal or cast-iron skillet over a medium-high flame. Add the tomatillos and plum tomatoes and cook until nicely browned on all sides, about 10 minutes, turning with tongs. Cook the garlic cloves (with skins on) and the piece of onion the same way. Alternatively, preheat the broiler and broil the vegetables.

2. Place the vegetables in a food processor. Add the chipotles, cilantro, salt, and sugar. Purée to a coarse paste. Correct the seasoning, adding salt or sugar to taste.

Makes 1¾ cups, enough to serve 6 to 8

27 CALORIES PER SERVING (BASED ON 6 SERVINGS); 1 G PROTEIN; 1 G FAT; 0 G SATURATED FAT; 5 G CARBOHYDRATE; 136 MG SODIUM; 0 MG CHOLESTEROL

CHILE DE ÁRBOL SALSA

This salsa from the north of Mexico may be simple to make, but it packs a wallop you can feel a thousand miles away.
The salsa owes its invigorating flavor—not to mention its lip-stinging bite—to a long, slender, dried chili called chile de árbol.
Serve this brute with carnitas, taquitos, grilled meats, or any dish in need of a decisive blast of heat.

PREPARATION TIME: 5 MINUTES (PLUS 1 HOUR FOR SOAKING THE CHILIES)

20 dried chiles de árbol, stemmed
1 cup warm water
¼ white onion
1 clove garlic

3 tablespoons chopped cilantro
1 tablespoon lime juice
½ teaspoon salt, or to taste

1. Place the chilies in a bowl and add warm water to cover, about 1 cup. Let soak until very soft, about 1 hour.

2. Place the chilies and soaking liquid in a blender with the onion, garlic, cilantro, lime juice, and salt. Purée to a smooth paste, scraping down the sides of the blender with a rubber spatula. Correct the seasoning, adding salt to taste.

Note: For a milder salsa, tear open the soaked chilies and remove the seeds.

Makes about 1 ½ cups, enough to serve 8 to 10

6 CALORIES PER SERVING (BASED ON 8 SERVINGS); 0 G PROTEIN; 0 G FAT; 0 G SATURATED FAT;
1 G CARBOHYDRATE; 2 MG SODIUM; 0 MG CHOLESTEROL

DOG'S-NOSE SALSA
(XNI PEC)

Warning: If you don't like fiery food, do not attempt this recipe. Don't even READ this recipe, for xni pec (pronounced "SHNEE-pek") from the Yucatán is one of the hottest salsas in the world. The name says it all: Xni is the Mayan word for "dog," pec means "nose." Whether this curious moniker refers to the salsa's ferocious bite or to its tendency to make your nose run (a dog's nose is always wet), I'll leave to your imagination. I've given a range of chilies. Use all six only if you dare!

PREPARATION TIME: 10 MINUTES

2 to 10 habanero chilies (or Scotch bonnets), stemmed and finely chopped (for a milder sauce, seed the chilies)

2 medium red tomatoes, cut into ¼-inch dice (with juices)

1 medium red onion, finely chopped (about 1 cup)

¼ cup chopped fresh cilantro

¼ cup sour orange juice, or to taste
   (or 3 tablespoons fresh lime juice, plus
   1 tablespoon fresh grapefruit juice)

Salt (about 1 teaspoon)

Combine all the ingredients in an attractive bowl and toss to mix. To correct the seasoning, add sour orange juice or lime juice to taste.

Note: Sour orange is a citrus fruit that resembles a bumpy orange but tastes like a lime. To approximate its flavor, I use regular lime juice mixed with a little grapefruit juice.

Makes about 2½ cups, enough to serve 6 to 8

24 CALORIES PER SERVING (BASED ON 6 SERVINGS); 1 G PROTEIN; 0 G FAT; 0 G SATURATED FAT; 5 G CARBOHYDRATE; 5 MG SODIUM; 0 MG CHOLESTEROL

GUACAMOLE SALSA
(SALSA DE GUACAMOLE)

Most of us in the United States are familiar with guacamole as a dip, but in Mexico it's also served as a sauce. (The term "guacamole" comes from the Nahuatl words ahuacatl, *meaning "avocado," and* milli, *for "mixture" or "sauce.") The sauce version is a smooth, creamy purée that you can spoon or drizzle over tacos, burritos, and salads. In an effort to cut out some of the fat, I've replaced some of the avocado with no-fat sour cream. The result makes an elegant sauce that you can squirt in decorative squiggles from a squeeze bottle.*

PREPARATION TIME: 5 MINUTES

1 ripe avocado, peeled, seeded, and diced
1 clove garlic, chopped
½ medium white onion, chopped
2 to 3 serrano chilies, chopped (for milder
    guacamole, seed the chilies before chopping)

¼ cup coarsely chopped fresh cilantro
½ cup no-fat sour cream
½ cup water
1 to 2 tablespoons fresh lime juice, or to taste
Salt and freshly ground white pepper

1. Combine all the ingredients in a blender and purée to a smooth paste. If using a food processor, purée the avocado, garlic, onion, chiles, and cilantro first, then add the sour cream, water, lime juice, and seasonings. Correct the seasoning, adding salt or lime juice to taste; the salsa should be highly seasoned.

2. Transfer the salsa to a bowl with a spoon for serving, or place it in a plastic squeeze bottle for squirting decorative squiggles.

Makes 2 cups, enough to serve 8

56 CALORIES PER SERVING; 2 G PROTEIN; 4G FAT; 1 G SATURATED FAT;
5 G CARBOHYDRATE; 13 MG SODIUM; 0 MG CHOLESTEROL

SWEET CORN SALSA
(SALSA DE MAÍZ)

There's only one word for this sauce, which was inspired by a Oaxacan corn soup: amazing—amazing in its sweet corn flavor; amazing in its creamy richness; and triply amazing that it contains only 1 gram of fat per serving. (The secret is to use evaporated skim milk instead of cream.) For the best results, use fresh corn, but frozen corn produces a surprisingly sweet, flavorful salsa. To cut off the kernels of fresh corn, lay the cob flat on a cutting board. Cut off the kernels with broad, lengthwise strokes of a knife. For a smoky dimension, you can grill the corn (see page 147) before puréeing. It's hard to imagine a dish that wouldn't go well with this salsa, which makes a particularly satisfying accompaniment to chiles rellenos.

PREPARATION TIME: 10 MINUTES   COOKING TIME: 10 MINUTES

2 cups corn kernels (fresh, frozen, or grilled)
3 tablespoons diced onion
½ clove garlic, minced
2 tablespoons chopped fresh cilantro

1 teaspoon sugar (or to taste)
1¼ cups evaporated skim milk
Salt and freshly ground white pepper

1. Combine all the ingredients in a saucepan and simmer over medium heat until the corn is very soft, 5 to 8 minutes.

2. Transfer the mixture to a blender and purée until smooth. Return to the pan and correct the season-ing, adding salt or sugar as necessary. For a particu-larly velvety-smooth sauce, pour the sauce through a fine-meshed china cap strainer.

Makes 1½ cups, enough to serve 4 to 6

137 CALORIES PER SERVING (BASED ON 4 SERVINGS); 8 G PROTEIN; 1 G FAT; 0 G SATURATED FAT; 26 G CARBOHYDRATE; 360 MG SODIUM; 3 MG CHOLESTEROL

SOUPS

TORTILLA SOUP
(SOPA DE TORTILLA)

Is there anything more comforting on a chilly night than a steaming bowl of tortilla soup, its broth smoky with roasted vegetables, warmed by pasilla chilies, fragrant with meaty chicken stock, and thick with tortilla "noodles"? Tradition calls for the tortillas to be deep-fried, but I've found that baking produces the requisite crispness with dramatically less fat—especially if you use stale tortillas. Note: Canadian bacon isn't traditional either, but I like the way it enhances the soup's smoke flavor.

PREPARATION TIME: 20 MINUTES   COOKING TIME: 40 MINUTES

10 corn tortillas
3 pasilla chilies
8 plum tomatoes (1¼ to 1½ pounds)
1½ medium white onions, quartered
6 cloves garlic
3 sprigs epazote (or cilantro)
3 tablespoons chopped flat-leaf parsley
1 tablespoon lard or olive oil

1 ounce Canadian bacon, minced
6 cups chicken broth (see page 178)
Salt and freshly ground black pepper
4 to 6 tablespoons no-fat sour cream
¼ cup coarsely grated queso fresco, white cheddar, or Monterey Jack cheese (about 1 ounce)
4 to 6 wedges fresh lime

1. Preheat the oven to 350°F. Cut the tortillas in half, then crosswise into ½-inch strips. Arrange the strips on a baking sheet in a single layer. Bake until lightly browned, 6 to 8 minutes. Remove from the oven and let cool; the tortillas will crisp as they cool.

2. Stem the chilies, tear open, and remove the veins and seeds. Place the chilies on a baking sheet and bake until they are aromatic and crisp but not burnt, 4 to 6 minutes. Transfer to a plate to cool; the chilies will crisp as they cool. Coarsely crumble the chilies.

3. In a comal or cast-iron frying pan or under the broiler, roast the tomatoes, onions, and garlic until nicely browned: 8 to 10 minutes for the tomatoes and onions; 4 to 6 minutes for the garlic. (See instructions on page 175.) In the blender, purée the tomatoes, onion, garlic, epazote, parsley, and one of the toasted chilies.

4. Heat the lard in a large saucepan. Fry the tomato purée and Canadian bacon over high heat, stirring well, until thick, dark, and fragrant, 5 to 10 minutes. Add the chicken broth and simmer for 10 minutes. Stir in the toasted tortilla strips and salt and pepper to taste. Cook for 2 minutes.

5. To serve, ladle the tortilla soup into bowls and garnish each with a dollop of sour cream. Sprinkle the cheese and remaining crumbled pasilla chilies on top and serve at once, accompanied by lime wedges for squeezing.

Serves 6 as an appetizer, 4 as a hearty main course

328 CALORIES PER SERVING (BASED ON 4 SERVINGS); 12 G PROTEIN; 9 G FAT; 2 G SATURATED FAT;
57 G CARBOHYDRATE; 312 MG SODIUM; 14 MG CHOLESTEROL

Tortilla Soup

MEXICAN GAZPACHO

Gazpacho is a Spanish soup, of course, not Mexican, but the ingredients—luscious, ripe red tomatoes, onions, garlic, and peppers—are shared by both countries. One day I had the idea to roast the vegetables in a comal Mexican-style before puréeing them to make gazpacho: The result was a revelation. I think you'll be amazed by the complex, charred, smoky flavors that result from roasting the vegetables.

PREPARATION TIME: 15 MINUTES   COOKING TIME: 10 MINUTES

2 corn tortillas
8 large ripe red plum tomatoes (about 2 pounds)
1 red bell pepper
1 poblano chili or green bell pepper
1 medium white onion, quartered
1 to 2 jalapeño peppers
4 cloves garlic, peeled
4 scallions, white part trimmed, green part finely chopped

1 cucumber, peeled and seeded
2 tablespoons extra-virgin olive oil
2 tablespoons red wine vinegar, or as needed
¼ cup finely chopped cilantro
Salt and freshly ground black pepper
6 lime wedges

1. Preheat the oven to 350°F. Cut the tortillas in half, then crosswise into ¼-inch strips. Arrange the strips on a baking sheet in a single layer. Bake until lightly browned, 6 to 8 minutes. Remove from the oven and let cool; the tortillas will crisp as they cool.

2. In a comal or cast-iron frying pan or under the broiler, roast the tomatoes, red pepper, poblano, onion, jalapeños, garlic, and scallion whites until nicely browned on all sides: 8 to 10 minutes for the tomatoes, peppers, and onions; 4 to 6 minutes for the jalapeños, garlic, and scallion whites. (Turn with tongs.) Transfer the vegetables to a plate and let cool.

Cut open the pepper and chilies and remove the veins and seeds, reserving the juices.

3. Combine the roasted vegetables, cucumber, olive oil, vinegar, and cilantro in a blender and purée until smooth. Add water to thin the gazpacho to pourable consistency (1 to 2 cups). Add salt, pepper, and more vinegar (if needed); the gazpacho should be highly seasoned.

4. Pour or ladle the gazpacho into bowls. Garnish each with the chopped scallion greens and crisped tortilla slivers. Serve with lime wedges for squeezing.

Serves 6

127 CALORIES PER SERVING; 4 G PROTEIN; 6 G FAT; 1 G SATURATED FAT;
20 G CARBOHYDRATE; 33 MG SODIUM; 0 MG CHOLESTEROL

YUCATÁN CHICKEN-LIME SOUP
(SOPA DE LIMA)

Delectably aromatic and tongue-tinglingly tart is this colorful chicken soup from the Yucatán. It takes only minutes to make:
Indeed, its immediacy is one of its virtues, yet the invigorating doses of chilies and lime juice make it one of the most flavorful
and satisfying soups ever to grace a bowl. Chicken soup is the universal remedy for a cold, and this one offers curative doses of
vitamin C (from the lime juice), fresh garlic (a traditional antiseptic and antibiotic), and fresh chilies, which have a
wonderful way of clearing stuffed sinuses. But even if you don't have a cold, you'll love the electrifying flavors.

PREPARATION TIME: 10 MINUTES   COOKING TIME: 10 MINUTES

1 boneless, skinless chicken breast (10 to 12 ounces)
4 corn tortillas, cut into matchstick slivers
1 tablespoon olive oil
1 medium onion, thinly sliced
8 cloves garlic, thinly sliced
2 to 4 serrano or jalapeño chilies, thinly sliced

5 cups chicken broth (see page 178), or use a good low-sodium canned broth
⅓ cup fresh lime juice, or to taste
1 large ripe tomato, peeled, seeded, and cut into ¼-inch dice
Salt and freshly ground black pepper
¼ cup coarsely chopped fresh cilantro

1. Preheat the oven to 350°F. Wash and dry the chicken breast and trim off any sinews or fat. Cut the chicken breast across the grain into matchstick slivers.

2. Spread the tortilla slivers on a baking sheet or on a piece of foil and bake until lightly browned, 5 to 8 minutes. Transfer the tortilla strips to a plate to cool.

3. Just before serving, heat the oil in a large saucepan. Add the onion, garlic, and chili slices and cook over medium heat until lightly browned, about 5 minutes. Stir in the chicken broth, lime juice, chicken, and tomatoes. Gently simmer the soup until the chicken is cooked, 3 to 5 minutes. Add salt and pepper to taste and extra lime juice if desired; the soup should be tart and highly seasoned. Stir in the cilantro. Ladle the soup into bowls and sprinkle with the toasted tortilla strips.   *Serves 4*

221 CALORIES PER SERVING; 19 G PROTEIN; 6 G FAT; 1 G SATURATED FAT;
23 G CARBOHYDRATE; 105 MG SODIUM; 41 MG CHOLESTEROL

CHICKEN GARBANZO BEAN SOUP WITH SMOKY CHILIES (CALDO TLALPEÑO)

I first tasted this soup at the sprawling Arroyo restaurant in Coyoacán outside Mexico City. The preparation comes from the community of Tlalpán, where an exuberant use of chipotles (smoked jalapeño chilies) gives the soup a heady smoke flavor and fiery bite. As elsewhere, I give a range of chilies: Two will give you a pleasantly warm caldo tlalpeño; four, a soup with volcanic intensity. Note: I like to cook the chicken on the bone for extra flavor, but you can certainly opt for the convenience of boneless breast.

PREPARATION TIME: 20 MINUTES　COOKING TIME: 40 MINUTES

FOR THE CHICKEN AND BROTH:
7 cups chicken stock
1 pound bone-in but skinless chicken breasts
1 bay leaf
¼ onion
1 clove
2 sprigs cilantro

TO FINISH THE SOUP:
4 plum tomatoes
1½ tablespoons lard or olive oil
1 medium white onion, finely diced

3 cloves garlic, finely chopped
4 scallions, trimmed and finely chopped (reserve the greens for garnish)
1 carrot, peeled and finely diced
1 large potato, peeled and finely diced
1 to 3 canned chipotle chilies, minced, with 1 to 3 teaspoons juice from the can
1 cup cooked garbanzo beans
2 sprigs epazote
Salt and freshly ground black pepper
6 wedges fresh lime

1. Place the stock and chicken breasts in a large saucepan. Pin the bay leaf to the onion quarter with the clove. Add this to the pot with the cilantro. Gradually bring the mixture to a boil, reduce the heat, and gently simmer the chicken until cooked, 8 to 10 minutes. Transfer the chicken to a plate to cool, then tear it off the bones into shreds and set aside. Strain the stock; you should have about 6 cups.

2. In a comal or cast-iron frying pan or under the broiler, roast the tomatoes until they are nicely browned, 8 to 10 minutes. Transfer them to a plate to cool. Purée the tomatoes in a blender.

3. Heat the lard in a large saucepan over medium heat. Cook the onion, garlic, and scallion whites until they're lightly browned, 5 minutes, stirring often. Increase the heat to high and add the tomato purée. Cook until thick and fragrant, about 5 minutes.

4. Stir in the chicken broth, carrot, potato, and chipotles with their juices and cook 5 minutes. Add the shredded chicken, garbanzo beans, epazote, and salt and pepper. Gently simmer the soup until it is richly flavored and the vegetables are tender, 5 minutes. Correct the seasoning, adding salt and pepper to taste. Ladle the soup into bowls and sprinkle with the scallion greens. Serve with the lime wedges.

Serves 6 to 8

247 CALORIES PER SERVING (BASED ON 6 SERVINGS); 22 G PROTEIN; 7 G FAT; 2 G SATURATED FAT; 27 G CARBOHYDRATE; 251 MG SODIUM; 51 MG CHOLESTEROL

CHICKEN SOUP WITH GARBANZO BEANS AND RICE (CONSOMÉ DE POLLO CON GARBANZOS Y ARROZ)

The whole world loves chicken soup, observes New York food writer Mimi Sheraton. Central Mexico's version is a stick-to-the-ribs melange of chicken, rice, and garbanzo beans. For the very best results, make the chicken broth from scratch, as instructed below. If you're in a hurry, use a good low-sodium canned chicken stock and start at step 3. (You'll need about 2 quarts of chicken broth and 2 cups of shredded chicken.)

PREPARATION TIME: 10 MINUTES   COOKING TIME: 1¼ HOURS

FOR THE CHICKEN AND BROTH:
1 (3½-pound) chicken
1 bay leaf
1 medium onion, quartered
1 clove
1 ripe tomato, quartered
1 carrot, cut into 1-inch chunks
1 stalk celery, cut into 1-inch chunks
2 sprigs parsley
2 sprigs cilantro
10 cups cold water

TO FINISH THE SOUP:
½ cup uncooked white rice
Salt and freshly ground black pepper
1 carrot, peeled and finely chopped
1 celery stalk, finely chopped
1 cup cooked garbanzo beans
¼ cup finely chopped flat-leaf parsley

1. Remove the skin and any visible fat from the chicken. Wash the chicken and blot it dry. Pin the bay leaf to one of the onion quarters with the clove. Place the chicken in a large pot with the onion, tomato, carrot, celery, parsley, and cilantro. Add 10 cups of cold water and bring to a boil. Using a ladle, skim off any fat and foam that rise to the surface. Reduce the heat and gently simmer the chicken until cooked, about 1 hour, skimming often. (It's important to skim the broth frequently to remove the fat.) Add cold water as needed to keep the bird covered.

2. Transfer the chicken to a plate and let cool. Strain the broth into a large saucepan, pressing the vegetables to extract the juices. You should wind up with about 8 cups of broth. Pull the chicken meat off the bones and finely shred. You should wind up with about 4 cups. You'll need 2 cups for this recipe. Reserve any remaining chicken for enchiladas.

3. Add the rice, salt, and pepper to the broth and simmer over medium heat for 10 minutes. Add the carrot, celery, shredded chicken, garbanzo beans, and half the parsley to the soup. Simmer for another 10 minutes, or until the rice and vegetables are tender. Correct the seasoning, adding salt and pepper to taste. Sprinkle the soup with the remaining parsley and serve at once.   *Serves 8*

159 CALORIES PER SERVING; 16 G PROTEIN; 2 G FAT; 1 G SATURATED FAT;
18 G CARBOHYDRATE; 148 MG SODIUM; 37 MG CHOLESTEROL

MEXICAN HERB SOUP

Supremely satisfying and offbeat is this silky green soup made with traditional Mexican herbs, such as cilantro, epazote, and hoja santa. The latter is a heart-shaped leaf with a delicate anise flavor (see Mail-Order Sources). If you can't find hoja santa, substitute two ¼-inch-thick slices of fresh fennel.

PREPARATION TIME: 10 MINUTES   COOKING TIME: 30 MINUTES

2 poblano chilies
½ medium white onion, cut in half
1 bunch scallions, trimmed, white part left whole, green part finely chopped
4 cloves garlic
5 cups chicken broth, or as needed
1 cup evaporated skim milk
1 medium potato (about 6 ounces), peeled and cut into ½-inch dice

Salt and freshly ground pepper
1 bunch fresh cilantro, washed and stemmed
1 bunch flat-leaf parsley, washed and stemmed
3 tablespoons chopped epazote
2 hoja santa leaves or 1 (2¼-inch-thick) slice fresh fennel
¼ cup no-fat sour cream
1 cup Garlic Parmesan Chili "Croutons" (optional; page 48)

1. In a comal or cast-iron frying pan over medium-high heat or under the broiler, roast the poblanos, onion, scallion whites, and garlic until nicely browned: 8 to 10 minutes for the poblanos and onion; 4 to 6 minutes for the scallions and garlic. (Turn with tongs.) Transfer to a plate to cool. When they're cool, peel the poblanos and remove the veins and seeds.

2. Place the roasted onion and scallion whites, the chicken broth, skim milk, potato, salt, and pepper in a large heavy saucepan and simmer over medium-high heat until the potatoes are soft, 8 minutes. (If you are using fennel slices instead of hoja santa, add them with the onion and potato.) Add the poblanos, cilantro, parsley, epazote, hoja santa, and most of the scallion greens, reserving 2 tablespoons for garnish. Boil the soup for 2 minutes.

3. Transfer the soup to a blender and purée until smooth, working in several batches as necessary. Add salt and pepper to taste.

4. To serve, ladle the soup into bowls and garnish each with a dollop of sour cream in the center. Sprinkle with the reserved scallion greens and serve at once. Serve the optional garlic chili Parmesan "croutons" on the side or sprinkle them over the soup.

Serves 6

87 CALORIES PER SERVING; 5 G PROTEIN; 0 G FAT; 0 G SATURATED FAT;
16 G CARBOHYDRATE; 74 MG SODIUM; 2 MG CHOLESTEROL

RED BEAN SOUP WITH ROASTED TOMATOES

Come winter, cold winds sweep across the high plains of central Mexico. Here's the perfect warm-up, a rich, silky red bean soup robustly flavored with roasted tomatoes and other vegetables and earthy pasilla chilies. To trim the amount of fat, I bake the tortilla "noodles" instead of frying, and have greatly reduced the amount of lard. Note: If you're using canned beans, you'll need two 15-ounce cans. Choose a low- or no-sodium brand and rinse the beans well under cold running water.

PREPARATION TIME: 20 MINUTES   COOKING TIME: 30 MINUTES

10 ripe red plum tomatoes (cut out the stem end)
1 large white onion, quartered
4 cloves garlic
3 scallions, white part trimmed, green part finely chopped
3 pasilla chilies
3 tablespoons finely chopped cilantro
1½ tablespoons lard or olive oil
3 cups cooked kidney beans (rinsed and drained in a colander)

5 cups chicken or vegetable stock, or as needed (pages 178, 180)
Salt and freshly ground black pepper

FOR SERVING:
1 flour tortilla
½ cup no-fat sour cream
3 tablespoons chopped fresh scallion greens (reserved from above)

1. Heat a comal or cast-iron skillet over medium-high heat. Roast the tomatoes, onion, garlic, and scallion whites until nicely browned on all sides: 8 to 10 minutes for the tomatoes and onion; 4 to 5 minutes for the garlic and scallion whites. Transfer the vegetables to a plate to cool. Toast the chilies on the comal until they are aromatic and crisp, 20 to 30 seconds per side. Do not let them burn. Alternatively, the vegetables and chilies can be browned under the broiler or on a barbecue grill. Preheat the oven to 350°F.

2. Tear open the chilies and discard the seeds and stems. Break the chilies into 1-inch pieces. Combine the tomatoes, onion, garlic, scallion whites and all but 3 tablespoons of the greens, the cilantro, and toasted chilies in a blender and purée until smooth.

3. Heat the lard in a large deep saucepan. Add the vegetable-chili mixture and fry over medium-high heat until it is thick, dark, and fragrant, 5 to 8 minutes, stirring with a wooden spoon. (Stir often to keep the mixture from spattering.) Add the beans, stock, salt, and pepper and cook until the soup is richly flavored, about 10 minutes.

4. Return the soup to the blender and purée until smooth. Thin to pourable consistency by adding a little extra stock if needed. Add salt and pepper to taste.

5. Meanwhile, prepare the tortilla "noodles." Cut the tortilla in half, then crosswise into ⅛-inch strips. Arrange the strips on a baking sheet in a single layer. Bake until lightly browned, 6 to 8 minutes. Remove the pan from the oven. The tortilla noodles will crisp as they cool.

6. To serve, ladle the soup into bowls. Place a dollop of sour cream in the center of each. Sprinkle the soup with the scallion greens and tortilla noodles. Serve at once.

Makes about 8 cups, enough to serve 8
as a first course, 4 to 6 as a light main course

183 CALORIES PER SERVING (BASED ON 8 SERVINGS); 9 G PROTEIN; 4 G FAT; 1 G SATURATED FAT;
31 G CARBOHYDRATE; 58 MG SODIUM; 2 MG CHOLESTEROL

MEXICAN NOODLE SOUP
(SOPA DE FIDEOS)

Every nation has its version of chicken noodle soup. Mexico's owes its ruddy complexion and rousing flavor to the addition of fried noodles and puréed tomatoes. Although it's not customary to roast the vegetables for this recipe, I like the depth of flavor that roasting imparts and so invite you to take a little extra time to roast the tomatoes, onion, and garlic—your pasta soup will be all the more tasty.

PREPARATION TIME: 15 MINUTES   COOKING TIME: 20 MINUTES

2 medium ripe red tomatoes
1 small white onion, quartered
4 cloves garlic
1½ tablespoons lard or olive oil
6 ounces vermicelli (or other slender pasta),
   broken into 3-inch lengths

3 tablespoons finely chopped flat-leaf parsley, plus
   6 sprigs for garnish
6 cups chicken stock
Salt and freshly ground black pepper

1. Heat a comal or cast-iron skillet over medium-high heat. Roast the tomatoes, onion, and garlic until nicely browned on all sides, 8 to 10 minutes for the tomatoes and onion, 4 to 5 minutes for the garlic. Transfer the vegetables to a blender and purée to a smooth paste.

2. Heat the lard in a large saucepan. Add the vermicelli and cook over medium-high heat until it is golden brown, stirring continuously, 2 to 3 minutes. Add the vegetable purée and chopped parsley and fry until thick and fragrant, 2 to 3 minutes. Stir in the stock and bring to a boil.

3. Reduce the heat and simmer the soup until the pasta is tender, 8 to 10 minutes, stirring occasionally. Add salt and pepper to taste. Ladle the soup into bowls and serve at once, garnishing each with a sprig of parsley.

*Makes 6 cups, enough to serve 6
as an appetizer, 4 as a light main course*

259 CALORIES PER SERVING (BASED ON 4 SERVINGS); 8 G PROTEIN; 6 G FAT; 2 G SATURATED FAT;

45 G CARBOHYDRATE; 37 MG SODIUM; 5 MG CHOLESTEROL

VEGETABLE SOUP WITH MEATBALLS

This is Mexican comfort food at its best, a steaming bowl of broth chock-full of vegetables and tiny meatballs fragrant with spices and enriched with rice. There are probably as many different meatball recipes in Mexico as there are cooks. These feature the aromatic accents of oregano, cumin, and, for a sweet touch, cinnamon and cloves. To decrease the amount of fat, I've replaced some of the pork and beef with boneless, skinless chicken breast and used egg whites instead of a whole egg.

PREPARATION TIME: 40 MINUTES   COOKING TIME: 20 MINUTES

FOR THE MEATBALLS:

6 ounces boneless, skinless chicken breast, cut into ½-inch cubes
6 ounces lean pork loin, cut into ½-inch cubes
6 ounces lean beef (like sirloin), cut into ½-inch cubes
1 teaspoon salt, or to taste
½ teaspoon freshly ground black pepper
½ teaspoon dried oregano
½ teaspoon ground cumin
¼ teaspoon cinnamon
Pinch of ground cloves
3 tablespoons minced onion
2 cloves garlic, minced
2 egg whites
1 cup cooked rice

TO FINISH THE SOUP:

9 cups chicken broth (page 178)
1 bay leaf
1 medium onion
2 carrots
2 stalks celery
¼ medium cabbage
1 baking potato
6 ounces green beans
½ cup cooked corn kernels
½ cup cooked green peas
½ cup cooked lima beans
Salt and freshly ground black pepper

1. To prepare the meatballs, place the chicken, pork, beef, salt, pepper, oregano, cumin, cinnamon, cloves, onion, and garlic in a food processor and grind to a fine paste. Add the egg whites and process to mix. Transfer the mixture to a large bowl and stir in the rice. To test for seasoning, fry a small piece of meatball mixture in a nonstick skillet. Correct the seasoning, adding salt, pepper, or any other spice to taste. Chill the meatball mixture for 30 minutes.

2. Meanwhile, prepare the soup. Bring the chicken broth with the bay leaf to a boil in a large pot. Cut the onion, carrots, celery, cabbage, potato, and green beans into ½-inch dice (the green beans will be in ½-inch pieces). Add them to the pot with the corn, peas, and lima beans. Briskly simmer the soup until the vegetables are almost cooked, 8 to 10 minutes.

3. Form the meatball mixture into 32 (¾-inch) balls. (It helps to dampen your hands when forming the balls.) Gently lower the meatballs into the soup and simmer until they are cooked through, 10 to 15 minutes. Season the broth to taste, adding salt and pepper. Ladle it into bowls and serve at once.

Serves 8 as an appetizer,
4 to 6 as a light main course

334 CALORIES PER SERVING (BASED ON 6 SERVINGS); 33G PROTEIN; 6 G FAT; 2 G SATURATED FAT; 39 G CARBOHYDRATE; 140 MG SODIUM; 69 MG CHOLESTEROL

SALADS

JÍCAMA-ORANGE SALAD WITH CHIPOTLE VINAIGRETTE

This colorful salad features two of the most refreshing foods on the planet: orange and jícama. The orange cools you with its juicy tartness; the jícama delights with its apply crunch. Put them together and you wind up with a salad that's short on preparation time but long and bold on taste. Note: This recipe calls for canned chipotles (smoked jalapeños); instructions for using dried chipotles are found on page 184.

PREPARATION TIME: 15 MINUTES

1 large bunch leaf spinach, stemmed, washed, and spun dry
4 fresh oranges (preferably navels)
8 ounces jícama, peeled and cut into ¼-inch dice
8 black olives, cut in half lengthwise
¼ cup fresh cilantro leaves, washed

FOR THE VINAIGRETTE:
1 or 2 canned chipotle chilies, minced
1 clove garlic, minced
½ teaspoon salt
¼ teaspoon freshly ground black pepper
3 tablespoons fresh orange juice
2 tablespoons fresh lime juice
1 tablespoon extra-virgin olive oil

1. Carpet four salad plates or a platter with spinach leaves. Cut the rind (both zest and pith) off each orange to expose the flesh. Cut each orange widthwise into ¼-inch slices, removing any seeds with the tines of a fork. Arrange the slices over the spinach, leaving ½ inch of green showing at the edges. Sprinkle the salads with jícama, olives (rounded side up), and cilantro.

2. To prepare the vinaigrette, in a mixing bowl combine the chipotles, garlic, salt, and pepper. Mash to a paste with the back of a wooden spoon. Stir in the orange juice, lime juice, and olive oil. Correct the seasoning, adding salt or lime juice to taste; the dressing should be highly seasoned. Spoon the dressing over the salad and serve at once. *Serves 4*

151 CALORIES PER SERVING; 4 G PROTEIN; 5 G FAT; 1 G SATURATED FAT;
26 G CARBOHYDRATE; 351 MG SODIUM; 0 MG CHOLESTEROL

Jícama-Orange Salad with Chipotle Vinaigrette

POSOLE SALAD

This salad has probably never been served in Mexico, but it's thoroughly Mexican in color, flavor, and spirit. Posole—parched, hulled, cooked corn—is traditionally served in soups and stews, but its malty flavor and softly chewy texture make it a delectable base for a salad. Here, as elsewhere in this book, for the sake of convenience I call for canned hominy (posole).

PREPARATION TIME: 5 MINUTES

1¾ cups cooked hominy (one 14-½-ounce can, drained and rinsed several times)
1 ripe red tomato, seeded and cut into ¼-inch dice
1 cucumber, peeled, seeded, and cut into ¼-inch dice
3 scallions, trimmed and finely chopped
½ cup chopped fresh cilantro

1 or 2 jalapeño chilies, seeded and minced (for a spicier salad, leave in the seeds)
½ teaspoon ground cumin
3 tablespoons fresh lime juice
Salt and freshly ground black pepper
4 to 6 lettuce leaves, washed and dried

1. Combine all the ingredients except the lettuce leaves in a mixing bowl and toss to mix.
2. Place a lettuce leaf on each salad plate. Mound the posole on each leaf and serve at once.

Serves 4 to 6

99 CALORIES PER SERVING (BASED ON 4 SERVINGS); 3 G PROTEIN; 1 G FAT; 0 G SATURATED FAT; 20 G CARBOHYDRATE; 224 MG SODIUM; 0 MG CHOLESTEROL

GRILLED CACTUS SALAD
(ENSALADA DE NOPALITOS)

Nopalitos—the tender young paddles (leaves) of the prickly pear cactus—are a popular salad fixing and vegetable in Mexico. You find them stacked in decorative mounds at markets throughout the country. The flavor of the nopalito is pleasingly earthy, somewhat like that of a green bean. The texture is soft and fleshy, like a roasted bell pepper. Add the smoke flavor that comes from grilling the cactus and other vegetables and you have a salad you won't soon forget. If grilling isn't practical, roast the vegetables under the broiler. If you live in an area with a large Mexican community, you may be able to buy fresh nopalitos: These are ideal for grilling. If not, use canned nopalitos and omit the grilling. Or substitute green beans for the cactus. (To grill green beans, thread five or six on a toothpick and grill.)

PREPARATION TIME: 15 MINUTES   COOKING TIME: 12 MINUTES

3 or 4 nopalitos (about 1 pound), or 1 (15-ounce) jar or can cooked nopalitos
1 yellow bell pepper
1 tomato
½ medium white onion
1 or 2 red serrano or other fresh hot chilies, finely chopped (for a milder salad, seed the chilies)

¼ cup coarsely chopped fresh cilantro
1 tablespoon fresh lime juice
1 tablespoon red wine vinegar
1 tablespoon olive oil
Salt and freshly ground black pepper
1 tablespoon crumbled queso fresco or feta cheese

1. Preheat your barbecue grill to high.

2. If you buy fresh nopalitos at a market, they're likely to be trimmed already. But if you see any spines, trim them off with a paring knife. Place the nopalitos on the grill and cook until they are lightly browned and tender, 4 to 6 minutes per side. Grill the yellow pepper, tomato, and onion until lightly browned, 4 to 6 minutes per side. Transfer the vegetables to a cutting board and let cool.

3. Cut the cactus paddles crosswise into ½-inch strips. Core the yellow pepper and cut the flesh into ½-inch strips. Finely dice the tomato and onion. Transfer the vegetables to a serving bowl and stir in the chili, cilantro, lime juice, vinegar, olive oil, and salt and pepper. Correct the seasoning, adding lime juice or salt to taste. The salad can be prepared several hours ahead and kept in the refrigerator. Just before serving, sprinkle the queso fresco on top, then serve at once. *Serves 4*

106 CALORIES PER SERVING; 4 G PROTEIN; 5 G FAT; 1 G SATURATED FAT;
14 G CARBOHYDRATE; 31 MG SODIUM; 3 MG CHOLESTEROL

WHITE BEAN SALAD WITH EPAZOTE AND ORANGE

This colorful salad was inspired by a dish I tasted at the central food market in Merida. I love the contrast of textures and flavors: the nutty crunch of pepitas (roasted pumpkin seeds), the creamy softness of the white beans, the succulent tartness of fresh orange. The epazote adds a unique astringent, aromatic flavor. If you can't find epazote, use cilantro or flat-leaf parsley, although the flavor won't quite be the same.

PREPARATION TIME: 10 MINUTES   COOKING TIME: 3 MINUTES

2 oranges
¼ cup pepitas (hulled pumpkin seeds)
2 cups cooked white beans (rinse well if using
    canned beans)
½ medium red onion, finely diced (about ½ cup)
1 clove garlic, minced

3 tablespoons chopped fresh epazote (or cilantro),
    plus 4 whole sprigs for garnish
3 tablespoons lime juice
Salt and freshly ground black pepper
4 Boston lettuce leaves, washed and spun dry

1. Cut the rind and pith off the oranges, working over a bowl to catch the juices. Cut the segments away from the pith. Cut each orange segment in half and remove any seeds. Place the orange segments in a mixing bowl, reserving four pieces for garnish.

2. Toast the pumpkin seeds in a dry skillet over medium heat until they are lightly browned, 2 to 3 minutes. Transfer the pumpkin seeds to the mixing bowl. Stir in the beans, onion, garlic, epazote, lime juice, reserved orange juice, and salt and pepper to taste.

3. Arrange the lettuce leaves on four plates and mound the salad mixture in the center of each. Garnish with an orange segment and a sprig of cilantro.

Serves 4

190 CALORIES PER SERVING; 11 G PROTEIN; 2 G FAT; 0 G SATURATED FAT;
34 G CARBOHYDRATE; 9 MG SODIUM; 0 MG CHOLESTEROL

CAESAR SALAD

Caesar salad may seem like an odd dish to find in a Mexican cookbook. The flavorings—garlic, anchovies, Romano cheese—are more Italian than Mexican and these days you're much more likely to find Caesar salad at a restaurant in the United States than south of the border. Withal, Caesar salad was first served at a restaurant called Caesar's Palace in Tijuana in 1924, the creation of an Italian immigrant turned restaurateur named Caesar Cardini. So how do you decrease the amount of fat in a salad whose main ingredients are olive oil, fried bread, cheese, and egg? My low-fat version features buttermilk in place of some of the olive oil and egg substitute instead of the coddled egg. (The egg substitute—optional here—has the added advantage of being pasteurized, so you needn't worry about the risks associated with eating raw eggs.) Cheese-and-chili-toasted tortilla chips stand in for the fried bread. Here, then, is a heart-healthy Caesar that would do Cardini proud.

PREPARATION TIME: 10 MINUTES   COOKING TIME: 10 MINUTES FOR THE CROUTONS

2 hearts romaine lettuce
Garlic Parmesan Chili "Croutons" (page 48)

FOR THE DRESSING:
1 large clove garlic, cut in half
4 anchovy fillets, rinsed with hot water, then
    drained, plus 4 to 6 fillets for garnish (optional)
1 teaspoon Dijon mustard

1 tablespoon egg substitute (optional)
1¼ teaspoons Worcestershire sauce
3 tablesoons low-fat buttermilk
1 tablespoon fresh lemon juice
1 tablespoon extra-virgin olive oil
Salt and freshly ground black pepper
¼ cup freshly grated Pecorino Romano cheese

1. Wash the lettuce and spin dry. Tear leaves into 2-inch pieces; you should have 6 to 8 cups. Prepare the "croutons."

2. Make the dressing. (For extra points, do this tableside before the admiring gaze of your guests.) Rub a large salad bowl with ½ clove of garlic. Mince the remainder of the garlic and the four anchovy fillets with a knife or cleaver. Place them in the salad bowl and mash to a paste with the back of a mixing spoon.

Whisk in the mustard, egg substitute (if using), Worcestershire sauce, buttermilk, lemon juice, and olive oil. Add salt and pepper to taste; the dressing should be highly seasoned. The dressing can be made up to 4 hours ahead.

3. Just before serving, add the lettuce, cheese, and croutons. Gently toss the salad to mix. Mound the Caesar on salad plates, crowning each with an optional anchovy fillet.   *Serves 6*

172 CALORIES PER SERVING; 7 G PROTEIN; 9 G FAT; 2 G SATURATED FAT;
17 G CARBOHYDRATE; 367 MG SODIUM; 9 MG CHOLESTEROL

GARLIC PARMESAN CHILI "CROUTONS"

I first created these garlicky, cheesy, chili-charged "croutons" to go with the Mexican-style Caesar salad on page 47.
People liked them so much that I started serving them with other salads, soups, and even as a finger food.
You can use either corn or flour tortillas; in my house, we prefer the latter.

PREPARATION TIME: 5 MINUTES   COOKING TIME: 8 TO 12 MINUTES

1 clove garlic, minced
1 tablespoon extra-virgin olive oil, melted lard, or
   melted butter
4 (8-inch) flour tortillas

1 tablespoon pure chili powder
Salt and freshly ground black pepper
3 tablespoons freshly grated Parmesan cheese

1. Preheat the oven to 350°F.

2. Stir the garlic into the olive oil. Using a pastry brush, paint the top of each tortilla with garlic oil. Sprinkle the tortillas with chili powder, salt, pepper, and Parmesan cheese. Cut each tortilla into eight wedges or other shapes, using a large knife.

3. Arrange the "croutons" on a baking sheet in a single layer. Bake until they are lightly browned, 8 to 12 minutes. Remove from the oven and let cool on the baking sheet; the croutons will crisp as they cool.

Makes 32 croutons, enough to serve 4 to 6

172 CALORIES PER SERVING (BASED ON 4 SERVINGS); 5 G PROTEIN; 8 G FAT; 2 G SATURATED FAT;
21 G CARBOHYDRATE; 274 MG SODIUM; 4 MG CHOLESTEROL

Jícama, Mango, and Watercress Salad with Pumpkin Seed–Orange Vinaigrette

This salad is simplicity itself (it takes about 10 minutes to prepare), but the contrast of colors (white, orange, and green), textures (crisp and juicy), and flavors (sweet, sour, fruity, nutty, and peppery) will take your breath away. And talk about refreshing! When choosing mangoes, let a squeezable softness and intense fruity smell be your guide: Some varieties remain green even when ripe.

PREPARATION TIME: 10 MINUTES   COOKING TIME: 3 MINUTES

FOR THE VINAIGRETTE:
1 tablespoon pumpkin seeds
½ teaspoon salt
½ teaspoon freshly ground black pepper
2 tablespoons fresh orange juice
2 tablespoons fresh lime juice
1 tablespoon olive oil

FOR THE SALAD:
1 (8- to 10-ounce) piece jícama, peeled
1 ripe mango, peeled and seeded
2 bunches watercress, washed, trimmed, and dried

1. To prepare the vinaigrette, lightly toast the pumpkin seeds in a comal or dry skillet over medium heat until they are fragrant and just beginning to brown, 2 to 3 minutes. Transfer the pumpkin seeds to a mixing bowl and set aside. Just before serving, add the salt, pepper, orange juice, and lime juice and whisk until the salt crystals dissolve. Whisk in the oil. Correct the seasoning, adding salt and pepper to taste.

2. To assemble the salad, cut the jícama and mango into matchstick slivers. To serve, mound the watercress on four salad plates and sprinkle the jícama and mango slivers on top. Whisk the vinaigrette again and spoon it over the salads. Serve at once.

Serves 4

103 CALORIES PER SERVING; 2 G PROTEIN; 4 G FAT; 1 G SATURATED FAT;
17 G CARBOHYDRATE; 275 MG SODIUM; 0 MG CHOLESTEROL

MEXICAN "SLAW"

Thinly sliced white cabbage accompanies countless Mexican dishes, from flautas (page 65) to tacos and taquitos. Its refreshing crispness and audible crunch make a pleasing counterpoint to stews and soft, moist tortilla dishes. From shredded cabbage, it's a short jump to slaw. This recipe owes its bite to that tangy Mexican triumvirate of flavors: lime juice, cilantro, and chilies.

PREPARATION TIME: 10 MINUTES

FOR THE DRESSING:
1 small clove garlic, minced
1 tablespoon sugar, or to taste
½ teaspoon salt, or to taste
½ teaspoon freshly ground black pepper
½ teaspoon toasted cumin seeds (optional)
⅓ cup fresh lime juice

FOR THE "SLAW":
3 cups white cabbage, finely shredded (about 5 ounces)
1 carrot, shredded
4 to 5 ounces jícama, shredded
1 tomato, seeded and cut into ¼-inch dice
1 or 2 jalapeño chilies, minced (for a milder slaw, seed the chilies)
⅓ cup coarsely chopped cilantro

1. In the bottom of a serving bowl, combine the garlic, sugar, salt, pepper, and cumin (if using) and mash to a paste with a wooden spoon. Stir in the lime juice.

2. Add the cabbage, carrot, jícama, tomato, jalapeños, and cilantro and toss to mix. Correct the seasoning, adding sugar or lime juice. The slaw should be a little sweet and a little sour.

Note: The sugar makes a U.S.-style slaw. To be more Mexican, you could certainly omit it.

Serves 4 to 6

56 CALORIES PER SERVING (BASED ON 4 SERVINGS); 2 G PROTEIN; 0 G FAT; 0 G SATURATED FAT; 13 G CARBOHYDRATE; 46 MG SODIUM; 0 MG CHOLESTEROL

ROASTED CHILI SALAD WITH PUMPKIN-SEED VINAIGRETTE (ENSALADA DE RAJAS CON SALSA DE PEPITAS)

It's hard to imagine Mexican cuisine without rajas, those smoky, spicy, electrifyingly flavorful strips of roasted poblano chilies. This salad features a colorful assortment of roasted peppers, topped with a nutty pumpkin-seed vinaigrette.

PREPARATION TIME: 10 MINUTES   COOKING TIME: 10 MINUTES

8 poblano chilies
2 yellow bell peppers
2 red bell peppers

FOR THE VINAIGRETTE:
2 tablespoons coarsely chopped pumpkin seeds
2 tablespoons fresh lime juice

½ teaspoon salt
½ teaspoon freshly ground black pepper
¼ teaspoon minced garlic
1½ tablespoons olive oil

1. Roast the chilies and peppers over a high flame, on a barbecue grill, or under the broiler (see page 177), until the skins are charred all over, 8 to 10 minutes. Place the chilies and peppers in a paper bag and seal the top, or put them in a bowl and cover with plastic wrap. Let cool for 15 minutes.

2. Scrape the burnt skin from the chilies and peppers, using a paring knife. Seed and devein the chilies and peppers, cutting each lengthwise into ¼-inch-wide strips. Work on a grooved cutting board to collect any pepper juices. Reserve these juices for the dressing.

3. Arrange the chili and pepper strips in a starburst pattern on round plates, alternating colors. The strips should radiate from the center of the plates like the spokes of a wheel.

4. To prepare the vinaigrette, roast the pumpkin seeds in a skillet over medium heat until they are lightly toasted and fragrant, about 2 minutes. Set aside. Combine the lime juice, salt, pepper, and garlic in a mixing bowl and whisk until the salt is dissolved. Whisk in the olive oil and pepper juices. Spoon this mixture over the salad and sprinkle with the pumpkin seeds. Serve at once. *Serves 4 to 6*

108 CALORIES PER SERVING (BASED ON 4 SERVINGS); 4 G PROTEIN; 7 G FAT; 1 G SATURATED FAT;
12 G CARBOHYDRATE; 272 MG SODIUM; 0 MG CHOLESTEROL

Egg Dishes and Crêpes

Huevos Motuleños
(eggs with salsa, ham, and tortillas)

I first tasted this rich, flavorful dish at a breakfast buffet in Mérida. Scarcely a day went by when I wasn't served some version of eggs in the style of the Yucatán town of Motul. This dish has something for everyone: smoky ham, habanero-heated salsa, fresh peas for a flash of green, and refried beans to keep up your strength. To decrease the amount of fat in the traditional recipe, I bake the tortillas instead of deep-frying them, use lean Canadian bacon instead of ham, and use scrambled egg substitute instead of fried eggs. There's still so much flavor that you won't miss the fat.

PREPARATION TIME: 15 MINUTES   COOKING TIME: 30 MINUTES

FOR THE SALSA:
3 medium ripe red tomatoes
½ medium white onion, cut in half
3 cloves garlic
1 habanero chili, cut in half and seeded (for an
   incandescent salsa, leave in the seeds)
½ teaspoon dried oregano
½ teaspoon ground cinnamon
Salt and freshly ground black pepper
4 corn tortillas
1 cup refried beans (page 138) or use a good brand
   of fat-free canned refried beans

FOR THE EGGS:
1 tablespoon lard or olive oil
½ medium white onion, thinly sliced
1 clove garlic, thinly sliced
1½ cups egg substitute (or 12 egg whites)
2 ounces Canadian bacon or country-style ham,
   cut into ¼-inch dice
½ cup cooked green peas
1 tablespoon crumbled queso fresco or feta cheese

1. To prepare the salsa, heat a comal or frying pan over a medium-high flame. Roast the tomatoes, onion, garlic, and habanero until lightly browned: 8 to 10 minutes for the tomatoes and onion; 4 to 5 minutes for the garlic and chili. Transfer the roasted vegetables to a food processor and grind to a coarse purée.

2. Transfer the purée to a saucepan. Add the oregano, cinnamon, salt, and pepper and simmer for

5 minutes, stirring with a wooden spoon. Correct the seasoning, adding salt and pepper to taste.

3. Preheat the oven to 400°F. Bake the tortillas until they are golden brown, about 5 minutes. Transfer the tortillas to plates or a platter; they'll crisp as they cool. Warm the refried beans in a saucepan.

4. Heat the lard or oil in a nonstick frying pan. Lightly brown the sliced onion and garlic over medium heat, 3 to 5 minutes. Add the egg substitute

Huevos Motuleños

53

and cook until scrambled, 2 minutes, stirring with a wooden spoon. Add salt and pepper to taste.

5. Warm the Canadian bacon and peas in a non-stick saucepan over medium heat.

6. To assemble the huevos motuleños, spread the refried beans on each of the tortillas. Mound the scrambled eggs on top. Spoon the salsa over the eggs and sprinkle with the bacon, peas, and queso fresco. Serve at once.

Serves 4

267 CALORIES PER SERVING; 21 G PROTEIN; 6 G FAT; 2 G SATURATED FAT;
33 G CARBOHYDRATE; 615 MG SODIUM; 13 MG CHOLESTEROL

HUEVOS RANCHEROS
(COUNTRY-STYLE EGGS)

Huevos rancheros are the quintessential Mexican breakfast. Talk about tasty—tortillas fried in lard or chorizo fat, topped with eggs (also fried in lard or chorizo fat), and slathered with zesty salsa ranchera. And talk about a good way to use up your weekly allotment of fat grams in a single sitting! To make healthier huevos rancheros, I've taken to "bake-frying" the tortillas and poaching the eggs instead of frying them. To make up for some of the lost richness, I spread the tortillas with refried beans.

PREPARATION TIME: 10 MINUTES, PLUS THE TIME IT TAKES TO MAKE THE REFRIED BEANS AND THE SALSA
COOKING TIME: 5 MINUTES

4 corn tortillas
1 tablespoon melted lard or olive oil (optional)
1 cup refried beans (page 138, or use a good no-fat
  commercial brand)
1 batch Salsa Ranchera (page 22)

2 quarts water
1 tablespoon distilled white vinegar
4 very fresh eggs
¼ cup coarsely chopped fresh cilantro

1. Preheat the oven to 350°F. Brush the tortillas with lard (if using) and arrange in a single layer on a baking sheet. Bake until they are lightly browned, 10 to 15 minutes. The tortillas will crisp as they cool.

2. Heat the refried beans and Salsa Ranchera.

3. Just before serving, bring the 2 quarts of water and the vinegar to a boil in a deep saucepan. Crack the eggs into the water and poach them until cooked to taste, about 2 minutes for whites that are set and yolks that are somewhat runny. (Try to crack the eggs into the most agitated spots in the water—the swirling bubbles help envelop the yolks in the whites.) With a slotted spoon, transfer the poached eggs to a plate lined with paper towels.

4. To assemble the huevos rancheros, arrange a crisp tortilla on each plate and spread it with ¼ cup of the refried beans. Set a poached egg on top and spoon the ranchera sauce over it and the tortilla. Sprinkle with cilantro and serve at once.   *Serves 4*

251 CALORIES PER SERVING; 12 G PROTEIN; 9 G FAT; 3 G SATURATED FAT;

32 G CARBOHYDRATE; 298 MG SODIUM; 216 MG CHOLESTEROL

MEXICAN EGG SCRAMBLE
(HUEVOS REVUELTOS A LA MEXICANA)

Mexicans aren't bashful when it comes to big-flavored breakfasts. This gutsy scramble—redolent with cilantro, garlic, and serrano chilies—will get your day off to a rousing start. To cut the fat in the traditional recipe, I call for egg substitute or a mixture of whole eggs and egg whites. Chorizo is a spicy Mexican sausage: If your fat budget allows, the little called for below adds a world of flavor. (I've made it optional.) But even without it, the eggs will be delectable.

PREPARATION TIME: 10 MINUTES   COOKING TIME: 10 MINUTES

4 corn tortillas
1 tablespoon lard or olive oil
2 tablespoons finely chopped chorizo sausage
   (optional)
½ medium white onion, finely diced
2 cloves garlic, thinly sliced
2 to 6 serrano or jalapeño chilies, finely chopped
   (for milder eggs, seed the chilies)

½ teaspoon ground cumin
2 ripe red tomatoes (10 to 12 ounces), seeded and
   finely diced
½ cup coarsely chopped cilantro
4 whole eggs plus 8 whites, or 2 cups egg
   substitute, or 16 egg whites, beaten lightly with
   a fork
Salt and freshly ground black pepper

1. Preheat the oven to 350°F. Cut each tortilla into six long strips. Arrange the strips on a baking sheet and bake until they are lightly browned and crisp, about 10 minutes. Transfer to a rack and let cool.

2. Heat the lard in a nonstick skillet over medium heat. Cook the chorizo (if using), onion, and garlic until lightly browned, about 3 minutes. Increase the heat to high and stir in the chilies, cumin, and tomatoes. Cook to evaporate the tomato juices, about 3 minutes. Stir in the cilantro and eggs and whites (or egg substitute or egg whites) and cook until scrambled, about 2 minutes, stirring with a wooden spoon. Add salt and pepper to taste.

3. To serve, spoon the eggs onto plates or a platter. Stand a few toasted tortilla strips upright in each portion. Serve at once.

Note: The more whole eggs you use, the creamier your scramble will be. When I make this dish, I like to use 4 whole eggs and 8 egg whites. You can cut the fat considerably by using egg substitute or egg whites.

Serves 4

215 CALORIES PER SERVING; 16 G PROTEIN; 9 G FAT; 3 G SATURATED FAT;
17 G CARBOHYDRATE; 182 MG SODIUM; 216 MG CHOLESTEROL

TEX-MEX TORTILLA EGG SCRAMBLE WITH CHILE VERDE AND SALSA VERDE (MIGAS)

Migas are Tex-Mex comfort food, a rib-sticking scramble of eggs and fried tortillas slathered with salsa verde or salsa ranchera. This may not sound like the best way to get your day off to a healthy start, but by bake-frying the tortillas and replacing the eggs with egg whites or egg substitute, you can make a great-tasting Tex-Mex breakfast that won't send you into coronary arrest.

PREPARATION TIME: 10 MINUTES, PLUS THE TIME IT TAKES TO MAKE THE SALSA VERDE
COOKING TIME: 15 MINUTES

8 corn tortillas
1 tablespoon lard or canola oil
1 medium white onion, thinly sliced
4 cloves garlic, thinly sliced
1 (4½-ounce) can chiles verdes (or 2 Anaheim or 1 large poblano chili, roasted, peeled, and diced)
2 cups egg substitute or 4 whole eggs and 8 whites

½ cup chopped cilantro, plus 4 sprigs for garnish
Salt and freshly ground black pepper
2 cups Salsa Verde (page 25)
½ cup no-fat sour cream
2 tablespoons crumbled queso fresco, sharp white cheddar, or feta cheese

1. Preheat the oven to 400°F. Arrange the tortillas on a baking sheet and bake until they are lightly browned, 5 to 8 minutes. Remove the tortillas from the oven; they'll crisp as they cool.

2. Heat the lard or oil in a nonstick frying pan. Lightly brown the onion over medium heat, 5 minutes, stirring often, adding the garlic and chiles verdes after 3 minutes

3. Beat the egg substitute (or whole eggs and whites), cilantro, and salt and pepper in a mixing bowl. Break the tortillas into 1-inch pieces and stir them into the egg mixture. Let soften for 5 minutes.

4. Add the egg mixture to the frying pan and cook until scrambled, 2 to 4 minutes, stirring with a wooden spoon. Correct the seasoning, adding salt and pepper to taste.

5. Transfer the migas to plates and carpet each with the salsa verde. Place a dollop of sour cream on top, sprinkle with cheese, and serve at once.

Serves 4

305 CALORIES PER SERVING; 22 G PROTEIN; 7 G FAT; 2 G SATURATED FAT;
39 G CARBOHYDRATE; 406 MG SODIUM; 10 MG CHOLESTEROL

LOW-FAT CRÊPES

You certainly know that Mexicans love wrapped foods (think tacos and burritos). What you may not be aware of is their unbridled enthusiasm for crêpes. These paper-thin pancakes are used as a wrapping for everything from shrimp (page 59) to cajeta (Mexican caramel; page 156). My low-fat crêpes contain one ingredient that's not traditionally Mexican, however: buttermilk. The thick, creamy consistency of this low-fat dairy product allows you to eliminate the butter and most of the egg yolks that are in the traditional recipe for crêpes.

PREPARATION TIME: 5 MINUTES   COOKING TIME: 20 MINUTES

1 egg
2 egg whites
½ cup low-fat buttermilk
¾ cup water
½ teaspoon sugar
½ teaspoon salt, or to taste

1 teaspoon canola oil
1 cup unbleached all-purpose flour
Spray oil
1 or more crêpe or omelet pans (approximately 7 inches in diameter)

1. Combine the whole egg and the whites in a bowl and whisk to mix. Whisk in the buttermilk, water, sugar, salt, and oil. Sift in the flour and gently whisk just to mix. (Do not overwhisk, or the crêpes will be rubbery.) If the batter looks lumpy, strain it into another bowl. It should be the consistency of heavy cream. If it's too thick, thin it with a little more water.

2. Lightly spray the crêpe pan(s) with oil and heat over a medium flame. (When the pan is the proper temperature, a drop of water will evaporate in 2 or 3 seconds.) Off the heat, add 3 tablespoons of the crêpe batter to the pan in one fell swoop. Gently tilt and rotate the pan to coat the bottom with a thin layer of batter. (Pour back any excess—the crêpe should be as thin as possible.)

3. Cook the crêpe until it is lightly browned on both sides, 30 to 60 seconds per side, turning with a spatula. As the crêpes are done, stack them on a plate. For the best results, spray the pans with oil between pouring batter.

Note: Don't worry if your first crêpe looks weird: That's usually the case. The crêpes will look better the more you make.

Makes 12 to 14 (7-inch) crêpes

40 CALORIES PER CRÊPE; 2 G PROTEIN; 1 G FAT; 0 G SATURATED FAT;
7 G CARBOHYDRATE; 78 MG SODIUM; 14 MG CHOLESTEROL

SHRIMP CRÊPES WITH ANCHO CHILI SAUCE

Tortillas aren't the only flatcakes used as a wrap in Mexican cooking. Crêpes may have entered the Mexican repertoire in the 1860s, when Mexico was virtually ruled by France. But there's nothing French about the following filling, which is built on toasted ancho and guajillo chilies, roasted tomatoes and onions, Mexican herbs, and shrimp stock. Shrimp crêpes make a surprisingly elegant entrée: Given their rich flavor, you'd never guess how low they are in fat.

PREPARATION TIME: 20 MINUTES (PLUS THE TIME IT TAKES TO MAKE THE CRÊPES)
COOKING TIME: 30 MINUTES, PLUS TIME FOR SOAKING THE CHILIES

1 pound medium shrimp in their shells
3 cups fish stock or bottled clam broth

FOR THE SAUCE:
4 ancho chilies
4 guajillo or dried New Mexican red chilies
1 ripe tomato
1 small onion, quartered
2 cloves garlic

4 sprigs cilantro
½ teaspoon oregano (preferably Mexican)
Salt and freshly ground black pepper
12 crêpes (page 58)
Spray oil
¼ cup grated jack or white cheddar cheese (optional)
¾ cup fat-free sour cream

1. Peel and devein the shrimp, reserving the shells. Combine the shrimp shells and fish stock in a saucepan and simmer gently until the shrimp shells turn orange, 8 to 10 minutes.

2. Heat a comal or cast-iron skillet over medium heat. Toast the chilies until they are fragrant but not burned, 20 seconds per side. Transfer to a plate to cool. Roast the tomato, onion quarters, and garlic in the hot comal until nicely browned on all sides: 8 to 10 minutes for the tomato and onion; 4 to 6 minutes for the garlic. Transfer to a plate to cool. Place the chilies in a bowl and strain the hot shrimp stock over them. Let soak until the chilies are soft and pliable, about 20 minutes.

3. With a slotted spoon, remove the chilies from the shrimp stock. Tear open the chilies and remove the veins and seeds. Combine the chilies, roasted tomato, onion, garlic, cilantro, oregano, and shrimp stock in a blender and purée until smooth. Add salt and pepper to taste; the sauce should be highly seasoned.

4. Transfer the sauce to a saucepan and cook over medium heat until it is thick and richly flavored, 6 to 8 minutes. (If the sauce becomes too thick, add a little more stock.) Stir in the shrimp and simmer until cooked, 2 to 3 minutes.

5. Preheat the oven to 400°F.

6. Assemble the crêpes. Place a crêpe, darker side down, on a plate. Place a large spoonful of shrimp and sauce along the bottom and roll the crêpe into a tube. Assemble all the crêpes in this fashion. Arrange the crêpes in an attractive baking dish you've lightly sprayed with oil. Spoon any excess sauce over the crêpes. Lightly sprinkle the crêpes with the grated cheese (if using) and place a spoonful of sour cream in the center of each. (Alternatively, whisk the sour cream in a bowl until smooth, transfer it to a squirt bottle, and squirt decorative squiggles of cream over the crêpes.)

7. Bake the crêpes until they are browned and bubbling, 10 to 15 minutes. Serve at once.

Serves 4

314 CALORIES PER SERVING; 33 G PROTEIN; 5 G FAT; 1 G SATURATED FAT;
35 G CARBOHYDRATE; 448 MG SODIUM; 213 MG CHOLESTEROL

TORTILLA DISHES

HOMEMADE CORN TORTILLAS

What would Mexican cuisine be without tortillas? These soft, ground-corn flatbreads have been the staff of life in Mexico virtually since the domestication of corn some 9,000 years ago. A meal simply isn't a meal in Mexico without fresh tortillas, and small indeed is the town that doesn't have a tortilla bakery, with its rickety chain-link conveyor belt carrying freshly pressed tortillas to be cooked over open flames. In villages women pat tortillas by hand; fancy restaurants employ special cooks who make tortillas to order. The good news is that if you have a tortilla press (available in Mexican grocery stores and cookware shops, or see Mail-Order Sources), fresh tortillas are a snap to make at home. You'll need to know about one special ingredient, masa harina (ground, hulled parched corn), which is available at most supermarkets. Don't be discouraged if your first few tortillas don't come out perfect: With a little practice, you'll be turning them out like a pro.

PREPARATION TIME: 10 MINUTES   COOKING TIME: 10 MINUTES

2 cups masa harina

1¼ cups hot water, or as needed

1. In a mixing bowl, combine the masa harina and water. Mix and knead with your fingers to obtain a smooth, pliable dough, about 3 minutes. (The consistency of the dough should be like that of soft ice cream. Add a spoonful or two of water if needed.) Cover the dough with plastic wrap and let it rest at room temperature for 20 minutes.

2. Heat a comal, griddle, or cast-iron frying pan over medium-high heat. To test the temperature, spatter a drop of water on the pan: It should evaporate in a few seconds. Pinch off a walnut-size piece of dough and roll it between the palms of your hands into a ball. Sandwich this ball between two sheets of plastic (a torn-open zip-top bag works well for this) and place it in the tortilla press. Close the press to flatten the dough into a 5-inch tortilla.

3. Peel off the top layer of plastic, then the bottom layer, and place the tortilla in the hot pan. Cook for about 1 minute per side, or until the top of the tortilla puffs and the bottom begins to brown. Transfer the tortilla to a basket lined with a cloth napkin. As you make and cook the tortillas, transfer them to the basket and keep them covered. The cloth keeps in the steam, so the tortillas remain soft and tender.

Makes 14 to 16 (5-inch) tortillas

52 CALORIES PER TORTILLA; 1 G PROTEIN; 1 G FAT; 0 G SATURATED FAT;
11 G CARBOHYDRATE; 1 MG SODIUM; 0 MG CHOLESTEROL

Mexican Chicken Salad Tostadas (page 62)

MEXICAN CHICKEN SALAD TOSTADAS

A good tostada combines the crispness of a cracker and the refreshing crunch of salad with the mouth-filling satisfaction of a sandwich. You might think that a dish whose main components are a deep-fried tortilla, refried beans, and a pile of grated cheese would be off-limits to a heart-healthy diet. But by bake-frying the tortilla and using a little strong-flavored cheese as an accent instead of a main ingredient, you wind up with a popular Mexican snack that's as good for you as it tastes good to eat.

PREPARATION TIME: 10 MINUTES, PLUS THE TIME IT TAKES TO MAKE THE CHICKEN AND REFRIED BEANS
COOKING TIME: 15 MINUTES

8 corn tortillas
1 tablespoon melted lard or olive oil

FOR THE DRESSING:
¾ cup no-fat sour cream
2 tablespoons fresh lime juice
¼ teaspoon ground cumin
2 tablespoons chicken or vegetable broth
Salt and freshly ground black pepper

1½ cups refried beans (page 138, or use a good fat-free canned brand)
1½ cups shredded cooked chicken (page 181)
2 cups shredded lettuce
⅓ medium onion, diced (about 5 tablespoons)
½ avocado, peeled and diced
8 (¼-inch-thick) slices ripe red tomato
¼ cup crumbled queso fresco, queso añejo, or feta cheese (or ¼ cup grated Romano cheese)

1. Preheat the oven to 350°F. Brush the tortillas on both sides with the lard or olive oil. Arrange them in a single layer on a baking sheet and bake until they're lightly browned, 10 to 15 minutes. Transfer the tortillas to a cake rack; they'll crisp as they cool.

2. Meanwhile, make the dressing. Combine the sour cream, lime juice, and cumin in a mixing bowl and whisk until smooth. Whisk in enough chicken broth to make a pourable dressing, then add salt and pepper to taste. Warm the refried beans in a saucepan.

3. Just before serving, spread 3 tablespoons of the refried beans on each tortilla. Top with the shredded chicken, shredded lettuce, onion, and avocado. Drizzle the dressing on top. Place a tomato flat on top of each tostada and sprinkle it with the crumbled cheese.

*Makes 8 tostadas, enough to
serve 8 as an appetizer, 4 as a light entrée*

214 CALORIES PER TOSTADA; 16 G PROTEIN; 7 G FAT; 1 G SATURATED FAT;
21 G CARBOHYDRATE; 251 MG SODIUM; 36 MG CHOLESTEROL

SHRIMP PANUCHOS

I like to think of this snack as a Yucatán Dagwood sandwich. Local legend credits its invention to one Señor Ucho, who ran a bar in Merida. One day, pressed by hungry customers but short on food, he piled leftover refries, turkey, and lettuce onto a puffed, fried tortilla. Today, Ucho's bread (for this is what panucho means) is a beloved Yucatán snack. In the following recipe I give the panuchos a maritime twist, topping them with marinated grilled shrimp or shark. In Mexico, the tortillas for panuchos are often cooked on a griddle and patted with a damp cloth to make them steam and puff before deep-frying. I opt here for bake-frying the tortillas to make them crisp, like tostadas.

PREPARATION TIME: 10 MINUTES, PLUS 30 MINUTES FOR MARINATING THE SHRIMP
COOKING TIME: 15 MINUTES

1 pound shrimp, peeled and deveined, or 1 pound
   shark steaks
1 habanero chili
2 tablespoons fresh lime juice
2 tablespoons chopped white onion
2 tablespoons chopped fresh cilantro
1 clove garlic, minced
½ teaspoon annatto seeds
Salt and freshly ground black pepper

8 corn tortillas
½ cup warm refried black beans
1 cup shredded lettuce
1 large ripe tomato, seeded and diced
2 to 3 tablespoons sliced pickled jalapeño peppers
1 cup Cooked Tomato Salsa (page 23; optional)
3 tablespoons crumbled queso fresco or Romano
   cheese

1. Place the shrimp or shark in a glass bowl. Make a slit in the side of the habanero, but otherwise leave the chili whole. Add the chili, lime juice, onion, cilantro, garlic, annatto, salt, and pepper to the shrimp. Toss to mix. Marinate for 30 minutes. Preheat the grill to high.

2. Thread the shrimp onto skewers and grill until cooked, 2 to 3 minutes per side. Remove from the skewers and let cool. (If you are using shark, grill until cooked, 3 to 4 minutes per side.) When cool, cut into bite-size pieces. Preheat the oven to 400°F.

3. Arrange the tortillas in a single layer on baking sheets. Bake until they are lightly browned, 6 to 8 minutes. Transfer the tortillas to a rack to cool; they'll crisp as they cool.

4. To assemble the panuchos, spread each tortilla with a little of the refried black beans. Top with the shrimp, tomato, pickled jalapeños, the optional salsa, and the cheese. Serve at once. *Serves 4*

316 CALORIES PER SERVING; 31 G PROTEIN; 7 G FAT; 1 G SATURATED FAT;
31 G CARBOHYDRATE; 321 MG SODIUM; 184 MG CHOLESTEROL

OAXACAN "PIZZAS"
(CLAYUDAS)

Clayudas are the Oaxacan version of tostadas—flour tortillas brushed with pork fat, crisped on a comal, and topped with beans, lettuce, tomatoes, onion, avocado, and queso fresco. The overall effect is rather like that of a pizza. To decrease the amount of fat, I've cut back on the lard, and I bake the tortillas instead of pan-frying them. (If you hate lard, you can use olive oil.) I've also increased the proportion of vegetables. Clayudas make a great snack, not to mention an unexpected hors d'oeuvre.

PREPARATION TIME: 15 MINUTES   COOKING TIME: 10 MINUTES

4 (8-inch) fat-free flour tortillas
1 tablespoon lard or olive oil
¾ cup refried beans or drained cooked pinto beans
1½ cups shredded lettuce
1 large ripe red tomato, seeded and diced

½ avocado, diced and tossed with 1 teaspoon fresh lime juice
¼ cup diced white or red onion
¼ cup crumbled queso fresco or rinsed and drained feta cheese

1. Preheat the oven to 350°F. Brush the tops of the tortillas with lard and arrange on a baking sheet. Bake them until they are just beginning to brown, 8 to 10 minutes. Let the tortillas cool on the baking sheet for 2 minutes, then arrange them on plates.

2. Spread the refried beans on top of the tortillas. Arrange the lettuce, tomato, avocado, and onion on top. Sprinkle the clayudas with queso fresco and serve at once.   *Serves 4*

236 CALORIES PER SERVING; 9 G PROTEIN; 12 G FAT; 2 G SATURATED FAT;
27 G CARBOHYDRATE; 396 MG SODIUM; 18 MG CHOLESTEROL

FLAUTAS
(TORTILLA "FLUTES")
WITH FRUIT AND NUT PICADILLO

Flautas (flutes) are one of the hundreds of variations on a theme of crisply fried tortillas garnished with vegetables, meat, and salsa. Tradition calls for the tortilla tubes to be deep-fried. To make a low-fat version, I brush the tortillas with lard (or olive oil) and bake them crisp in the oven: You get the same shattering crispness with just a fraction of the fat. The fillings for flautas are really limited to your imagination. I call for a fruit and nut picadillo here, but you could also use shredded chicken, shrimp, or tinga (page 126). Note: If you have Italian cannoli tubes, lightly spray them with oil and tie the tortillas around them. Bake until lightly browned, then gently twist the tortillas to unmold. Cannoli molds will give you perfectly tubular flautas.

PREPARATION TIME: 15 MINUTES, PLUS THE TIME IT TAKES TO MAKE THE PICADILLO AND SALSA
COOKING TIME: 15 MINUTES

12 corn tortillas
1½ tablespoons melted lard or olive oil
1 batch of Fruit and Nut Picadillo (page 144),
    warmed in a small saucepan
6 cups shredded lettuce (romaine or Boston)

3 cups Cooked Tomato Salsa (page 23) or salsa
    verde (page 25)
1 cup no-fat sour cream
1 tomato, seeded and diced
Sliced radishes, for garnish

1. Preheat the oven to 350°F. Bake the tortillas, a few at a time, until they are soft and pliable, 2 to 4 minutes. Roll up each tortilla into a cigarlike tube and tie with a piece of string.

2. Brush the tortilla tubes with lard and arrange them on a baking sheet. Bake the "flutes" until just beginning to brown, 15 to 20 minutes. Remove from the oven; the flutes will crisp as they cool.

3. Just before serving, with a small spoon stuff the picadillo into the tortilla tubes. Spread half the lettuce on a platter and arrange the flutes on top. Place the remaining lettuce atop the flutes and ladle the salsa on top. Garnish with dollops of sour cream, diced tomatoes, and the sliced radishes.

Note: To make vegetarian flautas, substitute an additional 1 cup of refried beans for the picadillo.

*Makes 12 flautas, enough to serve 6
as an appetizer, 4 as a light main course*

306 CALORIES PER SERVING (BASED ON 6 SERVINGS); 18 G PROTEIN; 9 G FAT; 2 G SATURATED FAT;
45 G CARBOHYDRATE; 68 MG SODIUM; 22 MG CHOLESTEROL

BARBARA'S MUSHROOM AND BLACK BEAN TACOS

These tacos have been a favorite in our family for decades. As my wife, Barbara, and stepdaughter, Betsy, became vegetarian, we switched from making them with chicken to using mushrooms. In the old days, we bought commercial, American-style taco shells (which are loaded with fat); we now bake our own shells in the oven. (In so doing, we drastically slash the number of fat grams.) To do this, you'll need a metal taco rack (available in cookware shops), or a French bread mold. Mushroom and black bean tacos make a great vegetarian party dish.

PREPARATION TIME: 15 MINUTES   COOKING TIME: 30 MINUTES

12 corn tortillas

FOR THE FILLING:
1 tablespoon olive oil
1 onion, finely chopped
1 clove garlic, finely chopped
1 pound button or shiitake mushrooms, trimmed
½ teaspoon ground cumin
½ teaspoon dried oregano
1 cup cooked black beans
½ cup roasted tomato salsa (or your favorite salsa)
3 tablespoons chopped fresh cilantro
Salt and freshly ground black pepper

TO FINISH THE TACOS,
use any or all of the following:
2 ounces sharp cheddar cheese, coarsely grated
1½ cups roasted tomato salsa (or your favorite salsa)
1 large ripe tomato, finely chopped
3 scallions, finely chopped
½ medium white onion, finely chopped
¼ head iceberg lettuce or green cabbage, thinly shredded
½ cup no-fat sour cream
¼ cup sliced pickled jalapeño peppers

1. To make the taco shells, preheat the oven to 350°F. Warm the tortillas on a baking sheet until soft and pliable, 2 to 3 minutes. Fold the tortillas in half to make U-shaped shells (U-shaped when viewed from the end) and place them in a taco rack or French bread mold, open side up. Bake until they're lightly browned and crisp, about 10 minutes. Let the shells cool to room temperature.

2. To prepare the filling, heat the olive oil in a nonstick frying pan over medium heat. Brown the onions and garlic, starting over medium heat, then reducing the heat to low, 8 to 10 minutes in all, stirring often. (The idea is to caramelize the onions without burning them.)

3. Wipe the mushrooms clean with a damp paper towel and finely dice. Return the heat to medium and add the mushrooms, cumin, and oregano. Cook the mushrooms until they are nicely browned and most

of the liquid has evaporated, 5 to 8 minutes. Stir in the black beans, salsa, and cilantro and boil for 2 minutes. Add salt and pepper to taste; the mixture should be highly seasoned. The recipe can be prepared up to 48 hours ahead to this stage. Store the taco shells in an airtight container at room temperature; refrigerate the filling.

4. To finish the tacos, preheat the oven to 400°F. Spoon the filling into the taco shells. Sprinkle the cheese on top of the filling. Bake the tacos until they are heated through and the cheese is melted, 5 to 8 minutes. Transfer to a platter. Arrange the remaining salsa, chopped tomato, scallions, onion, lettuce, sour cream, and pickled jalapeños in attractive bowls. Serve the tacos, letting each diner spoon on salsa, tomato, scallions, onion, lettuce, sour cream, and jalapeños to taste.

Makes 12 tacos, enough to serve 4 to 6

433 CALORIES PER SERVING (BASED ON 4 SERVINGS); 17 G PROTEIN; 11 G FAT; 4 G SATURATED FAT;
72 G CARBOHYDRATE; 503 MG SODIUM; 15 MG CHOLESTEROL

SOUTH-OF-THE-BORDER "LASAGNA" (BUDÍN AZTECA)

This recipe is Mexican comfort food at its best. I like to think of budín azteca (Aztec "pudding") as south-of-the-border lasagne. Tortillas stand in for the noodles and salsa verde for the tomato sauce. This version, lavished with shredded chicken and sour cream, tastes so rich and filling that you'd never dream it's low in fat. The recipe is really quite easy: Once you have the chicken and salsa verde, the budín takes only 10 minutes to assemble.

PREPARATION TIME: 20 MINUTES (PLUS THE TIME FOR PREPARING THE SALSA VERDE AND COOKING THE CHICKEN)   COOKING TIME: 30 MINUTES

3 cups salsa verde (page 25)
12 corn tortillas
1 cup hot chicken stock in a frying pan
2 cups cooked shredded chicken (about 12 ounces; see page 181)

2 poblano chilies, charred, peeled, seeded, and cut into strips (see page 177)
1½ cups no-fat sour cream
¾ cup grated sharp white cheddar cheese (about 3 ounces)

1. Preheat the oven to 400°F.

2. Spoon a little salsa verde (3 tablespoons) in the bottom of a 10-inch springform pan. Cut two tortillas in half. Cook them in the chicken stock for a few seconds to soften them, then use them to line the springform pan. (Place the cut edge of each tortilla at the top edge of the pan, bringing the rounded edge to and over the bottom.) Soften a third tortilla and place it on the bottom. The idea is to cover the sides and bottom of the pan.

3. Arrange one third of the chicken and chili strips in the pan and top with one quarter of the remaining salsa verde and sour cream. Sprinkle with 2 tablespoons of the cheese. Soften three more tortillas in the stock and use them to make a second layer.

Top with a second layer of chicken, chilies, salsa verde, sour cream, and a light sprinkling of cheese. Make a third layer of tortillas, followed by a third and final layer of chicken and chilies, using half the remaining salsa verde and sour cream and a sprinkling of cheese. Soften the remaining tortillas and use them to cover the top. Spoon the remaining salsa verde and sour cream on top and sprinkle with the remaining cheese. Breathe a sigh of relief: The hard part is over.

4. Bake the budín until it is lightly browned on top and bubbling and heated in the center, 15 to 25 minutes. Cut into wedges for serving.

Serves 6 as an appetizer, 4 as an entrée

339 CALORIES PER SERVING (BASED ON 6 SERVINGS); 29 G PROTEIN; 8 G FAT; 3 G SATURATED FAT; 39 G CARBOHYDRATE; 360 MG SODIUM; 63 MG CHOLESTEROL

BURRITOS AND ENCHILADAS

AMAZING BLACK BEAN BURRITOS

At first glance, burritos may seem an unlikely candidate for a heart-healthy makeover. After all, what could be worse for you than lard-laden refried beans or ground beef wrapped in flour tortillas and deep-fried? One day I tried brushing the burritos with a little lard (or canola oil) and baking them in the oven. Eureka! The burritos came out moist and creamy inside and crusty and crisp outside, with a tiny fraction of the traditional fat. The purist may want to make refried beans from scratch, following the recipe on page 138. If you're in a hurry, use a good low- or no-fat can of refries.

PREPARATION TIME: 20 MINUTES   COOKING TIME: 15 MINUTES

8 (8-inch) fat-free flour tortillas
2 cups refried beans (page 138)
¼ cup chopped red or white onion
8 sprigs fresh epazote (optional)
1 to 1½ teaspoons melted lard or canola oil

FOR SERVING THE BURRITOS:
½ avocado, diced
1 tablespoon fresh lime juice
1 medium red onion, diced
½ cup chopped fresh cilantro
1 cup nonfat sour cream
1 batch Salsa Mexicana (page 21)

1. Preheat the oven to 400°F. Warm the tortillas in the oven until they are soft and pliable, 2 to 4 minutes. (Alternatively, you can warm the tortillas in a comal.) Spoon ¼ cup of the refried beans in a short cigar shape along the line that would represent the bottom third of the tortilla. Place a little chopped onion and a sprig of epazote on top of the refries. Roll up the tortilla, folding in the sides, as you would an egg roll. Make the remaining burritos the same way.

2. Lightly brush the bottoms and sides of the burritos with lard; brush the tops more heavily. Arrange the burritos, seam side down, in an attractive baking dish. Bake the burritos until they are lightly browned and steaming hot, 10 to 15 minutes.

3. Meanwhile, place the avocado in a serving bowl and toss with the lime juice. Place the onion, cilantro, sour cream, and salsa in serving bowls. Let each diner spoon the garnishes and salsa over his burritos to taste.

Serves 8 as an appetizer, 4 as a light main course

414 CALORIES PER SERVING (BASED ON 4 SERVINGS); 19 G PROTEIN; 8 G FAT; 2 G SATURATED FAT;
75 G CARBOHYDRATE; 682 MG SODIUM; 7 MG CHOLESTEROL

Amazing Black Bean Burritos

ROASTED MUSHROOM BURRITOS

This dish takes its inspiration from a popular Mexican appetizer—mushrooms broiled with cheese.
Roasting intensifies the rich, woodsy flavor of the mushrooms; thus, you don't have to use as much cheese.
I liked the filling so much that I decided to fold it into a flour tortilla, burrito-style.

PREPARATION TIME: 10 MINUTES   COOKING TIME: 30 MINUTES

FOR THE FILLING:
12 ounces cremini or button mushrooms, wiped
    clean, trimmed, and quartered
½ medium onion, peeled and cut into quarters
2 cloves garlic, peeled
2 teaspoons lard or canola oil
Salt and freshly ground black pepper
¼ cup no-fat sour cream
¼ cup grated queso fresco or sharp cheddar cheese

TO FINISH THE BURRITOS:
8 large, low-fat flour tortillas
2 teaspoons lard or canola oil
¾ cup no-fat sour cream
1 tomato, seeded and cut into ¼-inch dice
½ white onion, cut into ¼-inch dice
½ cup chopped fresh cilantro

1. Preheat the oven to 400°F. Place the mushrooms, onion, and garlic in a nonstick roasting pan. Toss with the 2 teaspoons of lard and the salt and pepper. Roast the mushrooms until they're nicely browned, 15 to 20 minutes, stirring once or twice to ensure even cooking.

2. Transfer the mushrooms to a saucepan and stir in the ¼ cup of sour cream. Boil the mixture for 2 minutes, stirring well. Remove the pan from the heat and stir in the cheese. Correct the seasoning, adding salt and pepper to taste.

3. Warm the tortillas on a baking sheet in the oven until they are soft and pliable, about 1 minute. Arrange the tortillas on a work surface and place a mound of mushroom mixture in the center of each.

Roll the tortilla up as you would an eggroll—that is, roll the bottom around the filling, fold over the left and right sides, and continue rolling to obtain a compact cylinder. Make the remaining burritos the same way. Arrange them, seam side down, in a baking dish and brush with the remaining 2 teaspoons of lard or oil.

4. Bake the burritos until they are lightly browned and heated through, 5 to 8 minutes. Meanwhile, place the remaining sour cream and diced tomato in serving bowls. Combine the onion and cilantro in a serving bowl and toss to mix. Serve the burritos with the sour cream, tomatoes, and onion-cilantro mixture for spooning on top.   *Serves 4*

309 CALORIES PER SERVING; 16G PROTEIN; 9 G FAT; 2 G SATURATED FAT;
49 G CARBOHYDRATE; 704 MG SODIUM; 18 MG CHOLESTEROL

EVERYTHING-BUT-THE-KITCHEN-SINK BURRITOS

The burrito may have been born in Mexico, but it reached its apotheosis in San Francisco. As it traveled north, it grew in size and complexity, becoming a full meal wrapped in a flour tortilla. The burritos served at San Francisco burrito parlors were the inspiration for the wrap mania now sweeping the country, and they're a great way to use up leftovers. The following recipe is a rough guideline: Feel free to customize it with whatever filling ingredients you have on hand.

PREPARATION TIME: 10 MINUTES (PLUS THE TIME IT TAKES TO MAKE THE VARIOUS FILLINGS)
COOKING TIME: 5 MINUTES

8 large (14- to 16-inch) fat-free flour tortillas
3 cups cooked rice (use any of the rices on pages 129–132)
1 to 2 cups refried beans (page 138, or use a good fat-free commercial brand)
1 cup shredded cooked chicken or cooked baby shrimp
2 cups shredded lettuce or cabbage

1 tomato, seeded and finely chopped
½ white onion, diced
½ avocado, diced
¼ cup thinly sliced radishes
¼ cup chopped fresh cilantro
½ cup no-fat sour cream
2 cups of your favorite salsa (I like the salsa verde on page 25 or the Salsa Chipotle on page 27)

1. Warm the tortillas on a comal or in a preheated 350-degree oven until they are soft and pliable—1 to 2 minutes per side on the comal or 2 to 4 minutes in the oven. Heat the rice, beans, and chicken.

2. Arrange a tortilla on your work surface. Place a mound of rice in the center. Top it with the beans, chicken, lettuce, tomato, onion, avocado, radishes, cilantro, sour cream, and salsa (save half the salsa for dipping).

3. Roll the tortilla up as you would an egg roll; that is, roll the bottom around the filling, fold over the left and right sides, and continue rolling to obtain a compact cylinder. Make the remaining burritos the same way. If you like, roll up the burritos in aluminum foil or waxed paper, so you can eat them out of hand. Serve the remaining salsa on the side as a dip for the burritos.   *Serves 4*

488 CALORIES PER SERVING; 27 G PROTEIN; 7 G FAT; 1 G SATURATED FAT;
85 G CARBOHYDRATE; 665 MG SODIUM; 32 MG CHOLESTEROL

SPINACH ENCHILADAS

Say "enchilada" to most of us in the United States and you'll evoke visions of tortillas stuffed with melted cheese or chicken. Here's a colorful, offbeat spinach enchilada that is naturally high in flavor and low in fat. I like the smoky taste imparted by the Canadian bacon, but a vegetarian can certainly omit it. For the best results, use tender leaf spinach (the kind sold in bunches).

PREPARATION TIME: 15 MINUTES   COOKING TIME: 20 MINUTES

12 ounces fresh spinach, stemmed and washed, or
   1 (12-ounce) package frozen
Salt
3 cups salsa verde (page 25)
½ medium white onion, finely diced (about ½ cup)

1 slice (1 ounce) Canadian bacon, finely chopped
½ cup no-fat sour cream, plus ½ cup for garnish
1 cup chicken or vegetable stock
Freshly ground black pepper
12 corn tortillas

1. Cook the spinach in 2 cups of rapidly boiling salted water in a large pot until tender, 2 to 3 minutes. (If you are using frozen spinach, cook according to the directions on the package.) Drain the spinach in a colander, refresh it under cold water, and drain well. Wring the water out of the spinach by grabbing and squeezing bunches between your fingers. Coarsely chop the spinach with a knife.

2. Heat ¾ cup of the salsa verde in a nonstick frying pan. Add half the diced onion and all the Canadian bacon and simmer until the onion has lost its rawness, about 3 minutes. Stir in the spinach and ½ cup sour cream. Simmer for 2 minutes, or until thick and creamy. Add salt and pepper to taste.

3. Bring the chicken stock to a simmer in a shallow pan. Dip a tortilla in the stock for 10 seconds to soften it, then lay it on a plate. Place 3 tablespoons of the spinach mixture on top of the tortilla and roll it up. Continue stuffing and rolling the tortillas in this fashion until all are used up.

4. Spoon ¼ cup salsa verde over the bottom of a 12-inch baking dish (for ease in cleaning, first lightly spray the dish with oil). Arrange the enchiladas, seam side down, on top. Spoon over the enchiladas the remaining salsa verde and sprinkle with the remaining onion. Garnish with dollops of sour cream. The recipe can be prepared ahead to this stage and refrigerated.

5. Preheat the oven to 400°F. Bake the enchiladas until they are heated through and the salsa verde is bubbling, 10 to 15 minutes. Serve at once.

*Makes 12 enchiladas, enough to
serve 6 as an appetizer, 4 as a light entrée*

291 CALORIES PER SERVING (BASED ON 4 SERVINGS); 15 G PROTEIN; 4 G FAT; 0 G SATURATED FAT;
55 G CARBOHYDRATE; 292 MG SODIUM; 3 MG CHOLESTEROL

SQUASH AND MUSHROOM ENCHILADAS WITH RED CHILI SAUCE

In Mexico, enchiladas come with all sorts of fillings, including squash and mushrooms. This recipe makes a great vegetarian entrée. Roasting the vegetables creates great depth of flavor without extra fat. Fresh epazote will give you a clean, piny flavor, but don't worry too much if you can't find it: Cilantro provides plenty of taste, too.

PREPARATION TIME: 20 MINUTES   COOKING TIME: 1 HOUR

FOR THE FILLING:

12 ounces butternut squash or calabaza, trimmed, seeded, and cut into ¼-inch dice
12 ounces button mushrooms, trimmed and cut in quarters
2 cloves garlic, thinly sliced
½ medium white onion, thinly sliced
Salt and freshly ground black pepper
½ teaspoon dried oregano
½ teaspoon ground cumin

2 tablespoons chopped fresh epazote or cilantro
½ cup no-fat sour cream

3 cups Red Chili Salsa (page 74)
½ cup chicken or vegetable broth
12 (6-inch) corn tortillas
¼ cup finely chopped white onion
¼ cup grated white cheddar or Monterey Jack cheese

1. Preheat the oven to 400°F. Place the squash, mushrooms, garlic, and onion in a nonstick roasting pan and toss with the salt, pepper, oregano, and cumin. Roast the vegetables until they're browned and tender, about 20 minutes, stirring occasionally. Remove the pan from the oven and stir in the epazote or cilantro and no-fat sour cream. Correct the seasoning, adding salt and pepper to taste.

2. Pour a third of the red chili sauce in the bottom of a lightly oiled, 12-inch baking dish. (Choose a dish that's attractive enough for serving.)

3. Heat the ½ cup broth in a frying pan. Dip the tortillas, one by one, in the stock to soften them, then lay them on a plate. Place 3 tablespoons of the squash mixture on each tortilla and roll it up into a tube. Place the tube seam side down in the baking dish. Repeat until all the tortillas and filling are used up. Spoon the remaining sauce over the enchiladas and sprinkle the chopped onion and cheese on top. The recipe can be prepared ahead to this stage and stored in the refrigerator. (If you do make it ahead, let it cool to room temperature before refrigerating.)

4. Just before serving, preheat the oven to 400°F. Bake the enchiladas until the cheese is melted and the sauce is bubbling hot, 10 to 15 minutes.

Serves 6 as an appetizer, 4 as an entrée

351 CALORIES PER SERVING (BASED ON 4 SERVINGS); 13 G PROTEIN; 6 G FAT; 3 G SATURATED FAT;
65 G CARBOHYDRATE; 319 MG SODIUM; 15 MG CHOLESTEROL

RED CHILI SALSA

This handsome, rust-colored chili salsa is the lifeblood of Mexican-Americans living in Texas, Arizona, and New Mexico. It owes its earthy richness to the chile colorado—the dried New Mexican chili—which is flavorful but not particularly hot. You could also use guajillo chilies.

PREPARATION TIME: 20 MINUTES   COOKING TIME: 20 MINUTES

3 ounces chiles colorados (dried red New Mexican chilies) or guajillo chilies, 14 to 16 chilies in all
2½ cups warm chicken or vegetable broth, or as needed
1 medium ripe red tomato
¼ medium white onion
1 clove garlic, peeled
1 tablespoon chopped cilantro
½ teaspoon oregano
Salt and freshly ground black pepper

1. In a large saucepan, soak the chilies in the broth until they are pliable, 10 minutes. Stem the chilies, tear them open, and remove the veins and seeds. Return the chilies to the stock. Cook over low heat, uncovered, until the chilies are soft, about 10 minutes.

2. Meanwhile, preheat a comal or cast-iron skillet over a medium-high flame. Roast the tomato, onion, and garlic until nicely browned; 8 to 10 minutes for the tomato and onion; 4 to 6 minutes for the garlic. Transfer to a plate and let cool.

3. Place the chilies, with 2½ cups of the cooking liquid and the garlic, tomato, onion, cilantro, and oregano, into a blender and purée until smooth. Add cooking liquid as needed to obtain a pourable sauce. Correct the seasoning, adding salt and pepper to taste.

Makes 3 cups

53 CALORIES PER SERVING, BASED ON 6 SERVINGS (½ CUP); 2 G PROTEIN; 1 G FAT; 0 G SATURATED FAT; 10 G CARBOHYDRATE; 13 MG SODIUM; 0 MG CHOLESTEROL

ROASTED SWEET PLANTAIN ENCHILADAS WITH PUEBLA-STYLE MOLE (REBOZO CON MOLE)

I first tasted this dish at the chic La Valentina restaurant in Mexico City. The haunting contrast of flavors—the chili-chocolate earthiness of the mole, offset by the banana-like sweetness of the plantains—remains vivid to me to this day. Chef Oscar Rodriguez serves the dish as a botana (appetizer), using tiny, freshly made tortillas. I've reworked the recipe into an enchilada-style casserole; after all, if you're going to go to the trouble to make the mole, you might as well wind up with dinner.

A plantain is a cooking banana that becomes sweeter as it ripens. For maximum deliciousness, you'll want to use plantains so ripe (ripen them at room temperature) that the skins are completely black. Tradition calls for the plantains to be deep-fried, but a similar, candylike sweetness and texture can be obtained by roasting the plantains in a hot oven. The recipe for the mole poblano can be found on page 107. To make a vegetarian version, substitute olive oil for the lard and vegetable stock for the chicken stock.

PREPARATION TIME: 15 MINUTES (PLUS THE TIME IT TAKES TO MAKE THE MOLE POBLANO)
COOKING TIME: 30 MINUTES

FOR THE PLANTAINS:
2 very ripe plantains (the skins should be black)
Spray oil
1 batch Mole Poblano Sauce (page 107)

12 corn tortillas
1 cup warm chicken or vegetable stock
1 tablespoon toasted sesame seeds

1. Preheat the oven to 450°F. Cut the ends off the plantains. Cut each plantain sharply on the diagonal into 1½-inch pieces. Arrange the plantain pieces in a single layer in a roasting pan (preferably nonstick) that you've sprayed lightly with oil. Roast the plantains until they are tender and the cut edges are a deep golden brown, 15 to 20 minutes, turning with a spatula. Remove the pan from the heat and let cool.

2. When the plantains are cool, remove and discard the skins. Cut the plantains into ½-inch dice.

3. Spoon one third of the mole poblano sauce into a large baking dish. Dip a tortilla in the warm stock for 10 seconds to soften it, then lay it on a plate. Place 3 tablespoons of the diced plantain on top of the tortilla and roll it up. Set it, seam side down, on top of the mole in the baking dish. Continue stuffing and rolling the tortillas in this fashion until all are used up. Spoon the remaining mole over the enchiladas. The recipe can be prepared ahead to this stage.

4. Bake the enchiladas in a 400-degree oven until they are thoroughly heated, 10 to 15 minutes. Sprinkle the enchiladas with the sesame seeds and serve at once.

Makes 12 enchiladas, enough to serve 6 as an appetizer, 4 as a light entrée

415 CALORIES PER SERVING (BASED ON 4 SERVINGS); 9 G PROTEIN; 9 G FAT; 2 G SATURATED FAT; 82 G CARBOHYDRATE; 54 MG SODIUM; 2 MG CHOLESTEROL

TAMALES, POSOLES, AND OTHER CORN DISHES

Tamales are a prominent feature in Mexico's gastronomic landscape: a welcomed snack for the weary traveler, sold at markets, lunch counters, bus terminals—wherever people need to relieve their hunger in a hurry. They're also a tribute to Mexican culinary ingenuity, as both the kernels and the husk of the corn are used. The former go into the masa (dough); the latter becomes the cooking vessel and plate. Below are four of my favorite tamales. To decrease the amount of fat from the traditional recipe, I replace some of the lard with creamed corn and chicken broth. Tamales may seem tricky to make, but with a little practice, you'll be turning them out like a Mexican grandmother. The fillings are limited only by your imagination.

TAMALES WITH FRUIT AND NUT PICADILLO

Here's a twist on one of Mexico's most popular tamales, a masa dough stuffed with spicy picadillo sweetened with nuts and dried fruits. Note the use of puréed creamed corn to lighten and sweeten the masa.

PREPARATION TIME: 20 MINUTES, PLUS THE TIME IT TAKES TO MAKE THE PICADILLO
COOKING TIME: 1½ HOURS

24 dried corn husks, plus 6 for lining the steamer

FOR THE DOUGH:
2½ cups masa harina
1 teaspoon salt
1 teaspoon baking powder
1 cup hot chicken or vegetable broth, or as needed
1 cup puréed creamed corn (purée in a blender)
2 tablespoons softened lard or canola oil
1 batch Fruit and Nut Picadillo (page 144)

1. Soak the corn husks in a bowl with hot water to cover until they are soft and pliable, 2 hours.

2. To make the dough, place the masa, salt, and baking powder in a mixing bowl and combine with a wooden spoon. Stir in the broth, puréed corn, and lard or oil. The mixture should be soft and pliable, like soft ice cream. If it's too firm, add some broth. Beat the mixture until it is light and fluffy, 5 to 10 minutes. For ease in preparation, do the beating in a mixer fitted with a dough hook or paddle. Have the picadillo ready and cooled to room temperature. Drain the corn husks.

3. To assemble the tamales, lay one of the corn husks flat on a work surface, tapered end toward you. Mound ¼ cup of the masa mixture in the center of the top half of the corn husk. (The mound should be somewhat rectangular, running the length of the corn husk.) Using your fingertips, make a shallow

Tamales

groove the length of the corn mixture and place a spoonful of picadillo mixture in it. Pinch the sides of the groove together to seal in the filling. Fold the tapered half of the corn husk over the top to encase the filling.

4. Lay another corn husk flat on the work surface, tapered end away from you. Place the first husk (with the filling) in the center of the bottom half of the second husk. Fold the tapered end over the bottom to encase the tamale. Tie the bundle into a neat rectangle, using strips of corn husk or string. Continue forming the tamales in this fashion until all the filling and the 24 corn husks are used up. Take a deep breath: The hard part is over.

5. Set up a steamer in a large pot filled with 4 inches of boiling water. Line the steamer with the six remaining corn husks. Stand the tamales upright in the steamer. Cover the pot and steamer. Steam the tamales until the filling is firm and set and comes away easily from the corn husks, 1 to 1½ hours. To test, unwrap one tamale. If it is not done, rewrap and continue cooking.

6. Serve the tamales in the husk, cutting the strings to facilitate unwrapping. Have each diner unwrap the corn husks to eat the sweet masa and filling inside. *Makes 12, enough to serve 6 as an appetizer or light entrée, 4 as a main course*

136 CALORIES PER SERVING (BASED ON 4 SERVINGS); 4 G PROTEIN; 4 G FAT; 1 G SATURATED FAT; 24 G CARBOHYDRATE; 185 MG SODIUM; 5 MG CHOLESTEROL

OAXACAN CHICKEN MOLE TAMALES

I first tasted these chili-chocolate-flavored tamales at the Central Market in Oaxaca. It was love at first bite. The recipe isn't complicated, particularly if you make them when you have leftover mole poblano sauce (page 107). (Oaxacans would use a black mole sauce that's similar to mole poblano, but made with a chili that is difficult to find in the United States.) The traditional wrapper for this tamale is a banana leaf—available at Mexican and Hispanic markets and via mail order. If you can't find any use corn husks, or even cook the tamales in sheets of foil.

PREPARATION TIME: 30 MINUTES, PLUS THE TIME IT TAKES TO MAKE THE MOLE POBLANO
COOKING TIME: 1½ HOURS

12 (12-inch) banana leaf squares

FOR THE DOUGH:
**4½ cups masa harina
2 teaspoons salt
2 teaspoons baking powder**

**1¾ cups hot chicken or vegetable broth, or as needed
1 cup puréed creamed corn (purée in a blender)
2 cups Mole Poblano Sauce (page 107)
¼ cup softened lard or canola oil
2 cups cooked shredded chicken**

1. Thaw the banana leaves, if frozen. Cut into 12-inch squares.

2. To make the dough, place the masa, salt, and baking powder in a mixing bowl and combine well with a wooden spoon. Stir in the broth, puréed corn, 1¼ cups of the mole poblano sauce, and the lard or oil. The mixture should be soft and pliable, like soft ice cream. If it's too firm, add more broth. Beat the mixture until it's light and fluffy, 5 to 10 minutes. For ease in preparation, do the beating in a mixer fitted with a dough hook or paddle.

3. To assemble the tamales, lay one of the banana leaves flat on a work surface, dark, shiny side down. Mound ⅓ cup of the masa mixture in the center of the banana leaf and pat it into a flat rectangle. Using your fingertips, make a shallow groove running the length of the corn mixture and place some shredded chicken and 1 tablespoon of the mole poblano sauce in the center. Pinch the sides of the groove together to seal in the filling. Fold the sides of the banana leaf over the filling, then the top and bottom, creating a rectangular package. Tie with string. Prepare the remaining tamales the same way. Pat yourself on the back: The hard part is over.

4. Set up a steamer in a large pot filled with 4 inches of boiling water. Stand the tamales upright in the steamer. Cover the pot and steamer. Steam the tamales until the filling is firm and set and comes away easily from the banana leaves, 1¼ to 1½ hours. To test, unwrap one tamale. If it is not done, rewrap and continue cooking.

5. Serve the tamales in the banana leaves, cutting the strings to facilitate unwrapping. Have each diner unwrap the tamale to get to the masa and filling inside. *Makes 12, enough to serve 4 to 6*

274 CALORIES PER TAMALE; 10 G PROTEIN; 7 G FAT; 2 G SATURATED FAT;
45 G CARBOHYDRATE; 379 MG SODIUM; 15 MG CHOLESTEROL

SHRIMP AND GREEN CHILI TAMALES

These colorful tamales are modeled on the green chili tamales so popular in New Mexico and Arizona. There are several possibilities for chilies. You could roast your own New Mexican green or Anaheim chilies or even chiles poblanos. Alternatively, you could use canned green chilies. The shrimp simmered in salsa verde is my own touch: I think you'll like the resulting depth of flavor.

PREPARATION TIME: 20 MINUTES, PLUS THE TIME IT TAKES TO MAKE THE SALSA VERDE
COOKING TIME: 1½ HOURS

24 dried corn husks, plus 6 for lining the steamer

FOR THE DOUGH:
2½ cups masa harina
1 teaspoon salt
1 teaspoon baking powder
1 cup hot fish, chicken, or vegetable broth, or as needed
½ cup puréed creamed corn (purée in a blender)

½ cup salsa verde (plus what's needed below)
2 tablespoons softened lard or canola oil
1 cup finely chopped roasted green chilies

FOR THE FILLING:
1 cup (8 ounces) baby shrimp or chopped regular shrimp
1 cup salsa verde (page 25)

1. Soak the corn husks in a bowl with hot water to cover until they are soft and pliable, 2 hours.

2. To make the dough, place the masa, salt, and baking powder in a mixing bowl and combine with a wooden spoon. Stir in the broth, puréed corn, ½ cup of the salsa verde, the lard or oil, and the green chilies. Beat the mixture until it is light and fluffy, 5 to 10 minutes. The mixture should be soft and pliable, like soft ice cream. If it's too firm, add more broth. For ease in preparation, do the beating in a mixer fitted with a dough hook or paddle.

3. To prepare the filling, combine the shrimp and remaining 1 cup of salsa verde in a saucepan and simmer until the shrimp are cooked, about 3 minutes. Let the mixture cool to room temperature. Drain the corn husks.

4. To assemble the tamales, lay one of the corn husks flat on a work surface, tapered end toward you. Mound ¼ cup of the masa mixture in the center of the top half of the corn husk. (The mound should be somewhat rectangular, running the length of the corn husk.) Using your fingertips, make a shallow groove the length of the corn mixture and place a spoonful of the shrimp mixture in it. Pinch the sides of the groove together to seal in the filling. Fold the

tapered half of the corn husk over the top to encase the filling.

5. Lay another corn husk flat on the work surface, tapered end away from you. Place the first husk (with the filling) in the center of the bottom half of the second husk. Fold the tapered end over the bottom to encase the tamale. Tie the bundle into a neat rectangle, using strips of corn husk or string. Continue forming the tamales in this fashion until all the filling and 24 of the corn husks are used up. Congratulations: The hard part is over.

6. Set up a steamer in a large pot filled with 4 inches of boiling water. Line the steamer with the remaining six corn husks. Stand the tamales upright in the steamer. Cover the pot and steamer. Steam the tamales until the filling is firm and set and comes away easily from the corn husks, 1 to 1½ hours. To test, unwrap one tamale. If it is not done, rewrap and continue cooking.

7. Serve the tamales in the husk, cutting the strings to facilitate unwrapping. Have each diner unwrap the corn husks to eat the masa and filling inside.

Makes 12, enough to serve 6
as an appetizer or light entrée, 4 as a main course

154 CALORIES PER TAMALE; 7 G PROTEIN; 4 G FAT; 1 G SATURATED FAT;

25 G CARBOHYDRATE; 210 MG SODIUM; 31 MG CHOLESTEROL

RED CHILI CHICKEN TAMALES

These satisfying chicken tamales are popular in Texas and Arizona, where they're flavored with a rust-colored
salsa made from dried New Mexican chilies. You can also use guajillo chilies or even a mix of the two.
You'll love the way the earthy, piquant flavor of the chili sauce is in counterpoint to the sweetness of the corn.

PREPARATION TIME: 20 MINUTES, PLUS THE TIME IT TAKES TO MAKE THE
RED CHILI SALSA AND COOK THE CHICKEN   COOKING TIME: 1½ HOURS

24 dried corn husks, plus 6 for lining the steamer

FOR THE DOUGH:
2½ cups masa harina
1 teaspoon salt
1 teaspoon baking powder

1½ cups Red Chile Salsa (½ batch; page 74)
¾ cup hot chicken or vegetable broth, or as needed
¼ cup puréed creamed corn (purée in a blender)
2 tablespoons softened lard or canola oil
1 cup diced cooked chicken (page 181)

1. Soak the corn husks in a bowl with hot water to cover until they are soft and pliable, 2 hours.

2. To make the dough, place the masa, salt, and baking powder in a mixing bowl and combine with a wooden spoon. Stir in 1 cup of the red chili salsa, and the broth, corn, and lard or oil. The mixture should be soft and pliable, like soft ice cream. If it is too firm, add more broth. Beat the mixture until it's light and fluffy, 5 to 10 minutes. For ease in preparation, do the beating in a mixer fitted with a dough hook or paddle. In a small bowl, stir the remaining salsa into the diced chicken. Drain the corn husks.

3. To assemble the tamales, lay one of the corn husks flat on a work surface, tapered end toward you. Mound ¼ cup of the masa mixture in the center of the top half of the corn husk. (The mound should be somewhat rectangular, running the length of the corn husk.) Using your fingertips, make a shallow groove the length of the corn mixture and place a spoonful of the diced chicken mixture in it. Pinch the sides of the groove together to seal in the filling. Fold the tapered half of the corn husk over the top to encase the filling.

4. Lay another corn husk flat on the work surface, tapered end away from you. Place the first husk (with the filling) in the center of the bottom half of the second husk. Fold the tapered end over the bottom to encase the tamale. Tie the bundle into a neat rectangle, using strips of corn husk or some string. Continue forming the tamales in this fashion until all the filling and the 24 corn husks are used up. Well done!: The hard part is over.

5. Set up a steamer in a large pot filled with 4 inches of boiling water. Line the steamer with the remaining six corn husks. Stand the tamales upright in the steamer. Cover the pot and steamer. Steam the tamales until the filling is firm and set and comes away easily from the corn husks, 1 to 1½ hours. To test, unwrap one tamale. If it is not done, rewrap and continue cooking.

6. Serve the tamales in the husk, cutting the strings to facilitate unwrapping. Have each diner unwrap the corn husks to get to the masa and filling inside.
Makes 12, enough to serve 6 as an
appetizer or light entrée, 4 as a main course

131 CALORIES PER TAMALE; 5 G PROTEIN; 3 G FAT; 1 G SATURATED FAT;
21 G CARBOHYDRATE; 187 MG SODIUM; 8 MG CHOLESTEROL

POSOLE A LA MEXICANA

Few people in the United States have tasted hominy (posole) if they don't live in the South or Southwest. Even in these regions, this hulled parched corn is generally served for breakfast (grits are nothing more than ground-up hominy). Here's a Mexican-style hominy—electrified with garlic and cilantro—that you can serve as a starch or a side dish. For the sake of convenience, I call for canned hominy (which is available at select supermarkets).

PREPARATION TIME: 10 MINUTES   COOKING TIME: 10 MINUTES

1¾ cups cooked hominy (one 14½-ounce can)
1 tablespoon canola oil
½ white onion, thinly sliced
2 cloves garlic, minced
3 scallions, white part minced, green part thinly sliced
½ teaspoon ground cumin

½ teaspoon dried oregano
¼ teaspoon ground cinnamon
1 tomato, peeled, seeded, and chopped
¼ cup chopped fresh cilantro
½ cup chicken stock
Salt and freshly ground black pepper
1 lime, cut into wedges

1. If you are using canned hominy, drain it well in a strainer, rinse with cold water, drain well again, and set aside.

2. Heat the oil in a nonstick frying pan. Add the onion, garlic, scallion whites, cumin, oregano, and cinnamon and cook over medium heat until the onions are lightly browned, 4 to 6 minutes, stirring with a wooden spoon. Increase the heat to high and add the tomato. Cook for 1 minute.

3. Stir in the cilantro, scallion greens, stock, and hominy. Cook over high heat until most of the stock is absorbed and the hominy is richly flavored, about 4 minutes. Add salt and pepper to taste. Serve at once, with lime wedges for garnish.   *Serves 4*

116 CALORIES PER SERVING; 3 G PROTEIN; 5 G FAT; 1 G SATURATED FAT;
19 G CARBOHYDRATE; 216 MG SODIUM; 0 MG CHOLESTEROL

RED PORK AND CHICKEN POSOLE (HOMINY STEW)

Posole (hominy) is one of the most satisfying corn preparations ever to grace a fork. Popular in Mexico and the American South and Southwest, it's virtually ignored in the rest of the United States. This is a shame, for few grains offer a more inviting texture (softly chewy) or flavor (starchy and cornlike, with a pleasing grainy sweetness). Here's a traditional northern Mexican way of serving posole: stewed with chicken and pork and spiced up with cinnamon, cumin, and chili powder. For speed and convenience, this recipe calls for canned hominy, which is available at select supermarkets.

PREPARATION TIME: 15 MINUTES   COOKING TIME: 40 MINUTES

1 tablespoon lard or vegetable oil
1 medium white onion, finely chopped
3 cloves garlic, finely chopped
1 tablespoon pure New Mexican or guajillo chili powder
1 teaspoon dried oregano (preferably Mexican)
½ teaspoon ground cumin (or to taste)
¼ teaspoon ground cinnamon
⅛ teaspoon ground cloves
1 bay leaf
1 tomato, cut in half, seeded, and grated
6 ounces boneless, skinless chicken breast, cut into 1-inch cubes
6 ounces pork loin or tenderloin, cut into 1-inch cubes

5 cups chicken broth or water, or as needed
3½ cups cooked hominy or 2 (14½-ounce) cans hominy, drained and rinsed
Salt and freshly ground black pepper

FOR THE GARNISH:
½ ripe avocado, cut into ½-inch dice
1 teaspoon fresh lime juice
1 ripe tomato, seeded and cut into ¼-inch dice
½ white onion, cut into ¼-inch dice
¼ cup chopped scallions (green part only)
¼ cup chopped cilantro
¼ cup sliced radishes
1 lime, cut into wedges

1. Heat the lard or oil in a large, nonstick sauté pan. Add the onion and garlic and cook over medium heat until the onions begin to brown, 3 to 4 minutes. Add the chili powder, oregano, cumin, cinnamon, cloves, and bay leaf and cook for 1 minute. Increase the heat to high and add the tomato. Cook until the tomato juices evaporate, 1 minute. Stir in the chicken and pork and cook until lightly browned, 3 to 4 minutes more.

2. Add the chicken broth and bring to a boil. Reduce the heat and gently simmer the mixture until the chicken and pork are tender, 20 to 30 minutes. Stir in the hominy for the last 10 minutes. Remove and discard the bay leaf. Correct the seasoning, adding salt and pepper to taste; the posole should be highly seasoned.

3. Meanwhile, toss the avocado with the lime juice and place in a small bowl. Arrange the tomatoes, onion, scallions, cilantro, and radishes in small individual bowls. Alternatively, arrange the vegetables in small mounds on a platter.

4. Serve the posole in shallow bowls, garnishing each serving with a wedge of lime. Serve the avocado, tomato, onion, scallions, cilantro, and radishes on the side with spoons for sprinkling the garnishes over the posole. *Serves 4*

345 CALORIES PER SERVING; 27 G PROTEIN; 10 G FAT; 3 G SATURATED FAT; 36 G CARBOHYDRATE; 377 MG SODIUM; 63 MG CHOLESTEROL

Shellfish Dishes

Seafood Cocktail in the Style of Veracruz

Served in oversize wine goblets, these seafood cocktails are guaranteed show-stoppers. You can pretty much use any seafood you fancy: shrimp, crabmeat, and squid rings if you like your seafood cooked; oysters, clams, and raw scallops if your taste runs to sushi and ceviche. Whatever seafood you choose, it will benefit greatly from the dual sauces: a piquant mixture of lime and orange juice and a smoky tomato salsa fired up with chipotle chilies. Serve this in the biggest wine- or martini glasses you have and prepare to wow your guests.

PREPARATION TIME: 15 MINUTES   COOKING TIME: 15 MINUTES

FOR THE SMOKY TOMATO SALSA:
2 tomatoes
¼ white onion
1 clove garlic
2 canned chipotle chilies
Salt

FOR THE LIME-ORANGE MARINADE:
⅓ cup fresh lime juice
⅓ cup fresh orange juice
½ teaspoon salt

½ pound lump crabmeat, picked through to remove any shell
½ pound cooked baby shrimp (or diced large shrimp)
½ pound cooked squid rings
12 shucked oysters (optional)
2 ripe tomatoes, seeded and cut into ¼-inch dice
1 medium red onion, cut into ¼-inch dice
1 to 2 jalapeño chilies, seeded and minced (for a hotter cocktail, leave in the seeds)
½ cup chopped fresh cilantro
½ avocado, peeled and diced

1. To prepare the smoky tomato salsa, heat a comal or cast-iron skillet over medium-high heat. Roast the tomatoes, onion, and garlic until they are lightly charred on all sides: about 8 minutes for the tomatoes and onions, 4 minutes for the garlic. Transfer to a plate and let cool. Purée the charred vegetables and chilies in a blender, adding salt to taste.

2. To make the lime-orange marinade, combine the lime juice, orange juice, and salt in a mixing bowl and whisk until the salt is dissolved. Add the crab, shrimp, squid, the optional oysters, the tomatoes, red onion, jalapeños, cilantro, and avocado and gently stir to mix.

3. Spoon the seafood mixture into four wine goblets. Spoon a little smoky tomato salsa over each. Serve at once, instructing each guest to lightly mix the cocktail in the glass with a fork before eating.

Serves 4

259 CALORIES PER SERVING; 33 G PROTEIN; 6 G FAT; 1 G SATURATED FAT; 18 G CARBOHYDRATE; 652 MG SODIUM; 276 MG CHOLESTEROL

Seafood Cocktail in the Style of Veracruz

SPICY CRAB SALPICÓN (SALPICÓN DE JAIBA)

Salpicón is the Spanish word for "hodgepodge" or "medley." Depending on where you order it in Mexico, you might get an appetizer of spiced shredded beef (in central Mexico) or a fiery onion and habanero chili relish (in the Yucatán). I'm partial to the coastal version, made with fresh sweet crab teased into tiny shreds and spiced up with celery, onions, cilantro, and chilies. This recipe makes a wonderful summertime appetizer or salad.

PREPARATION TIME: 10 MINUTES   COOKING TIME: 5 MINUTES

1 pound backfin crabmeat
2 red ripe tomatoes, thinly sliced
12 large basil leaves, washed and stemmed
1 tablespoon olive oil
½ small onion, finely chopped
1 clove garlic, finely chopped
1 stalk celery with leaves, finely chopped

1 to 3 serrano chilies, finely chopped (for a milder salpicón, seed the chilies)
1 tomato, peeled, seeded, and finely diced
¼ cup coarsely chopped fresh cilantro, plus 4 sprigs for garnish
1 tablespoon lime juice, or to taste
Salt and black pepper

1. Pick through the crabmeat, discarding any pieces of shell. Tease large pieces into fine shreds. Line four salad plates with tomato slices (three or four slices to a plate) and arrange three large basil leaves in the center of each, points facing out.

2. Heat the oil in a nonstick skillet. Add the onion, garlic, celery, and chilies and cook over medium heat until the vegetables are soft but not brown, about 2 minutes.

3. Increase the heat to high and stir in the crab, diced tomato, and cilantro. Cook until the crab is hot, about 3 minutes. Stir in the lime juice and salt and pepper to taste.

4. Mound the crab mixture in the center of the tomato slices on top of the basil. (Let a little basil peek out from the edges.) Garnish each salpicón with a sprig of cilantro and serve at once.   *Serves 4*

161 CALORIES PER SERVING; 21 G PROTEIN; 5 G FAT; 1 G SATURATED FAT;
8 G CARBOHYDRATE; 353 MG SODIUM; 67 MG CHOLESTEROL

SEAFOOD CHILES RELLENOS

In the United States, chiles rellenos means poblano chilies stuffed with artery-clogging globs of melted cheese and soggily fried in egg batter—hardly the stuff of a healthy diet. You might be surprised to learn that Mexicans have dozens of different types of stuffed chilies—some filled with seafood, others with chicken or vegetables, and not all of them deep-fried. Consider the following seafood chiles rellenos, which make an inviting light entrée. I owe a special thanks to my friend Elida Proenza, for it was she who had the idea of adding rice to thicken the cooking liquid without using cream or cornstarch.

PREPARATION TIME: 20 MINUTES   COOKING TIME: 40 MINUTES

8 large poblano chilies

FOR THE FILLING:
1 tablespoon canola oil
1 medium onion, finely chopped
2 cloves garlic, minced
1 jalapeño chili, seeded and minced
8 ounces button mushrooms, trimmed, wiped clean with a damp cloth, and cut into ½-inch dice
8 ounces shrimp, peeled, deveined, and cut into ½-inch dice

8 ounces scallops, cut into ½-inch dice
2 tablespoons chopped fresh cilantro
1½ cups fish stock or bottled clam broth
½ cup evaporated skim milk
½ cup Valencia-style or arborio rice (short-grain rice)
Salt and freshly ground black pepper

1 batch Cooked Tomato Salsa (page 23) or Salsa Ranchera (page 22)

1. Roast the chilies over a high flame or under the broiler, as directed on page 177, until the skins are charred all over. This will take 8 to 10 minutes. Place the chilies in a bowl and cover with plastic wrap. Let cool for 15 minutes. Scrape the burnt skin off each chili, using a paring knife.

2. Cut the top (the stem end) three fourths of the way off each chili. (Leave it attached at the bottom.) Fold back the top and, using a grapefruit spoon or paring knife, scrape out the seeds and veins.

3. Meanwhile, prepare the filling. Heat the oil in a saucepan. Add the onion, garlic, and jalapeño and cook over medium heat until soft but not brown, about 4 minutes. Stir in the mushrooms, shrimp, scallops, and cilantro and cook for 2 minutes. Stir in the fish stock, evaporated milk, and rice.

4. Gently simmer the seafood mixture over medium-low heat, uncovered, until the rice is soft, the shellfish is cooked, and most of the liquid has been absorbed, 18 to 20 minutes. Add salt and pepper to taste.

5. Fill each chili with the seafood mixture, using a spoon, and arrange the chilies in a nonstick baking dish. Spoon any excess filling over the chilies. The recipe can be prepared ahead to this stage.

6. Preheat the oven to 400°F. Bake the chiles rellenos until they are thoroughly heated, 10 to 15 minutes. Spoon the salsa on plates or a platter and arrange the chiles rellenos on top. (Alternatively, spoon the salsa over them.)

Serves 8 as an appetizer, 4 as an entrée

349 CALORIES PER PEPPER; 42 G PROTEIN; 6 G FAT; 1 G SATURATED FAT;
36 G CARBOHYDRATE; 382 MG SODIUM; 194 MG CHOLESTEROL

SHRIMP IN GARLIC TOMATO SAUCE (CAMARONES AL AJILLO)

Shrimp in garlic sauce is a popular Mexican entrée. Most versions are awash in a sea of butter. Mexico City–born Los Angeles restaurateur Frank Romero offers a low-fat twist on this fat-laden favorite, flavoring his sauce with fried garlic and roasted tomatoes and onion. It lets you enjoy a rich garlic flavor with only a fraction of the fat. Note: This preparation works equally well with fish.

PREPARATION TIME: 10 MINUTES   COOKING TIME: 15 MINUTES

1½ pounds ripe red tomatoes (3 to 4 tomatoes)
1 small onion, peeled and quartered
1 to 2 jalapeño chilies
3 tablespoons chopped cilantro, plus 2 tablespoons
    for garnish

½ teaspoon oregano (preferably Mexican)
1 tablespoon olive oil
6 cloves garlic, peeled and thinly sliced widthwise
Salt and freshly ground black pepper
1¼ pounds large shrimp, peeled and deveined

1. Heat a comal or cast-iron frying pan over medium-high heat. Roast the tomatoes, onion, and chilies until nicely browned on all sides: 8 to 10 minutes for the tomatoes and onion; 4 to 6 minutes for the jalapeños. Transfer to a plate and let cool.

2. Seed the chilies. (For a more fiery sauce, leave in the seeds.) Purée the tomatoes, onion, chilies, 3 tablespoons of the cilantro, and the oregano in a food processor.

3. Heat the olive oil in a nonstick frying pan. Add the garlic and cook over medium heat until it is lightly browned, stirring steadily, 2 to 3 minutes. Do not let the garlic burn. Stir in the tomato purée and simmer until it is slightly thickened and richly flavored, about 5 minutes. Add salt and pepper to taste. The recipe can be prepared ahead to this stage.

4. Just before serving, stir in the shrimp. Gently simmer until the shrimp are firm and pink, about 3 minutes. Correct the seasoning, adding salt and pepper to taste. Sprinkle the shrimp with the remaining cilantro and serve at once.   *Serves 4*

209 CALORIES PER SERVING; 25 G PROTEIN; 7 G FAT; 1 G SATURATED FAT;
14 G CARBOHYDRATE; 185 MG SODIUM; 172 MG CHOLESTEROL

Cascabel Chili and Orange–Marinated Shrimp Fajitas

The first fajitas were made with beef (skirt steak, to be exact). Indeed, faja *is the Spanish word for skirt steak (literally, it means "girdle"). These days, anything goes when it comes to fajitas. Consider the following, made with shrimp marinated with fiery cascabel chilies. The cascabel is a cherry-shaped dried chili whose seeds rattle when you shake it. (*Cascabel *means "sleighbell.") Orange juice and annatto (a small, orange, squarish, seed spice that has an earthy, iodiney flavor. It's often used in the cooking of the Yucatán) round out the flavor of this fiery chili to make a shrimp fajita you won't soon forget.*

PREPARATION TIME: 25 MINUTES, PLUS THE TIME FOR MAKING THE SALSA
COOKING TIME: 15 MINUTES

FOR THE MARINADE:
1 cup fresh orange juice
2 cascabel chilies or 2 small dried hot red peppers, stemmed
2 cloves garlic
½ teaspoon annatto seeds
2 teaspoons chopped fresh marjoram, or 1 teaspoon dried
½ teaspoon salt, or to taste (optional)
¼ teaspoon freshly ground black pepper
¼ teaspoon ground cumin

TO SERVE THE FAJITAS:
1 cup no-fat sour cream
1 large ripe tomato, seeded and finely chopped
½ avocado, diced and sprinkled with a few drops of lime juice to prevent browning
1½ cups Chipotle Salsa (page 27), or your favorite salsa
2 poblano chilies
1 red bell pepper
1 yellow bell pepper
1 large white onion, peeled and cut lengthwise in eighths (leave the furry root end intact)
2 bunches of scallions, roots trimmed off
1 pound large shrimp, peeled and deveined
8 (8-inch) fat-free flour tortillas

1. To prepare the marinade, in a small saucepan combine the orange juice, chilies, garlic, and annatto seeds. Briskly simmer over medium-high heat until the chilies have softened and only ½ cup of juice remains, 5 to 8 minutes. Transfer the mixture to a blender and add the marjoram, salt, pepper, and cumin. Purée until smooth. Strain the mixture through a fine strainer into a large bowl and let cool completely. Correct the seasoning, adding salt and pepper to taste. The marinade should be very spicy. Stir the shrimp into the marinade and let marinate for 20 minutes.

2. Meanwhile, build a hot fire in your barbecue grill. Place the sour cream, tomato, avocado, and salsa in separate serving bowls.

3. Grill the poblano chilies and bell peppers until they are nicely charred on all sides, 2 to 3 minutes per side, 8 to 12 minutes in all. Transfer to a cutting board. Grill the onion wedges until they are nicely browned, 3 to 4 minutes per side. Transfer to the cutting board. Grill the scallions until they are charred and wilted, 2 minutes per side. Transfer to the cutting board. Scrape any really burnt skin off the peppers and cut the flesh off the cores and seeds. Cut the flesh into long, thin strips. Thinly slice the onions, discarding the furry root end. Leave the scallions whole. Arrange the vegetables on a platter and keep warm.

4. Thread the shrimp onto skewers and grill until cooked, 2 to 3 minutes per side. Transfer the shrimp to the platter and remove them from the skewer.

5. Warm the tortillas on the grill until they're soft and pliable, 10 to 20 seconds per side.

6. To serve the fajitas, invite each guest to place a few shrimp and grilled vegetables on a tortilla. Spoon the tomato, avocado, and salsa on top and roll the tortilla into a tube for eating.

Note: Fajitas are often served on theatrically sizzling skillets. To achieve this at home, preheat a cast-iron skillet in a 400-degree oven for about 30 minutes. Just before serving, transfer the grilled shrimp and vegetables to the skillet: They will sizzle at once. Warn your guests not to touch the skillet.

Makes 8 fajitas, enough to serve 4

439 CALORIES PER SERVING; 37 G PROTEIN; 7 G FAT; 1 G SATURATED FAT; 66 G CARBOHYDRATE; 790 MG SODIUM; 172 MG CHOLESTEROL

MUSSELS STEAMED WITH CHIPOTLES AND TEQUILA

This recipe is simplicity itself, but it never fails to elicit raves. I use canned chipotles, adding a tablespoon of the adobo (can juices) to the broth. I also like to use small mussels: They're sweeter and more tender than the large ones.

PREPARATION TIME: 15 MINUTES   COOKING TIME: 10 MINUTES

4 pounds mussels
1 cup dry white wine
½ cup water
¼ cup tequila
2 tablespoons fresh lime juice
1 large ripe red tomato, diced

1 medium white onion, finely chopped
2 cloves garlic, thinly sliced
1 to 3 chipotle chilies, minced
1 to 3 teaspoons chipotle juices
½ cup chopped fresh cilantro

1. Scrub the mussels, discarding any with cracked shells or shells that fail to close when tapped. Remove the cluster of threads at the hinge of the mussels. (Pinch the threads between your thumb and the back of a paring knife and pull, or use needle-nose pliers.)

2. To prepare the broth, combine the wine, water, tequila, lime juice, tomato, onion, garlic, chipotles, chili juices, and cilantro in a large pot and bring to a boil.

3. Add the mussels and cook, covered, over high heat until the shells open wide, about 8 minutes, stirring the mussels once or twice to give the ones on the bottom room to open.

4. With a slotted spoon, transfer the mussels to a serving bowl. Spoon most of the broth over them, leaving behind any sandy dregs. Serve at once with tortillas or bread for dunking in the broth, and extra bowls for the empty mussel shells.   *Serves 4*

208 CALORIES PER SERVING; 17 G PROTEIN; 3 G FAT; 0 G SATURATED FAT;
11 G CARBOHYDRATE; 333 MG SODIUM; 64 MG CHOLESTEROL

FISH DISHES

MESQUITE-GRILLED TUNA WITH FLAME-CHARRED TOMATO SALSA

If you like smoke and fire, you'll love this simple grilled tuna dish from the north of Mexico. The mesquite gives the fish a heady smoke flavor—a flavor reinforced by the northern Mexico–style fire-charred tomato salsa. Chiles de árbol are long, slender, fiery, dried red chilies.

PREPARATION TIME: 15 MINUTES   COOKING TIME: 15 TO 20 MINUTES

6 chiles de árbol, stemmed
1½ pounds fresh tuna, cut into 4 (½-inch-thick) steaks
2 cloves garlic, minced
1 teaspoon salt
½ teaspoon black pepper
2 tablespoons chopped cilantro, plus a few sprigs for garnish
¼ cup fresh lime juice

FOR THE FLAME-CHARRED SALSA:

2 large ripe red tomatoes
½ small white onion, cut in half lengthwise
1 clove garlic, peeled
¼ cup coarsely chopped cilantro
1 to 2 tablespoons fresh lime juice
Salt and black pepper

1 teaspoon oil for the grill grate
Warm flour tortillas for serving
Mesquite wood chunks for building your fire, or
    1½ cups mesquite chips to toss on the coals

1. Place the chiles de árbol in a small bowl with warm water to cover. Let soak until they are soft and pliable, about 30 minutes.

2. Rinse the tuna and blot dry. With a pestle in a mortar or in a small bowl, mash together the garlic, salt, pepper, and chopped cilantro. Coarsely chop two of the soaked chiles de árbol and add them to the garlic mixture with the lime juice. Arrange the tuna steaks in a baking dish just large enough to hold them, and pour the marinade over the fish. Marinate in the refrigerator for 20 minutes, turning once.

3. If you are using mesquite chunks, build a brisk fire. If you're using a charcoal or gas grill, preheat to high. Toss ½ cup of the mesquite chips on the coals.

4. To make the salsa, grill the tomatoes until the skins are dark and blistered, 8 to 10 minutes, turning with tongs. Thread the onion and garlic onto a skewer and grill until lightly browned, 4 minutes per side. Transfer the tomatoes, onion, and garlic to a plate and let cool. Scrape any really burnt bits off the tomatoes. Drain the remaining chiles de árbol and tear them into pieces. (For a milder salsa, discard the seeds.) Combine the chilies, tomatoes, onion, garlic, cilantro, and lime juice in a blender and purée until smooth. Add salt, pepper, and lime juice to taste; the salsa should be highly seasoned.

5. Oil the grill grate. Toss the remaining 1 cup of mesquite chips (if using) on the charcoal or in the

Smoky grilled tuna in the style of Chihuahua

smoker box of a gas grill. Grill the tuna until it's cooked to taste: about 3 minutes per side for medium-rare. (That's how I like my tuna.) Warm the tortillas on the grill. (You'll need about 20 seconds per side.) Serve the tuna with the salsa and tortillas.

Note: Grill shops and hardware stores sell chunks of mesquite wood that you can light and use like charcoal. (Light them in a chimney starter, just as you would charcoal.) If you can't find these, use mesquite chips, which are available at gourmet shops and cookware shops. I suppose you could use oak or hickory, but the flavor wouldn't be quite the same.

Serves 4

289 CALORIES PER SERVING; 41 G PROTEIN; 9 G FAT; 2 G SATURATED FAT;
9 G CARBOHYDRATE; 609 MG SODIUM; 64 MG CHOLESTEROL

MAHIMAHI TIKEN-XIK
(WITH A MAYAN MARINADE OF
SOUR ORANGE AND ANNATTO)

The cooking of the Yucatán is unlike that of anywhere else in Mexico. Consider tiken-xik ("tee-ken-SHEEK"). Named for the Mayan words for "marinated" and "turned" (as in flipped with a spatula), this ancient preparation features a fish flavored with a Mercurochrome orange recado (spice paste) flavored with annatto seeds and sour orange juice, then cooked on a griddle or grill. Annatto is a rust-colored Caribbean seed that has the sort of tangy, iodiny flavor one associates with French oysters. Sour orange is a citrus fruit that looks like an orange but tastes like a cross between a lime and a grapefruit. Put them together and you get a dish that screams with exotic Caribbean flavors, yet is immediately accessible to anyone who likes fish. Note: I call for mahimahi here, but you could also use snapper, pompano, or another mild whitefish.

PREPARATION TIME: 10 MINUTES, PLUS 30 MINUTES FOR MARINATING   COOKING TIME: 20 MINUTES

FOR THE RECADO:
½ teaspoon annatto seeds
½ teaspoon black peppercorns
2 allspice berries
2 cloves
1 (½-inch) piece cinnamon stick
½ teaspoon dried oregano
1 bay leaf
¼ cup sour orange juice or lime juice
2 tablespoons fresh orange juice
¼ medium white onion
2 cloves garlic

1 teaspoon salt
¼ cup water

1½ pounds boneless, skinless mahimahi fillets, cut sharply on the diagonal into 4 pieces

1 tablespoon olive oil
½ medium white onion, thinly sliced
1 clove garlic, thinly sliced
1 tomato, peeled, seeded, and diced
1 tablespoon chopped epazote or cilantro, plus 4 whole sprigs for garnish
Salt and freshly ground black pepper
4 lime wedges for garnish

1. To prepare the recado, place the annatto seeds, peppercorns, allspice, cloves, cinnamon, oregano, and bay leaf in a coffee grinder or spice mill and grind to a fine powder. Transfer the mixture to a blender and add the sour orange juice, fresh orange juice, onion, garlic, salt, and water. Purée to a smooth paste.

2. Arrange the fish in a nonreactive baking dish. Pour the recado over it, turning once or twice to coat both sides. Marinate in the refrigerator for 1 hour.

3. Preheat your barbecue grill to high.

4. Shortly before serving, heat the oil in a nonstick skillet. Add the sliced onion and garlic and cook over medium heat until they're soft but not brown, 3 minutes. Increase the heat to high and add the tomato and chopped epazote. Cook for 1 minute. Add salt and pepper to taste.

5. Grill the fish until done, 4 to 6 minutes per side, turning with a spatula. Place the fish on a platter. Spoon the onion-tomato mixture on top. Garnish each piece of fish with an epazote sprig and serve at once with wedges of lime for squeezing.   *Serves 4*

218 CALORIES PER SERVING; 33 G PROTEIN; 5 G FAT; 1 G SATURATED FAT;

11 G CARBOHYDRATE; 690 MG SODIUM; 124 MG CHOLESTEROL

Sea Bass a la Veracruzana
(in a spicy sauce of fresh tomatoes, olives, capers, and pickled peppers)

This is one of the most famous fish dishes in Mexico, and it's easy to see why. You start with the freshest possible fish. You bake or simmer it in a sauce that jolts your taste buds with electrifying bursts of flavor from salty capers, tangy olives, pickled jalapeño peppers, and even sweet spices, such as cinnamon and cloves. Despite the large number of ingredients, Veracruz-style fish is relatively quick and easy to make. (I wouldn't hesitate to prepare it on a week night.) There are many possibilities for fish here, including sea bass, snapper, and pompano. Any mild whitefish will do.

PREPARATION TIME: 20 MINUTES   COOKING TIME: 30 MINUTES

4 (6-ounce) boneless, skinless sea bass fillets
Salt and freshly ground black pepper
1 clove garlic, minced
3 tablespoons fresh lime juice

FOR THE SAUCE:
8 to 10 ripe red plum tomatoes or 4 regular
  tomatoes (about 2 pounds)
1 tablespoon olive oil
1 medium white onion, finely chopped
2 cloves garlic, finely chopped

1 tablespoon drained capers
1 tablespoon chopped pitted green olives
1 to 2 pickled jalapeño chilies, finely chopped
1 to 2 tablespoons pickled jalapeño juice
2 tablespoons chopped fresh flat-leaf parsley, plus
  4 sprigs for garnish
½ teaspoon dried oregano
1 bay leaf
1 (2-inch) piece cinnamon stick
⅛ teaspoon ground cloves
1 cup fish broth (page 179) or bottled clam juice

1. Rinse the fish and blot it dry. Season the fillets with salt and pepper and arrange them in a baking dish. Sprinkle with the garlic, pour the lime juice over the fish, and let marinate for 15 minutes. Preheat the oven to 400°F. Bring 2 quarts of water to a boil in a large saucepan.

2. Place the tomatoes in the boiling water for 30 seconds. Dip them in a bowl of cold water, drain well, then pull off the skins. Cut the tomatoes in half and squeeze out the seeds. Coarsely chop the tomatoes.

3. Heat the oil in a large, nonstick frying pan. Add the onions and cook over medium heat until they are just beginning to brown, 4 to 5 minutes, adding the garlic halfway through. Increase the heat to high and add the tomatoes. Cook until most of the tomato juices are evaporated, 3 minutes. Stir in the

capers, olives, jalapeños, jalapeño juice, parsley, oregano, bay leaf, cinnamon stick, cloves, and fish broth. Simmer the sauce until it is thick and richly flavored, 5 to 8 minutes, stirring with a wooden spoon. Correct the seasoning, adding salt and pepper to taste. For extra heat and sharpness, add a little more pickled jalapeño juice.

4. Spoon one third of the sauce over the bottom of a baking dish. Arrange the fish on top and spoon the remaining sauce over it. Bake the fish until it is cooked (when done, it will break into clean flakes when pressed with your finger), 10 to 15 minutes. Remove and discard the bay leaf and cinnamon stick. Serve the fish at once, garnishing each fillet with a sprig of parsley.   *Serves 4*

285 CALORIES PER SERVING; 38 G PROTEIN; 7 G FAT; 1 G SATURATED FAT;

18 G CARBOHYDRATE; 398 MG SODIUM; 62 MG CHOLESTEROL

BAKED SALMON WITH MINTED SALSA VERDE

Salmon isn't particularly traditional or even popular in Mexico, but many Mexican preparations lend themselves to this dark, rich, widely available fish. Consider the following recipe—salmon baked under a blanket of mint-flavored salsa verde. I love the contrast of colors and flavors in this recipe: the bright green of the salsa against the electric pink of the salmon, and the way the piquancy of the salsa cuts the richness of the fish.

PREPARATION TIME: 10 MINUTES   COOKING TIME: 30 MINUTES

FOR THE MINTED SALSA VERDE:
8 to 10 tomatillos (8 ounces), husked
1 small onion, peeled and quartered
3 cloves garlic
1 poblano chili, stems, seeds, and veins removed
1 to 2 serrano chilies, stems and seeds removed
　　(for a hotter salsa, leave in the seeds)
4 scallions, trimmed, white part cut into 1-inch
　　pieces, green part finely chopped
3 tablespoons chopped fresh spearmint or
　　peppermint, plus 4 whole sprigs

3 tablespoons chopped fresh cilantro
3 tablespoons chopped fresh flat-leaf parsley
½ teaspoon ground cumin
¼ teaspoon sugar
1 tablespoon olive oil
Salt and freshly ground black pepper
4 (6-ounce) salmon steaks or fillets
Spray oil
¼ cup no-fat sour cream

1. To prepare the salsa verde, bring 3 cups of water to a boil in a large saucepan. Add the tomatillos, half the onion, and the garlic, chilies, and scallion whites. Simmer until tender, about 5 minutes. Remove the pan from the heat.

2. With a slotted spoon, transfer the tomatillos, onion, garlic, chilies, and scallion whites to a blender, reserving the cooking liquid. Add the scallion greens, chopped mint, cilantro, parsley, cumin, sugar, and 1 cup of the cooking liquid. Purée until smooth. The salsa should be thick but pourable; add the reserved cooking liquid as needed.

3. Finely chop the remaining onion. Heat the oil in a large saucepan. Add the onion and cook over medium heat until soft but not brown, about 3 min-utes. Add the salsa verde and boil until it's richly fla-vored, 3 to 5 minutes, stirring with a wooden spoon. Add salt and pepper to taste.

4. Preheat the oven to 400°F.

5. Spray with oil an attractive baking dish just large enough to hold the fish. Spoon one third of the salsa verde on the bottom. Arrange the salmon on top. Spoon the remaining salsa verde over the fish. Place a dollop of sour cream in the center of each piece of fish. Bake the salmon until it is cooked and the salsa verde is bubbling, 12 to 15 minutes. (To test for doneness, insert a skewer in the center of a piece of fish: It will come out very hot to the touch when the fish is cooked.) Garnish each portion of fish with a mint sprig and serve at once.　　　　*Serves 4*

397 CALORIES PER SERVING; 37 G PROTEIN; 22 G FAT; 5 G SATURATED FAT;
12 G CARBOHYDRATE; 96 MG SODIUM; 112 MG CHOLESTEROL

POACHED STRIPED BASS WITH POBLANO CORN SALSA

I didn't catch her name, but she sure looked like she was in showbiz. We were flying to Mexico City and she was reading a book on low-fat cooking, so we got to chatting. It turned out she was a Mexican soap opera star, and she told me that one of the secrets to her trim figure was poaching her food instead of frying or sautéing it. A case in point: the following fish dish, which she poaches in an aromatic mixture of vegetables, chilies, and vinegar. My own contribution to this dish is the salsa, a colorful and spectacularly flavorful blend of fire-roasted corn and poblano chilies. If you live on the eastern seaboard, you should make this dish with striped bass: Its soft flesh absorbs the flavors of the poaching liquid splendidly. Other possibilities include sea bass, salmon, and bluefish.

PREPARATION TIME: 15 MINUTES   COOKING TIME: 20 MINUTES

1½ pounds skinless striped bass, sea bass, or other
fish fillets

FOR THE SALSA:
2 poblano chilies
2 ears of corn, husked
2 plum tomatoes
4 scallions
3 tablespoons chopped cilantro
3 tablespoons fresh lime juice
Salt and freshly ground black pepper

FOR THE POACHING LIQUID:
4 cups water
2 tablespoons distilled white vinegar
1 medium white onion, thinly sliced
1 carrot, thinly sliced
1 tomato, thinly sliced
2 stalks celery, thinly sliced
2 cloves garlic, thinly sliced
2 serrano chilies, seeded and thinly sliced
1 (2-inch) piece poblano chili
2 sprigs cilantro
1 bay leaf
2 allspice berries

1. Run your fingers over the fish, feeling for bones. Pull out any you find with pliers or tweezers. Rinse the fish and blot it dry.

2. To prepare the salsa, preheat a grill to high. Cook the chilies, corn, tomatoes, and scallions until nicely browned on all sides, 2 to 3 minutes per side (8 to 12 minutes in all). Transfer to a plate and let cool.

3. Scrape any really burnt bits off the poblanos, then core, seed, and cut them into ¼-inch dice. (A little black is fine.) Transfer to a mixing bowl. Cut the kernels off the corn and add them to the bowl. Dice the tomatoes and scallions and add them to the bowl. Add the cilantro, lime juice, and salt and pepper to taste. Toss to mix. Set aside the salsa.

4. Combine the ingredients for the poaching liquid in a fish poacher or sauté pan and bring to a boil. Reduce the heat and simmer the poaching liquid until richly flavored, about 10 minutes. Add salt and pepper to taste.

5. Lower the fish into the poaching liquid. Poach over medium heat (the liquid should be barely simmering) until the fish is cooked, about 10 minutes. Drain off the poaching liquid and carefully transfer the fish to a platter or plates, using a spatula. The fish can be served hot or chilled.

6. Mound the salsa in the center of the fish and serve at once.   *Serves 4*

290 CALORIES PER SERVING; 35 G PROTEIN; 5 G FAT; 1 G SATURATED FAT;
30 G CARBOHYDRATE; 156 MG SODIUM; 136 MG CHOLESTEROL

ANNATTO-GLAZED "GRIDDLED" POMPANO

Mexicans love foods that are cooked on a plancha (griddle). The proof of this assertion lies no farther than the nearest sidewalk food vendor or market. The problem from the health-conscious eater's point of view is the fat used to oil the griddle: often margarine, sausage drippings, or pork fat. That set me thinking about a low-fat method for giving foods the buttery crisp crust associated with griddling without a lot of fat. I took to doing my "griddling" on a lightly oiled, preheated baking sheet in a superhot oven. The following recipe calls for pompano, but you could really use any thin fish fillet or even thin fish steaks. As for the recado (seasoning), it owes its piquancy to vinegar and orange juice; its fragrance to cumin, cloves, and oregano; and its distinctive flavor and bright orange color to a Caribbean spice called annatto.

PREPARATION TIME: 10 MINUTES (PLUS 6 HOURS FOR MARINATING THE FISH)
COOKING TIME: 20 MINUTES

FOR THE RUB AND RECADO (MARINADE):
½ teaspoon annatto seeds
½ teaspoon black peppercorns
½ teaspoon cumin seeds
3 cloves
2 allspice berries
½ teaspoon dried oregano
½ teaspoon salt, plus salt for the salsa

1 large red ripe tomato
½ medium white onion

3 cloves garlic
⅓ cup fresh orange juice
1 tablespoon fresh lime juice
1 tablespoon red wine vinegar
Freshly ground black pepper

4 (6-ounce) pompano fillets
Spray oil or 1 tablespoon olive oil
¼ cup chopped fresh cilantro

1. To prepare the rub and the recado, in a comal or dry skillet, roast the annatto seeds, peppercorns, cumin, cloves, and allspice over medium heat until they are toasted and fragrant, 2 to 3 minutes. Transfer to a coffee grinder or spice mill and grind to a fine powder. Add the oregano and ½ teaspoon salt. Rub this mixture into the fish fillets and place them in a roasting pan. Marinate for 15 minutes. Bring 1 quart of water to a boil in a saucepan.

2. Cook the tomato, onion, and garlic in the boiling water until tender, about 5 minutes. Drain well. Combine the tomato, onion, garlic, orange juice, lime juice, and vinegar in a blender and purée to a smooth paste. Add salt and pepper to taste. Pour half this mixture over the pompano and marinate in the refrigerator for 4 to 6 hours, turning the fillets two or three times.

3. Preheat the oven to 400°F. Place a baking sheet (preferably nonstick) in the oven, preheating it as well. Remove the fish from the marinade and let it drain.

4. Just before serving, spray the preheated baking sheet with oil or drizzle with olive oil. Arrange the fish fillets on top. Spray or drizzle the fish with more oil. Bake the fish until it's cooked, 6 to 8 minutes per side, turning once with a spatula. Transfer the fish to plates or a platter and spoon the remaining tomato mixture on top. Sprinkle with cilantro and serve at once.

Serves 4

317 CALORIES PER SERVING; 33 G PROTEIN; 17 G FAT; 6 G SATURATED FAT;
8 G CARBOHYDRATE; 384 MG SODIUM; 86 MG CHOLESTEROL

GRILLED SNAPPER WITH AVOCADO SAUCE

You may not find this dish in traditional Mexican cookbooks, but the flavors of the smokily grilled fish served with a silken salsa of avocado, chilies, and fried garlic are as ancient as the country itself. I've called for snapper here, but you can really use any fish. For ease in turning the fish on the grill, cook it in a wire fish basket.

PREPARATION TIME: 15 MINUTES   COOKING TIME: 20 MINUTES

4 (6-ounce) boneless, skinless snapper fillets
Salt and freshly ground black pepper
2 cloves garlic, minced
¼ cup fresh orange juice
¼ cup fresh grapefruit juice

FOR THE SALSA:
1 poblano chili
1 jalapeño chili
½ medium white onion, cut in half
5 cloves garlic (2 cloves peeled, 3 cloves thinly sliced)

1 tablespoon olive oil
1 small or ½ large avocado, peeled and seeded
3 tablespoons chopped cilantro, plus 4 sprigs for garnish
¼ teaspoon ground cumin
½ cup no-fat sour cream
½ cup water, fish broth, or bottled clam juice
1 tablespoon fresh lime juice, or to taste
Spray oil

1. Season the fish fillets with the salt and pepper and sprinkle with the garlic. Arrange the fillets in a baking dish and pour the orange and grapefruit juice over them. Marinate for 1 hour, turning once or twice.

2. Meanwhile, prepare the salsa. Heat a comal or cast-iron skillet over a medium-high flame. Roast the chilies, onion, and the 2 peeled garlic cloves until nicely browned: 8 to 10 minutes for the poblano and onion; 4 to 6 minutes for the garlic and chilies. Transfer to a plate and let cool. Seed the chilies.

3. Heat the oil in a small skillet over medium heat. Fry the sliced garlic until it is lightly browned, 1 to 2 minutes. Do not let it burn. Drain the fried garlic in a colander.

4. Place the roasted chilies, onion, and garlic in a blender with the avocado, chopped cilantro, cumin, sour cream, water or fish broth, and lime juice. Purée until smooth, adding water as needed to obtain a thick but pourable sauce. Correct the seasoning, adding salt, pepper, and lime juice to taste. Add the fried garlic and pulse the blender just to mix.

5. Preheat the grill to high. Place the fish in an oiled fish basket. (Spray it with oil.) Grill the fish until it's cooked to taste, about 4 minutes per side. Arrange the fish fillets on plates or a platter and pour the salsa over them. Garnish with cilantro sprigs and serve at once.   *Serves 4*

249 CALORIES PER SERVING; 36 G PROTEIN; 7 G FAT; 1 G SATURATED FAT;
9 G CARBOHYDRATE; 118 MG SODIUM; 62 MG CHOLESTEROL

GRILLED SHARK AND PINEAPPLE IN THE STYLE OF TACOS AL PASTOR

The taco al pastor is one of Mexico's national snacks: thin slices of rotisseried pork served with sweet grilled pineapple on soft corn tortillas, with diced cabbage and onions for crunch. (A pastor is a shepherd and, by extension, someone from the Middle East. The taco al pastor is the Mexican version of Middle Eastern shwarma or Turkish donner kebab: The Arabic roots of this dish are obvious.) Here's a seafood taco al pastor made with shark that's been marinated with spices, chilies, and pineapple juice and grilled smokily over coals. We in the United States are just now discovering what Mexicans have known for centuries: that shark is a delectable, economical, low-fat seafood. You can also make this dish with tuna, snapper, grouper, or halibut.

PREPARATION TIME: 20 MINUTES, PLUS 20 MINUTES FOR HEATING THE GRILL
COOKING TIME: 10 MINUTES

2¼ pounds shark steaks
1 fresh pineapple

FOR THE SPICE MIX:
2 tablespoons pure chili powder (preferably guajillo chili powder)
1 teaspoon salt (or to taste)
1 teaspoon fresh black pepper
1 teaspoon ground cumin
1 teaspoon dried oregano

3 cloves garlic, minced
1 cup pineapple juice (reserved from cutting the pineapple)

2 cups finely shredded green cabbage
1 large white onion, finely chopped
1 bunch cilantro, washed, dried, and stemmed
1 batch of your favorite salsa (I like the Salsa Chipotle, page 27)
32 small corn tortillas (preferably fresh)

1. Cut the shark into ¼-inch-thick steaks. Peel the pineapple and cut widthwise into ½-inch slices. (Reserve any juice.) Combine the chili powder, salt, pepper, cumin, oregano, and garlic in a mixing bowl and blend well. Rub the shark slices with this mixture and place them in a nonreactive baking dish. Pour the pineapple juice over the shark and let marinate for 1 hour. Place the cabbage, onion, cilantro, and salsa in individual serving bowls.

2. Preheat the grill to high. Grill the shark and pineapple slices over high heat until the shark is cooked through and the pineapple is lightly browned. (This will take 2 to 3 minutes per side for the shark, 4 to 5 minutes per side for the pineapple.) Transfer the shark to a platter and cut it into slivers. Place in a serving bowl and keep warm. Sliver the pineapple and place it in a bowl. Warm the tortillas on the grill (10 to 20 seconds per side) or in the oven until they are soft and pliable, and place them in a cloth-lined basket.

3. To serve, have each guest place a spoonful of shark and pineapple on a tortilla. Sprinkle the shark and pineapple with cabbage, onion, cilantro, and salsa, then roll the tortillas into tubes or fold them in half. And pop in your mouth. *Serves 8*

446 CALORIES PER SERVING; 34 G PROTEIN; 9 G FAT; 2 G SATURATED FAT;
62 G CARBOHYDRATE; 856 MG SODIUM; 65 MG CHOLESTEROL

POULTRY

CHICKEN A LA MEXICANA

This robust stew contains only six main ingredients, but the finished dish fairly bursts with flavor. The secret is to use bone-in chicken breasts (the bones add extra flavor), cooking them in a sealed pot in the oven. To slash the overall fat, I remove the chicken skin. Note: If you don't like bones with your chicken, feel free to use boneless breasts.

PREPARATION TIME: 10 MINUTES   COOKING TIME: 1 HOUR

1¾ pounds bone-in but skinless chicken breasts (or 1½ pounds boneless, skinless breasts)
2 ripe tomatoes, peeled and quartered
1 large baking potato, peeled and cut into 2-inch pieces
1 medium white onion, peeled and cut into 8 wedges
4 cloves garlic, peeled and cut in half

1 poblano chili or green bell pepper, seeded and cut into 1-inch pieces
2 jalapeño chilies, cut in half and seeded
1 bay leaf
½ teaspoon oregano
½ teaspoon cumin
¼ teaspoon ground cinnamon
Salt and freshly ground black pepper

1. Preheat the oven to 350°F.

2. Cut each chicken breast into 2-inch pieces, using a cleaver to chop through the bones. Place the chicken, tomatoes, potato, onion, garlic, poblano, jalapeños, bay leaf, oregano, cumin, and cinnamon in a deep casserole or pot and stir to mix. Add 1 cup of water, and the salt and pepper to taste.

3. Tightly cover the pot and place it in the oven. Bake the chicken until done, about 45 minutes, stirring once or twice to ensure even cooking. Correct the seasoning, adding salt and pepper to taste.

Serves 4

352 CALORIES PER SERVING; 55 G PROTEIN; 7 G FAT; 2 G SATURATED FAT;
16 G CARBOHYDRATE; 135 MG SODIUM; 144 MG CHOLESTEROL

Chicken Almendrada in Oaxacan Almond Sauce (page 104)

CHICKEN ALMENDRADA
(IN OAXACAN ALMOND SAUCE)

Her nickname was La Abuelita ("Little Grandmother") and her lunch counter in the November 20 Market in Oaxaca was always crowded with locals. When she saw my notebook, she insisted I sit down to try her almendrada, a soulful stew flavored with toasted almonds, sesame seeds, and roasted vegetables. (This dish takes its name from the Spanish word for almond, almendra.) Little Grandmother makes her almendrada with chicken, but you could also use pork or veal. For that matter, you could serve the sauce over any type of grilled seafood. In terms of the flavor profile, we're playing sweet against sour here: the sweetness of almonds, raisins, and cinnamon in counterpoint to the acid tang of the tomatoes and tomatillos. To reduce the fat in the traditional recipe, I use a fraction of the lard and almonds, boosting the nutty taste of the latter with a few drops of almond extract. To further boost the flavor, I cook the chicken right in the sauce. (A Mexican would cook it separately.) Even with these modifications, you'll find this an irresistible dish with a delectably creamy consistency, bursting with unexpected flavors. Note: I know we're a little high on the fat grams here (although the fat still accounts for less than 30 percent of the calories). Make this a splurge dinner.

PREPARATION TIME: 20 MINUTES   COOKING TIME: 30 MINUTES

FOR THE ALMOND SAUCE:
4 medium tomatoes, stemmed (about 1¼ pounds)
3 tomatillos, peeled and washed (about 3 ounces)
6 cloves garlic, peeled
½ small onion, peeled and cut in half lengthwise
3 tablespoons slivered almonds (about ⅔ ounce)
2 tablespoons sesame seeds
1 slice white bread (with crust), lightly toasted
2 sprigs cilantro
2 sprigs parsley
½ teaspoon cinnamon
½ teaspoon dried oregano
⅛ teaspoon dried cloves
1 teaspoon salt, or to taste

½ teaspoon black pepper, or to taste
½ to 1 teaspoon sugar, or to taste
1 tablespoon lard or olive oil
¼ teaspoon almond extract
½ cup chicken stock, or as needed

TO FINISH THE ALMENDRADA:
1½ pounds boneless, skinless chicken breasts
2 tablespoons raisins
1 tablespoon sliced pickled jalapeño chilies
1 tablespoon sliced pimiento-stuffed olives
1 tablespoon drained capers
4 tortillas, warmed

1. Heat a comal or cast-iron skillet over medium-high heat. Cook the tomatoes and tomatillos until they are darkly browned on all sides, about 10 minutes. Transfer to the bowl of a blender. Roast the garlic and onion until they're darkly browned on all sides, about 6 minutes. Transfer to the blender. Toast the almonds until they are lightly browned, shaking the pan, 2 to 3 minutes. Transfer to the blender. Toast the sesame seeds until they're lightly browned, 1 to 2 minutes. Transfer half the sesame seeds to the blender. Set aside the remaining seeds for garnish.

2. Add the bread, cilantro, parsley, cinnamon, oregano, cloves, salt, pepper, and ½ teaspoon of the sugar to the blender. Purée until smooth.

3. Heat the lard or oil in a deep pot over high heat. Add the sauce and fry it until it's thick and flavorful, about 10 minutes, stirring often. Lower the heat to medium if the sauce spatters too much. Add the almond extract and ½ cup of stock after 5 minutes. The sauce should be thick but pourable: Add additional stock as needed. The recipe can be prepared up to a day ahead to this stage. (If preparing ahead, let the sauce cool to room temperature, then refrigerate.)

4. Trim any fat from the chicken. Wash each breast and blot dry. Cut each breast into 2-inch

pieces. Add the chicken, raisins, pickled jalapeños, olives, and capers to the sauce. Gently simmer over medium heat until the chicken is cooked, about 10 minutes. Correct the seasoning, adding salt and pepper to taste. Check the sweetness, adding sugar if needed; the sauce should have just the tiniest bit of sweetness. Transfer the chicken and sauce to a platter or plates and sprinkle with the remaining sesame seeds. Serve at once with the warm tortillas.

Serves 4

435 CALORIES PER SERVING; 58 G PROTEIN; 13 G FAT; 3 G SATURATED FAT;
21 G CARBOHYDRATE; 773 MG SODIUM; 145 MG CHOLESTEROL

CHICKEN IN PUEBLA-STYLE MOLE

Until you have feasted on this dish, you haven't experienced Mexican cuisine. Hyperbole, perhaps, but this dark, rich, sonorous sauce—bitter with cocoa powder, sweet with raisins and honey, nutty with almonds and sesame seeds, earthy and gently piquant with five different types of dried chilies—is one of the glories of Mexican cookery. The chocolate (cocoa powder in this case) acts more like a spice than a sweetener. I've eliminated more than ½ cup of lard from the traditional recipe, but the mole is still so flavorful that you won't for a moment miss the fat.

PREPARATION TIME: 10 MINUTES, PLUS THE TIME IT TAKES TO MAKE THE MOLE
COOKING TIME: 25 MINUTES

TO COOK THE CHICKEN:
8 half chicken breasts (6 to 7 ounces each),
   trimmed of all fat and sinew
1 bay leaf
¼ white onion

1 clove
1 clove garlic
1 sprig cilantro
1 batch of mole poblano (see below)
1 tablespoon toasted sesame seeds

1. To cook the chicken, arrange the breasts in a single layer in a large sauté pan. Pin the bay leaf to the onion quarter with a clove. Add it to the chicken with the garlic, cilantro, and water to cover by 1 inch (4 to 6 cups). Gently simmer the chicken over medium heat until it is cooked through, about 10 minutes. Remove the pan from the heat and let the chicken cool in the broth.

2. Prepare the mole, following the instructions on page 107. Preheat the oven to 400°F.

3. Just before serving, spoon one third of the mole into an attractive baking dish. Arrange the chicken breasts on top and spoon the remaining mole over them. Bake the chicken until it's thoroughly heated, 10 to 15 minutes. Sprinkle the chicken with sesame seeds and serve at once. *Serves 8*

444 CALORIES PER SERVING; 80 G PROTEIN; 10 G FAT; 3 G SATURATED FAT;
4 G CARBOHYDRATE; 202 MG SODIUM; 216 MG CHOLESTEROL

CHOCOLATE CHILI MOLE FROM PUEBLA (MOLE POBLANO)

Mole poblano is one of the most notorious and misunderstood dishes in the Mexican repertoire. It usually occasions squeals of incredulity (chocolate and chilies?), followed by sighs of pleasure upon actually tasting it. Yes, it contains chocolate (cocoa powder in this recipe, to keep a lid on the fat grams). But it also contains five different kinds of chilies, six different spices, raisins, nuts, tomatoes, toasted tortillas—in short, more than twenty ingredients whose sole purpose is to create a thick, creamy, dark, fragrant sauce with a symphonic range of flavors. The addition of chocolate to what is basically a savory sauce isn't as strange as it sounds. In pre-Columbian times, chocolate was used as a spice, not as a sweet. Its fruity, bitter flavor goes well with the pungency of the chilies. Note: Several recipes in this book call for mole poblano, so I'll often make a double batch and freeze it in 1-cup containers, to always have some on hand.

PREPARATION TIME: 30 MINUTES
COOKING TIME: 20 MINUTES (PLUS 30 MINUTES FOR SOAKING THE CHILIES)

3 ancho chilies
3 pasilla chilies
2 mulato chilies (or more anchos)
2 guajillo chilies
1 dried chipotle chili (optional)
1 teaspoon coriander seeds
½ teaspoon black peppercorns
½ teaspoon anise seeds
¼ teaspoon cumin seeds
4 cloves
1 (1-inch) piece cinnamon stick (or ½ teaspoon ground)
1 bay leaf
3 tablespoons slivered almonds

2 tablespoons sesame seeds
2 corn tortillas, torn into 1-inch pieces
1 medium white onion, quartered
5 cloves garlic, peeled
3 medium ripe red tomatoes
¼ cup chopped fresh cilantro
¼ cup yellow raisins
1½ tablespoons lard or vegetable oil
2 cups chicken or vegetable stock, or as needed
2½ tablespoons unsweetened cocoa powder
1 tablespoon honey, or to taste
2 teaspoons red wine vinegar, or to taste
Salt

1. Stem the chilies, tear them in half, and remove the veins and seeds. Place the chilies in a bowl with warm water to cover. (You may need to place a saucer on top of the chilies to keep them submerged.) Soak the chilies until they are soft and pliable, about 30 minutes. Drain off the water.

2. Meanwhile, place the coriander, peppercorns, anise seeds, cumin, cloves, cinnamon, and bay leaf in a comal or dry frying pan. Roast over medium heat until toasted and fragrant, 2 to 3 minutes, shaking the pan to keep the spices from burning. Place the roasted spices in a spice mill or coffee grinder and grind to a fine powder. **Note:** If you're in a hurry, use preground spices but roast them in a skillet briefly to boost their flavor.

3. Place the almonds in the comal or frying pan. Roast over medium heat until they are toasted and fragrant, 2 to 3 minutes, shaking the pan to prevent scorching. Transfer to a plate. Roast the sesame seeds and tortilla pieces separately the same way.

4. Roast the onion pieces, garlic, and tomatoes in the comal or frying pan until nicely browned on all sides: 8 to 10 minutes for the onion and tomatoes, 4 to 6 minutes for the garlic. Transfer the vegetables to a plate to cool.

5. Place the tomatoes, onion, garlic, soaked chilies, ground spices, almonds, sesame seeds, tortillas, cilantro, and raisins in a blender. Purée to a smooth paste, adding a little stock if needed. (You may need to work in several batches. Scrape down

the sides of the blender bowl as you work.) **Note:** You must use a blender for puréeing; a food processor does not produce a fine enough purée.

6. Heat the lard in a large saucepan. Add the mole mixture and fry it over high heat, stirring with a wooden spoon, for 5 minutes. Stir in the stock, cocoa powder, honey, vinegar, and salt to taste. Reduce the heat to medium and briskly simmer the mole until it is thick and flavorful, about 10 minutes. If the mole thickens too much, add a little more stock; it should remain pourable. Correct the seasoning, adding salt, vinegar, or honey to taste—the mole should be very flavorful. (The honey serves more to round off any sharp edges than to actually sweeten the mole.)

Makes about 4 cups, enough to serve 8 to 12

128 CALORIES PER SERVING (BASED ON 8 SERVINGS); 3 G PROTEIN; 5 G FAT; 1 G SATURATED FAT; 18 G CARBOHYDRATE; 26 MG SODIUM; 2 MG CHOLESTEROL

CHICKEN GRILLED IN HOJA SANTA LEAVES AND SERVED WITH OAXACAN MOLE VERDE

This exact dish may never have been served in Mexico, but it features a uniquely Mexican ingredient, an herb so divinely flavored that its Spanish name is hoja santa, *meaning "holy leaf." Imagine a soft, silky, emerald green, heart-shaped leaf with a peppery anise flavor that may remind you a little of sassafras. Then simply take your imagination to a Mexican market or to one of the mail-order sources at the back of this book and you'll have a gustatory experience that borders on the religious. If you can't find fresh* hoja santa, *you can approximate the flavor by grilling the chicken wrapped in lettuce leaves with sprigs of fresh fennel leaves or thin slices of bulb fennel. Note: I like to serve the grilled chicken over Oaxacan Mole Verde (in the following recipe), but if you're pressed for time, the chicken is quite tasty without it.*

PREPARATION TIME: 10 MINUTES, PLUS 30 MINUTES FOR MARINATING THE CHICKEN
COOKING TIME: 12 MINUTES

FOR THE CHICKEN AND MARINADE:
1½ pounds boneless, skinless chicken breasts
1 tablespoon extra-virgin olive oil
2 cloves garlic, minced
Salt and freshly ground black pepper

½ cup fresh orange juice
8 fresh hoja santa leaves or 8 large Boston lettuce leaves, 8 sprigs fennel leaves, or 8 paper-thin slices fennel
1 batch Oaxacan Mole Verde (page 110) (optional)

1. Trim any sinews or fat off the chicken breasts. Cut each half breast section in half lengthwise to obtain pieces about 4 inches long and 1½ inches wide.

2. Toss the chicken breasts with the oil and garlic in a shallow baking dish. Season generously with salt and pepper. Pour the orange juice over the chicken and marinate for 30 minutes, turning once or twice. Meanwhile, light your grill and build a hot fire.

3. If you are using hoja santa leaves, wash them and blot dry, but don't blanch. If you're using lettuce leaves, you'll need to blanch them in rapidly boiling salted water for 30 seconds, then refresh them under cold water, drain, and blot dry. Wrap each piece of chicken in one hoja santa leaf and tie shut with string or secure with a toothpick. If you're using lettuce leaves, place a sprig of fennel or fennel slice on top of a piece of the chicken and wrap in the lettuce leaf. Tie with string or pin shut with a toothpick.

4. Grill the chicken bundles until the meat is cooked, 4 to 6 minutes per side, turning with tongs. If you are serving the chicken with mole verde, spoon it onto four plates and set two chicken bundles on top of each. Be sure to remove the string or toothpicks.

Serves 4

331 CALORIES PER SERVING (BASED ON 4 SERVINGS); 54 G PROTEIN; 10 G FAT; 2 G SATURATED FAT;
5 G CARBOHYDRATE; 127 MG SODIUM; 144 MG CHOLESTEROL

CHICKEN IN MOLE VERDE
(GREEN HERB MOLE FROM OAXACA)

This chicken dish features the lightest and most refreshing of the seven great Oaxacan moles, a handsome green sauce built on roasted tomatillos and onions, lightly thickened with masa, and enlivened with fresh Mexican herbs. (The herbs are puréed and added to the mole at the end to preserve their bright green color.) To be completely authentic, you'll need to ferret out a few special ingredients, including epazote and hoja santa ("holy leaf"—a large flat leaf with a pleasant licoricy flavor). Fortunately, these can be ordered by mail. If unavailable, omit the epazote and substitute fresh basil for the hoja santa. Although I call for the mole to be served with poached chicken here, you could certainly serve it with grilled chicken or fish, shrimp, veal, or pork.

PREPARATION TIME: 10 MINUTES　　COOKING TIME: 20 MINUTES

2¼ pounds boneless skinless chicken breasts
5 cups chicken stock (see page 178)

FOR THE MOLE:
6 large tomatillos (about 8 ounces), peeled and
　halved
6 cloves garlic
4 jalapeño chilies (for a milder mole, seed the
　chilies)
1 small white onion, quartered

1 teaspoon salt, or to taste
1 teaspoon dried oregano
½ teaspoon dried thyme
½ teaspoon ground cumin
¼ teaspoon ground cloves
½ cup masa harina
1 bunch flat-leaf parsley, washed and stemmed
1 bunch fresh cilantro, washed and stemmed
2 tablespoons chopped epazote, fresh or dried
4 hoja santa leaves or 16 fresh basil leaves

1. Wash the chicken and blot dry. Cut the breasts into 2-inch diamonds. Heat the chicken stock in a large saucepan. Add the chicken and gently simmer until cooked, 3 to 5 minutes. Transfer the chicken to a plate with a slotted spoon. Reserve the broth.

2. In a blender, purée the tomatillos, garlic, chilies, onion, salt, oregano, thyme, cumin, cloves, and 1 cup stock. Transfer the mixture to a saucepan and cook over high heat until thick and aromatic, about 3 minutes, stirring with a wooden spoon.

3. Add 2 cups stock and boil the sauce for 5 minutes.

4. Combine the masa and 1 cup stock in a bowl and whisk until smooth. Whisk this mixture into the

mole. Simmer the mole until thick and creamy, 5 to 10 minutes.

5. Combine the parsley, cilantro, epazote, hoja santa leaves, and remaining 1 cup stock in the blender. Purée until smooth. Stir this purée into the mole and simmer for 3 minutes, or until the herbs have lost their rawness, but kept their bright green hue. Correct the seasoning, adding salt and pepper to taste.

6. Return the chicken pieces to the mole and simmer until heated through, 3 to 5 minutes. Serve at once.

Makes about 5 cups, enough to serve 4 to 6

358 CALORIES PER SERVING (BASED ON 4 SERVINGS); 56 G PROTEIN; 7 G FAT; 2 G SATURATED FAT;
15 G CARBOHYDRATE; 501 MG SODIUM; 144 MG CHOLESTEROL

CHICKEN BAKED IN PARCHMENT PAPER WITH AVOCADO LEAVES AND CHILIES (MIXIOTES)

Let the French have their papillotes, the Italians their cartuccias. I raise my fork for mixiotes. Mexicans have a longstanding tradition of roasting or grilling foods wrapped in plant leaves. (See the pibil on page 121.) The mixiote—native to central Mexico—may be the most ingenious such preparation of all. The term (pronounced "mee-she-OH-tay") refers to a paperlike membrane that covers the maguey cactus leaf, which is traditionally used to wrap meats marinated in chili paste for pit roasting or steaming. Cactus membranes are hard to come by in the United States, but you can use parchment paper or even aluminum foil with similar results. You'll need to know about one other offbeat ingredient here—avocado leaves, which have a smoky, licorice flavor. You can find them at Mexican grocery stores, but a thin slice of fresh fennel makes an acceptable substitute. This dish may sound complicated, but the actual cooking time is quite brief and the presentation is off the charts in wow power. Few dishes can compete with these dramatically puffed paper pouches, which release a heady scent of chilies and anise when opened before your guests at the table. Note: As parchment paper can be hard to find in some parts of the country, I call for aluminum foil below.

PREPARATION TIME: 15 MINUTES, PLUS 20 MINUTES FOR SOAKING THE CHILIES AND 2 HOURS FOR MARINATING THE CHICKEN   COOKING TIME: 15 TO 20 MINUTES

6 boneless skinless chicken breast halves (5 to 6 ounces each)

FOR THE ADOBO:
8 guajillo chilies (about 2 ounces) or 2½ tablespoons sweet paprika
1 ancho chili
1 pasilla chili
6 cloves garlic, peeled
¼ onion
½ teaspoon dried oregano (preferably Mexican)

¼ teaspoon dried thyme
¼ teaspoon ground cumin
¼ teaspoon ground cinnamon
¼ teaspoon ground allspice
⅛ teaspoon ground cloves
1 teaspoon salt
½ cup chicken broth
2 tablespoons distilled white vinegar
6 avocado leaves or thin (⅛-inch-thick) slices fresh fennel
6 (13- by 24-inch) rectangles of aluminum foil

1. Wash the chicken breasts and blot them dry. Trim off any excess fat or sinews.

2. To prepare the adobo, stem the chilies, tear them open, and remove the veins and seeds. Soak the chilies in warm water to cover until they are soft and pliable, about 20 minutes. Drain the chilies and place them in a blender with the garlic, onion, oregano, thyme, cumin, cinnamon, allspice, cloves, salt, broth, and vinegar. Purée to a smooth paste. Place the chicken pieces in a roasting pan and pour the adobo over them. Marinate for 2 hours, turning once or twice.

3. Preheat the oven to 400°F.

4. Place a sheet of foil (the shiny side should be down) on your work surface and place an avocado leaf or slice of fennel in the center of one half. Place a piece of chicken on top. Spoon one sixth of the adobo mixture on top. Fold the long side of the foil over the chicken, matching up the edges. Pleat (tightly fold over) the edges to form a hermetic seal. Prepare the other mixiotes the same way.

5. Arrange the mixiotes on baking sheets and bake until dramatically puffed and the chicken is cooked, 15 to 20 minutes. Slide the mixiotes onto six plates and present them this way to your guests. Have handy a pair of scissors and use them (or have your

guests use them) to open the mixiotes. (Keep your face and hands averted to avoid the escaping steam.) Slide the chicken and sauce out of the foil before eating. Serve with white rice, Mexican rice, or tortillas.

Note: Sometimes this dish is prepared with parchment paper. You'll need six 20-inch squares. Place the avocado leaf, chicken, and adobo in the center. Bring the sides of the parchment up over the chicken to encase it. Twist the raised ends of the parchment paper to seal in the chicken and tie with string: The idea is to create a hermetically sealed package. What results will look like a giant beggar's purse.

Serves 6

307 CALORIES PER SERVING; 54 G PROTEIN; 6 G FAT; 2 G SATURATED FAT;
5 G CARBOHYDRATE; 485 MG SODIUM; 144 MG CHOLESTEROL

CHICKEN WITH TOMATILLOS AND CILANTRO

I first tasted this dish—or one very much like it—at a charming Mexican restaurant in Boston called the Casa Romero. The Casa was one of the nation's first upscale Mexican restaurants, and this dish epitomizes its light approach to Mexican cooking. If you like cilantro, you'll love the explosive flavors of this simple stovetop sauté.

PREPARATION TIME: 15 MINUTES   COOKING TIME: 20 MINUTES

1 pound tomatillos, husked
1¼ pounds boneless skinless chicken breasts, trimmed of any fat
Salt and freshly ground black pepper
1 tablespoon olive oil
½ white onion, finely chopped (about ½ cup)

4 scallions, finely chopped
1 jalapeño chili (seeded and minced)
1 tablespoon fresh lime juice, or to taste
½ teaspoon sugar, or to taste
¼ cup chopped fresh cilantro

1. Heat a comal or cast iron skillet over a medium flame. Roast the tomatillos until lightly browned and soft, about 8 minutes in all, turning with tongs. Transfer the tomatillos to a food processor and grind to a coarse purée.

2. Wash the chicken breasts, blot dry, and cut into 2-inch diamonds. Season with salt and pepper.

3. Heat the olive oil in a nonstick skillet. Add the onion, scallions, and chili and cook over medium heat until soft but not brown, 4 minutes, stirring as needed. Increase the heat to high, add the chicken, and cook until lightly seared, 2 minutes. Stir in the tomatillos, lime juice, and sugar and simmer until the chicken is cooked, 2 minutes.

4. Stir in the cilantro and cook for 1 minute. Correct the seasoning, adding salt or sugar to taste. (Use the sugar to balance the tartness of the tomatillos.) Serve with white or Mexican rice.   *Serves 4*

314 CALORIES PER SERVING; 46 G PROTEIN; 10 G FAT; 2 G SATURATED FAT;
10 G CARBOHYDRATE; 105 MG SODIUM; 120 MG CHOLESTEROL

MEAT DISHES

GRILLED PORK TENDERLOIN IN THE STYLE OF THE YUCATÁN (POC CHUK)

Thinly sliced, brine-cured pork, smokily grilled, served with grilled pickled onions and a fiendishly hot salsa of grilled tomatoes and habanero chilies: Such is the legendary poc chuk—a specialty of the restaurant Los Almendros in the Yucatán. Mexican pork dishes aren't usually the stuff of heart-healthy diets, but this one fairly bursts with flavor and is naturally low in fat. For the best results, grill the pork and vegetables over charcoal. Note: Don't be put off by the seemingly large amount of salt used for curing the pork; most of it will be discarded.

PREPARATION TIME: 30 MINUTES   COOKING TIME: 30 TO 40 MINUTES

3 pork tenderloins (about 1½ pounds)
3 tablespoons salt
1 cup water

FOR THE PICKLED ONIONS:
1 large red onion, peeled and quartered (leave the furry root intact)
½ cup fresh lime juice
2 tablespoons fresh grapefruit juice
½ teaspoon salt

FOR THE SALSA:
2 ripe red tomatoes
1 to 2 habanero or Scotch bonnet chilies
3 tablespoons chopped fresh cilantro
2 tablespoons fresh lime juice
Salt

1 teaspoon oil for the grill grate
4 warm corn or flour tortillas for serving

1. Preheat the grill or broiler to high.

2. Cut each pork tenderloin in half widthwise. Cut each half almost in half lengthwise through the side and open it up like a book. Place each opened piece of tenderloin between two sheets of plastic wrap and pound with a scaloppine pounder or the side of a cleaver to a thickness of ¼ inch. The idea is to create broad, thin sheets of pork.

3. Arrange the pork in a baking dish. Combine the salt and water in a jar with a tightly fitting lid and shake until the salt crystals are dissolved. Pour the salt water over the pork and marinate for 15 minutes.

4. Meanwhile, prepare the pickled onions. Grill the onion quarters until they are nicely charred on all sides, 4 to 5 minutes per side. Transfer the onions to a cutting board and let cool. Thinly slice the onions widthwise and place them in a serving bowl. Stir in the lime juice, grapefruit juice, and salt. Marinate for 10 minutes.

5. To prepare the salsa, grill the tomatoes and habaneros until nicely charred on all sides: 8 to 10 minutes for the tomatoes, 4 to 6 minutes for the chilies. Transfer to a plate and let cool. Scrape any burnt bits of skin off the tomatoes and cut the tomatoes in

Grilled Pork Tenderloin in the Style of the Yucatán

quarters. For a milder salsa, seed the chilies; for an authentically fiery salsa, leave them in. Finely chop the tomatoes and chilies in a food processor. Add the cilantro, lime juice, and salt to taste. Okay: You've done the hard part.

6. Remove the pork from the brine and blot it dry with paper towels. Lightly oil the grill grate. Grill the pork until cooked, about 2 minutes per side. Transfer the pork to plates or a platter and top with the grilled onions. Warm the tortillas on the grill, about 20 seconds per side. Serve the pork with the salsa and tortillas on the side.

Serves 4

342 CALORIES PER SERVING; 40 G PROTEIN; 9 G FAT; 3 G SATURATED FAT;
22 G CARBOHYDRATE; 382 MG SODIUM; 99 MG CHOLESTEROL

OAXACAN-STYLE PORK IN RED MOLE
(PUERCO EN MOLE COLORADO)

This simple pork recipe features one of the seven great moles (sauces) of Oaxaca—mole colorado, a thick, dark red gravy made with ground nuts, dried chilies, and roasted vegetables. Like most moles, this one plays to every taste bud on your tongue: There are raisins and cinnamon for sweetness, ancho chilies for gentle heat, almonds and sesame seeds for a nutty flavor, onions and garlic for pungency, even avocado leaves for a touch of smoke and licorice sweetness. Thanks to all these flavorings, I was able to eliminate most of the lard used in the traditional recipe and still wind up with a dish that's bursting with richness.

PREPARATION TIME: 30 MINUTES   COOKING TIME: 1 HOUR

FOR COOKING THE PORK:
2 pounds boneless pork loin, cut into
   1½-inch cubes
4 cups chicken broth
1 bay leaf
¼ white onion
1 clove
Salt and freshly ground black pepper
2 baking potatoes, peeled and cut into 1½-inch
   cubes

FOR THE MOLE:
5 ancho chilies
4 guajillo chilies
2 tablespoons raisins
2 large or 3 medium ripe red tomatoes (about 1¼
   pounds)

½ large white onion, cut in half again
4 cloves garlic, peeled
1 corn tortilla
2 to 3 tablespoons sesame seeds
2 to 3 tablespoons slivered almonds
1 slice white bread, darkly toasted
½ teaspoon dried oregano
½ teaspoon dried marjoram
¼ teaspoon dried thyme
¼ teaspoon ground allspice
⅛ teaspoon ground cloves
1 tablespoon lard or olive oil
1 (2-inch) piece cinnamon stick
1 avocado leaf (optional)

1. Place the pork in a saucepan with the chicken broth. Pin the bay leaf to the onion quarter with a clove and add it to the broth. Add a little salt and pepper. Simmer the pork over medium heat for 20 minutes. Add the potatoes and continue simmering until the pork and potatoes are tender, 10 to 15 minutes more. With a slotted spoon, transfer the pork and potatoes to a plate and keep warm. Strain the broth and set aside.

2. To prepare the mole, stem the chilies, tear them open, and discard the seeds. Place the chilies and raisins in a bowl with hot water to cover. Let soften for 30 minutes.

3. Meanwhile, heat a comal or cast-iron skillet over a medium-high flame. Roast the tomatoes, onion, and garlic until nicely browned: 8 to 10 min-

utes for the tomatoes and onion, 4 to 6 minutes for the garlic. (Alternatively, you can roast the vegetables under the broiler, following the instructions on page 175.) Transfer the roasted vegetables to a blender.

4. Roast the tortilla in the pan until it is nicely browned, 2 to 4 minutes, turning with tongs. Tear the tortilla into pieces and transfer to the blender. Roast the sesame seeds and almonds until they are lightly browned, 2 to 3 minutes. Set aside 1 tablespoon of the sesame seeds for garnish. Add the remaining sesame seeds and almonds to the blender. Drain the chilies and raisins and add them to the blender. Add the bread, oregano, marjoram, thyme, allspice, and cloves and purée to a smooth paste.

5. Heat the lard in a deep saucepan over medium

heat. Add the puréed vegetable mixture, cinnamon stick, and the optional avocado leaf. Fry until thick, dark, and fragrant, 5 to 8 minutes, stirring with a wooden spoon to prevent splattering. Add 2½ cups of the reserved pork cooking liquid and simmer until thick and richly flavored, 5 to 8 minutes. The mole should be thick, but pourable; if it's too thick, add a little more stock or water. Correct the seasoning, adding salt and pepper to taste.

6. Just before serving, warm the pork and potatoes in the mole. Discard the cinnamon stick and avocado leaf. Transfer to plates or a platter. Sprinkle the pork with the remaining sesame seeds and serve at once.

Serves 6

452 CALORIES PER SERVING; 43 G PROTEIN; 18 G FAT; 5 G SATURATED FAT;
30 G CARBOHYDRATE; 155 MG SODIUM; 103 MG CHOLESTEROL

PORK IN MEXICAN GREEN PUMPKIN-SEED SAUCE (PUERCO EN PIPIÁN VERDE)

Here's another of the great moles of Oaxaca—this one made nutty with pumpkin seeds, tangy and tart with tomatillos and green chilies, and fragrant with fresh green herbs. Pumpkin seeds are a traditional flavoring and thickener in Mexican cuisine, and there's nothing quite like the rich, earthy, nutty flavor they impart to a sauce. Men, take note: There's growing scientific evidence that pumpkin seeds can help relieve prostate woes.

PREPARATION TIME: 20 MINUTES   COOKING TIME: 45 MINUTES

FOR COOKING THE PORK:
2¼ pounds pork loin, cut into 1-inch-thick slices
4 cups chicken stock (page 178)
1 bay leaf
¼ medium white onion
1 clove
1 clove garlic
2 sprigs cilantro
Salt and freshly ground pepper

FOR THE PIPIÁN VERDE:
⅓ cup hulled pumpkin seeds
12 fresh or canned tomatillos (about 1 pound), husked
¾ medium white onion, cut into quarters

1 poblano chili
3 to 6 fresh jalapeño chilies, cut in half lengthwise and seeded
4 scallions, trimmed and cut into 1-inch pieces
3 cloves garlic
3 leaves romaine lettuce, thinly sliced
½ cup finely chopped fresh cilantro, plus 6 sprigs for garnish
½ cup finely chopped flat-leaf parsley, plus 6 sprigs for garnish
½ teaspoon ground cumin
2 to 3 tablespoons fresh lime juice
1½ tablespoons lard or olive oil
3 sprigs epazote, finely chopped (optional)

1. To cook the meat, place the pork slices in a large frying pan with the chicken stock. Pin the bay leaf to the onion wedge with a clove. Add it to the pork with the garlic, cilantro, and a little salt and pepper. Gently simmer the pork over medium heat until it is tender, 20 to 30 minutes. Let the pork cool in the broth. Strain the broth.

2. Prepare the pipián (green pumpkin-seed sauce). Roast the pumpkin seeds in a comal or dry frying pan over medium heat until they begin to brown and pop, about 3 minutes, shaking the pan to ensure even cooking. Set aside 1 tablespoon of the pumpkin seeds for garnish and transfer the remainder to a blender.

3. Roast the tomatillos, onion, poblano and jalapeño chilies, scallions, and garlic in the comal or frying pan until nicely browned: 8 to 10 minutes for the tomatillos, onions, and poblanos; 4 to 6 minutes

for the jalapeños, scallions, and garlic. (Turn with tongs.) You'll need to work in several batches. Place the roasted vegetables in the blender. Add the lettuce leaves, half the cilantro, half the parsley, the cumin, and 2 tablespoons of the lime juice. Purée until smooth.

4. Heat the lard in a large saucepan or sauté pan over medium-high heat. Add the pumpkin seed–tomatillo mixture and fry until it is thick and fragrant, 5 minutes, stirring often. Strain in 3 cups of the reserved pork broth and simmer until it is somewhat thickened and richly flavored, about 10 minutes. The last 3 minutes, stir in the optional epazote and the remaining chopped cilantro and parsley. The mole should be highly seasoned: Add salt, pepper, and additional lime juice to taste.

5. Just before serving, warm the pork in the pump-

kin-seed sauce. Transfer to plates or a platter. Sprinkle the pork with the remaining 1 tablespoon of pumpkin seeds and garnish with the sprigs of cilantro and parsley. Serve at once.   *Serves 6*

347 CALORIES PER SERVING; 40 G PROTEIN; 15 G FAT; 5 G SATURATED FAT;
13 G CARBOHYDRATE; 122 MG SODIUM; 103 MG CHOLESTEROL

"Pit"-Roasted Pork Tenderloin in the Style of the Yucatán (Pibil)

Mention pibil to someone from the Yucatán and his mouth will water and his eyes light with pleasure. Pibil describes an ancient Mayan method of cooking: Pork or other meat is slathered with a rich recado (spice paste), wrapped in banana leaves, then roasted in a pib, a flame-heated hole in the ground. Visit the market in Merida and you can still find pit-roasted pibil, although most cooks today bake their pork in the oven. (I've also done the preparation on my barbecue grill.) If you can find banana leaves for wrapping, your pibil will have an even richer flavor, but foil wrapping produces a highly tasty pibil too.

PREPARATION TIME: 20 MINUTES (BUT ALLOW 4 HOURS FOR MARINATING THE PORK)
COOKING TIME: 1 HOUR

FOR THE RECADO (SPICE PASTE):
½ medium white onion, cut in half
4 cloves garlic
½ teaspoon annatto seeds
½ teaspoon black peppercorns
3 cloves
2 allspice berries
1 (½-inch) piece cinnamon stick
1 bay leaf

½ teaspoon oregano
⅓ cup fresh orange juice
⅓ cup fresh grapefruit juice
1 tablespoon red wine vinegar
1 teaspoon salt
1½ pounds pork tenderloin (3 tenderloins)
3 (8- by 16-inch) pieces banana leaf or aluminum foil

1. To prepare the recado, heat a comal or frying pan over a medium-high flame. Roast the onion and garlic until they are nicely browned on all sides: 8 to 10 minutes for the onion, 4 to 6 minutes for the garlic. Set aside.

2. Add the annatto, peppercorns, cloves, allspice, cinnamon, and bay leaf to the comal and roast until all are fragrant and toasted, 2 to 3 minutes. Transfer the spices to a coffee grinder or spice mill and grind to a fine powder. Place the roasted spices in a blender with the oregano, roasted onion and garlic, the orange and grapefruit juices, vinegar, and salt. Purée until smooth.

3. Trim any fat off the pork and arrange the tenderloins in a baking dish. Pour the recado over them and marinate for at least 4 hours or even overnight, turning two or three times. Preheat the oven to 350°F.

4. Wrap the tenderloins in banana leaves or foil (securing the ends with toothpicks if using leaves). Place the pork on a baking sheet. Bake until cooked, 30 to 40 minutes. (Use an instant-read thermometer to test for doneness. The internal temperature should be 165°F.) Transfer the pibils to a cutting board and let them sit for 5 minutes.

5. Unwrap the pibils and cut the pork, on the diagonal, into ¼-inch slices. (Take care not to burn yourself on the escaping steam as you open the packages.) Serve the pibils with warm tortillas and the xni pec (fiery dog's nose salsa) on page 29.   *Serves 4*

287 CALORIES PER SERVING; 38 G PROTEIN; 10 G FAT; 4 G SATURATED FAT;
8 G CARBOHYDRATE; 643 MG SODIUM; 99 MG CHOLESTEROL

GUAJILLO CHILI–MARINATED PORK TAQUITOS

These tangy taquitos (baby tacos) turn up everywhere in Mexico: at markets, bus stations, sidewalk stalls—wherever an enterprising cook has room to set up a grill or griddle. The meat ranges from beef to pork to innards. The following recipe features pork marinated in a Oaxacan-style adobo. An adobo is an aromatic but not particularly fiery paste of guajillo chilies, garlic, and vinegar. What's remarkable from a healthy eater's point of view is the modest proportion of meat to grains and vegetables. For taquitos are eaten on corn tortillas mounded with shredded cabbage, onions, cilantro, and salsa. A few shreds of meat per tortilla is all it takes to create a perfect dish.

PREPARATION TIME: 30 MINUTES   COOKING TIME: 10 MINUTES,
BUT ALLOW 2½ HOURS FOR SOAKING THE CHILIES AND MARINATING THE PORK

FOR THE ADOBO:
4 guajillo chilies
3 tablespoons distilled white vinegar
2 tablespoons chopped onion
2 cloves garlic
½ teaspoon salt
½ teaspoon freshly ground black pepper
½ teaspoon dried oregano
¼ teaspoon ground cinnamon
Pinch of ground cloves

2 pounds lean pork loin, thinly sliced across the
　grain

⅓ head green cabbage, thinly shredded (2 to 3
　cups)
1 medium red onion, finely diced
1 bunch cilantro, washed, stemmed, and coarsely
　chopped
8 radishes, washed and finely diced
2 cups of your favorite salsa (good options include
　the roasted Tomato Salsa on page 24 and the
　Salsa Chipotle, page 27)
24 corn tortillas

1. Tear open the chilies and remove the veins and seeds. In a bowl, soak the chilies in warm water to cover until soft, about 30 minutes. Drain the chilies and place them in a blender with the vinegar, onion, garlic, salt, pepper, oregano, cinnamon, and cloves. Purée to a smooth paste. Arrange the pork in a baking dish and pour the chili mixture over it. Marinate in the refrigerator for 2 hours, turning the pork once or twice.

2. Place the shredded cabbage in a serving bowl. Place the onion, cilantro, and radishes in another serving bowl and toss to mix. Place the salsa in a third serving bowl. Place spoons in each bowl.

3. Preheat the grill to high. (Mexicans grill over wood or charcoal, but you can also use gas.) Grill the pork until it is browned and well done, 2 to 3 minutes per side. Transfer it to a cutting board and chop into thin slivers with a cleaver. Place the pork in a serving bowl and keep warm. Warm the tortillas on the grill until they are soft and pliable, 1 to 2 minutes per side. Arrange the tortillas in a cloth-lined basket.

4. To eat the taquitos, each guest takes a tortilla, folds it in half, and spoons in pork, cabbage, some of the onion-cilantro-radish mixture, and salsa.

Serves 8

431 CALORIES PER SERVING (THREE TAQUITOS); 33 G PROTEIN; 9 G FAT; 3 G SATURATED FAT;
57 G CARBOHYDRATE; 668 MG SODIUM; 66 MG CHOLESTEROL

MEXICAN-STYLE PICADILLO
(FLAVORED WITH OLIVES, RAISINS, AND ALMONDS)

Picadillo is Mexican hash—finely chopped meat spiced up with onions, tomatoes, spices, and chilies. (Picar is the Spanish word for "to chop" or "mince.") Like picadillos throughout Latin America, this recipe offers an intricate interplay of sweet and salty flavors—sweet in the form of raisins, almonds, cinnamon, and cloves, salty in the capers and olives. What results is one of the most flavorful mincemeats ever to grace a tortilla or be stuffed into a roasted pepper. To lighten the traditional recipe, I combine lean ground pork and turkey, and I've dramatically slashed the cooking fat. But thanks to all the spices and seasonings, this picadillo still fairly explodes with flavor.

PREPARATION TIME: 10 MINUTES   COOKING TIME: 30 MINUTES

12 ounces lean pork loin, ground
12 ounces turkey breast, ground
1 teaspoon salt
½ teaspoon freshly ground black pepper
½ teaspoon dried oregano
½ teaspoon ground cumin
½ teaspoon ground cinnamon
⅛ teaspoon ground cloves
3 tablespoons slivered almonds
4 to 6 ripe red plum tomatoes or 2 large ripe
　　tomatoes (about 1 pound)
1 tablespoon lard or olive oil

1 medium white onion, finely chopped
　　(about 1 cup)
3 cloves garlic, minced
1 to 2 jalapeño or serrano chilies, finely chopped
　　(for a milder picadillo, seed the chilies)
2 tablespoons chopped cilantro, plus 1 tablespoon
　　for garnish
4 pimiento-stuffed green olives, finely chopped
1 to 2 pickled jalapeño chilies, finely chopped
　　(optional)
½ cup raisins
1 tablespoon drained capers

1. Combine the pork, turkey, salt, pepper, oregano, cumin, cinnamon, and cloves in a bowl and mix with a spoon. Let stand for 10 minutes.

2. Meanwhile, heat a comal or cast-iron skillet over medium-high heat. Roast the almonds until they are lightly browned, shaking the pan to ensure even cooking, 3 minutes. Transfer the almonds to a plate and let cool. Roast the tomatoes until they are browned and blistered on all sides, 8 to 10 minutes, turning with tongs. Core the tomatoes, scrape off any really burned bits of skin, and purée in a blender or food processor. Set aside.

3. Heat the lard in a large, nonstick frying pan over medium heat. Add the onion, garlic, and fresh jalapeño pepper. Cook until just beginning to brown, 4 to 5 minutes. Add the meat mixture, breaking it up

with a wooden spoon, and cook until it starts to turn white, about 3 minutes. As it cooks, chop the meat mixture into small pieces with the end of the spoon.

4. Stir in 2 tablespoons of the almonds, the puréed tomato mixture, cilantro, olives, pickled jalapeño (if using), and the raisins and capers. Gently simmer the picadillo until the meat is cooked through and the mixture is richly flavored, about 10 minutes. The picadillo should be moist but not soupy; if necessary, add a few tablespoons of water. Correct the seasoning, adding salt or pepper to taste.

Serve the picadillo with warm tortillas.

Note: Some cooks like to add a further element of sweetness in the form of a diced ripe plantain or banana.

Serves 6 to 8 on tostadas or in tortillas

288 CALORIES PER SERVING (BASED ON 6 SERVINGS); 32 G PROTEIN; 10 G FAT; 3 G SATURATED FAT;
18 G CARBOHYDRATE; 477 MG SODIUM; 83 MG CHOLESTEROL

CHIPOTLE CHILI–MARINATED PORK LOIN

Here's yet another adobo-marinated pork dish, this one featuring pork loin marinated in a fiery paste of chipotles (smoked jalapeño chilies). To balance the heat, I like to serve the pork on a sweet corn salsa. If you use dried chipotles, soak them in warm water until they are soft and pliable, about 30 minutes, then drain, stem, and seed.

PREPARATION TIME: 15 MINUTES   COOKING TIME: 25 MINUTES, BUT ALLOW 4 HOURS FOR MARINATING THE PORK

FOR THE ADOBO:
4 canned chipotle chilies with 1 tablespoon can juices (or 4 dried chipotles)
2 cloves garlic
½ teaspoon grated orange zest
½ cup fresh orange juice
½ cup fresh grapefruit juice (or more orange juice)
2 tablespoons red wine vinegar
2 tablespoons tomato paste

1 teaspoon dried oregano
½ teaspoon ground cumin
Salt and freshly ground black pepper

1¼ pounds lean pork loin, cut into ½-inch-thick steaks
Sweet Corn Salsa (page 31)
4 sprigs cilantro, for garnish

1. To prepare the adobo, combine the chilies, garlic, orange zest, orange juice, grapefruit juice, vinegar, tomato paste, oregano, and cumin in a saucepan and boil until reduced by a third, about 3 minutes. Transfer the mixture to a blender and purée to a smooth paste. Add salt and pepper to taste. Let the mixture cool to room temperature.

2. Arrange the pork slices in a roasting pan and generously spread them with adobo on both sides. Cover with plastic wrap and marinate in the refrigerator for at least 4 hours, or as long as overnight. Prepare the corn salsa.

3. The pork can be grilled or broiled. Preheat the grill or broiler to high. Grill or broil the pork loin until it is cooked through, 2 to 3 minutes per side, or until done to taste.

4. To serve, spoon the corn sauce on plates or a platter. Arrange the pork slices on top. Garnish with the cilantro sprigs and serve at once.   *Serves 4*

375 CALORIES PER SERVING; 39 G PROTEIN; 9 G FAT; 3 G SATURATED FAT; 35 G CARBOHYDRATE; 587 MG SODIUM; 85 MG CHOLESTEROL

CARNITAS
(FIRE-SEARED BEEF ON TORTILLAS)

Carnitas were the first dish I ever ate in Mexico. To this day, these robustly spiced, fire-seared bits of beef, served on flame-softened tortillas with salsa and onions, remain one of the quickest routes I know to gastronomic nirvana. And few dishes are better suited to a cookout or to summer entertaining. I like to cook the carnitas on the barbecue grill, but you can also use a broiler or nonstick frying pan.

PREPARATION TIME: 20 MINUTES   COOKING TIME: 10 MINUTES
(BUT ALLOW 1 HOUR TO MARINATE THE MEAT)

1 pound skirt steaks or thinly sliced sirloin

FOR THE SPICE MIX AND SEASONING:
1 tablespoon pure chili powder
1 teaspoon salt
½ teaspoon ground cumin
½ teaspoon dried oregano
½ teaspoon cayenne (or to taste)
1 small onion, thinly sliced
2 cloves garlic, thinly sliced
½ cup fresh lime juice
1½ cups of your favorite salsa (I use the Salsa

Chipotle on page 27 or fire-charred tomato
Chile de Árbol Salsa on page 28)
1 bunch cilantro, washed, dried, stemmed, and
coarsely chopped
1 tomato, seeded and cut into ¼-inch dice
1 cup jícama, cut into ¼-inch dice
½ ripe avocado, cut into ½-inch dice
1 teaspoon fresh lime juice

3 medium white onions, peeled and cut crosswise
into ½-inch slices
16 corn tortillas (preferably homemade)

1. Trim any fat off the steaks. Combine the chili powder, salt, cumin, oregano, and cayenne in a mixing bowl and rub this mixture on the meat. Place the meat in a nonreactive baking dish with the sliced onion and garlic. Add the lime juice and marinate 1 to 2 hours, turning the steaks once to ensure even seasoning.

2. Place the salsa, cilantro, tomato, and jícama in separate serving bowls. Place the avocado in a serving bowl and toss with the teaspoon of lime juice to prevent discoloring.

3. Preheat the grill or broiler to high. Place the onions on the grate and grill until they're nicely browned, about 4 minutes per side, turning carefully with a spatula. Add the steaks and cook to taste, about 4 minutes per side for medium-well. (Mexicans tend to eat their carnitas well done.) Transfer the meat and onions to a cutting board and cut or chop into ¼-inch pieces. Arrange the meat and onions on a platter. Warm the tortillas on the grill (or in the oven), until they are soft and pliable, 1 to 2 minutes per side, and place them in a cloth-lined basket.

4. To serve, have each guest spoon some carnitas and grilled onions onto a tortilla and top with cilantro, tomato, jícama, avocado, and salsa. The tortilla is folded in half or rolled up into a tube, ready to eat.

Serves 4

135 CALORIES PER SERVING; 9 G PROTEIN; 4 G FAT; 1 G SATURATED FAT;
18 G CARBOHYDRATE; 313 MG SODIUM; 12 MG CHOLESTEROL

SPICY STEW OF SHREDDED VEAL AND CHIPOTLE CHILIES (TINGA POBLANA)

Tinga is one of those versatile dishes you always want to have in your kitchen. (It stores well in the refrigerator and freezer.) Left whole or coarsely shredded, tinga makes the sort of rib-sticking stew that's great to serve on a cold winter evening. Finely shred the meat, as is done at street stalls throughout Mexico, and it becomes a succulent, flavorful, chili-fired filling for tacos and tortillas. To decrease the amount of fat, I've cut back on the chorizo and lard used in the traditional recipe. But I think you'll find the rich, meaty taste of the pork and the smoky sting of chipotle chilies and roasted tomatoes to be right on the money. Note: Here, as in other recipes, I call for a range of chilies and chipotle can juices. Adjust the heat to suit your taste. Also, this is a rather upscale tinga, using veal instead of pork. But pork would certainly be fine, too.

PREPARATION TIME: 15 MINUTES   COOKING TIME: 1 TO 1¼ HOURS

TO COOK THE MEAT:
1¼ pounds lean veal, cut into 1½-inch cubes
1 bay leaf
¼ medium white onion
1 clove
2 sprigs fresh thyme, or ½ teaspoon dried
2 sprigs fresh marjoram, or ½ teaspoon dried
2 sprigs fresh oregano, or ½ teaspoon dried

TO FINISH THE TINGA:
8 to 10 plum tomatoes (about 2 pounds)
¾ medium white onion (remaining from above), quartered
6 cloves garlic
3 tablespoons chopped fresh cilantro or parsley

1 tablespoon lard
1 (1-inch) piece chorizo sausage, finely chopped
1 teaspoon fresh oregano, chopped, or ½ teaspoon dried
1 teaspoon fresh marjoram, chopped, or ½ teaspoon dried
1 teaspoon fresh thyme, chopped, or ½ teaspoon dried
¼ teaspoon ground cinnamon
1 to 3 canned chipotle chilies, minced
1 to 3 teaspoons canned chipotle juices (adobo), or to taste
Salt and freshly ground black pepper
½ teaspoon sugar (optional)

1. Place the veal in a pot with 8 cups of water to cover. Pin the bay leaf to the onion with the clove and add it to the veal. Add the sprigs of thyme, marjoram, and oregano. Bring the water to a boil. Skim off any foam that rises to the surface. Reduce the heat to medium and gently simmer the veal until very tender, 40 minutes to 1 hour.

2. Remove the pan from the heat and let the veal cool in the cooking liquid. When the veal is cool, transfer it to a platter or cutting board with a slotted spoon. Tear it into shreds with a fork or your fingers. Reserve the cooking liquid.

3. Meanwhile, heat a comal or cast-iron frying pan over a medium-high flame. Roast the tomatoes, onion, and garlic in the comal until they are nicely browned: 8 to 10 minutes for the tomatoes and onion, 4 to 6 minutes for the garlic. Transfer the roasted vegetables to a food processor, add half the cilantro, and coarsely chop.

4. Heat the lard in a large sauté pan. Add the chorizo and cook until it's fragrant and browned, 3 minutes. Add the shredded veal and cook for 3 minutes. Add the chopped tomato mixture, the chopped oregano, marjoram, and thyme, the cinnamon, and the chipotles with their juices. Fry the mixture until it is very fragrant and the tomato juices have been absorbed by the meat, about 5 minutes. Add 1 cup of the reserved veal cooking liquid and simmer to ob-

tain a rich moist stew, 5 to 10 minutes. (Add more cooking liquid as needed; the tinga should be very moist.) Season with salt and pepper to taste. To round out the flavor, add a pinch of the optional sugar. For a hotter tinga, add more chipotle chilies or chili juices. Stir in the remaining cilantro and serve at once.

Makes about 4 cups, enough to stuff 16 tortillas or to top 16 tostadas, or to serve 4 as a light main-course stew

325 CALORIES PER SERVING (BASED ON 4 SERVINGS); 35 G PROTEIN; 14 G FAT; 5 G SATURATED FAT; 17 G CARBOHYDRATE; 362 MG SODIUM; 89 MG CHOLESTEROL

RICE DISHES

WHITE RICE
(ARROZ BLANCO)

White rice is, of course, a staple throughout Latin America. Even in its most basic incarnation, Mexicans give it distinction in the form of sautéed onion and garlic. Sautéing the rice imparts a nutty flavor. Now get ready for some of the tastiest basic white rice in the western hemisphere.

PREPARATION TIME: 5 MINUTES   COOKING TIME: 25 MINUTES

1 tablespoon olive oil or vegetable oil
1 small onion, finely chopped
1 clove garlic, minced

1½ cups long-grain white rice (like Uncle Ben's)
2½ cups chicken or vegetable stock
½ teaspoon salt

1. Heat the oil in a large heavy saucepan. Add the onion and cook over medium heat for 2 minutes, stirring with a wooden spoon. Add the garlic and continue cooking until the onion is soft and translucent but not brown, 2 minutes more, stirring as needed. Add the rice and cook until the grains are shiny and aromatic, 2 minutes.

2. Add the stock and salt and bring to a boil. Reduce the heat to the lowest setting. Cover the pan and cook until the rice is tender, 18 minutes. Do not stir. Check the rice after 15 minutes: If it appears too wet, partially uncover the pot to let some of the liquid evaporate.

3. Remove the rice from the heat and uncover. Drape a dishcloth over the pot and cover the rice again. Let stand for 2 minutes. Fluff the rice with a fork and serve at once.   *Serves 4*

309 CALORIES PER SERVING; 6 G PROTEIN; 4 G FAT; 1 G SATURATED FAT;
62 G CARBOHYDRATE; 282 MG SODIUM; 0 MG CHOLESTEROL

Mexican Green Rice (page 131), White Rice, and Mexican-Style Rice (page 130)

MEXICAN-STYLE RICE
(ARROZ A LA MEXICANA)

It's hard to imagine a Mexican meal without a mound of this red-hued rice. And if you're accustomed to restaurant versions—made with bottled salsa—this one, bursting with the brash flavors of fresh tomato, garlic, onion, cilantro, and chilies, will come as a revelation. Remember that the rice will only be as good as the raw materials, so try to use luscious ripe tomatoes. If you like your rice with a little heat, don't bother to seed the chili. Note: The cinnamon stick isn't traditional, but I like its spicy sweetness. I've made it optional.

PREPARATION TIME: 5 MINUTES   COOKING TIME: 20 MINUTES

1 ripe red tomato, stemmed and quartered
¼ white onion (about 2 ounces)
1 clove garlic
1 fresh jalapeño chili, seeded
3 sprigs cilantro

1 teaspoon salt
1 tablespoon canola oil
1½ cups long-grain white rice
1 (1-inch) piece cinnamon stick (optional)
1½ cups chicken stock or water

1. Place the tomato, onion, garlic, jalapeño, cilantro, and salt in a blender and purée to a smooth paste.

2. Heat the oil in a large pot. Add the rice and cinnamon stick and cook over medium heat until the rice grains are shiny, 2 to 3 minutes, stirring with a wooden spoon.

3. Increase the heat to high. Stir in the tomato mixture and bring to a boil. Reduce the heat to medium and cook the rice without stirring until most of the tomato liquid has evaporated and holes appear in the surface of the rice. Add the stock or water and bring to a boil.

4. Tightly cover the pot and reduce the heat to low. Cook the rice, without stirring, until it is tender, about 18 minutes. Check the rice after 15 minutes: If it looks too wet, leave the lid ajar to allow some of the excess liquid to evaporate. If it looks too dry, add a tablespoon or so of stock or water.

5. Remove the pan from the heat and uncover. Drape a dishcloth over the pot and cover the rice again. Let the rice stand for 2 minutes. Fluff the rice with a fork and serve at once.   *Serves 4*

303 CALORIES PER SERVING; 6 G PROTEIN; 4 G FAT; 1 G SATURATED FAT;

60 G CARBOHYDRATE; 547 MG SODIUM; 0 MG CHOLESTEROL

GREEN RICE
(ARROZ VERDE)

Rice is a relatively recent import to Mexico (it arrived with the Spanish), but few cuisines make such extensive or colorful use of this nourishing grain. Here's a green rice traditionally served at festivals and celebrations. The rice owes its offbeat hue and distinctive flavor to the addition of spinach, parsley, cilantro, and scallions.

PREPARATION TIME: 10 MINUTES   COOKING TIME: 20 MINUTES

Salt
10 spinach leaves, washed and stemmed (or ¼ cup cooked frozen spinach)
¼ cup fresh parsley leaves
¼ cup fresh cilantro leaves
1 poblano chili, roasted, peeled, and seeded (see page 177)

2¼ cups chicken stock
Freshly ground black pepper
1½ tablespoons olive oil
4 scallions, finely chopped
1 stalk celery, finely chopped
1 clove garlic, minced
1 cup long-grain white rice

1. Bring 2 cups of salted water to a rolling boil. Add the spinach, parsley, and cilantro and cook for 1 minute. Drain in a colander, rinse well with cold water, and drain again. Squeeze the spinach and herbs between your fingers to wring out any excess liquid.

2. Place the herbs in a blender with the chili and ¼ cup of the chicken stock. Purée until smooth. Add the remaining chicken stock and salt and pepper to taste.

3. Heat the oil in a nonstick sauté pan. Add the scallions, celery, and garlic and cook over medium heat until soft but not brown, about 3 minutes. Add the rice and cook until the grains are shiny, about 1 minute. Stir in the stock-herb mixture and bring to a boil.

4. Reduce the heat to the lowest setting and cover the pan. Cook the rice until it's tender, about 18 minutes. Check after 15 minutes: If the rice looks too soupy, set the lid ajar to allow the excess cooking liquid to evaporate. If the rice seems too dry, add a little water. Remove the rice from the heat and uncover. Drape a dishcloth over the pot and cover the rice again. Let stand for 2 minutes. Fluff the rice with a fork, adding salt and pepper to taste, and serve at once.

Serves 4

238 CALORIES PER SERVING; 5 G PROTEIN; 6 G FAT; 1 G SATURATED FAT; 42 G CARBOHYDRATE; 35 MG SODIUM; 0 MG CHOLESTEROL

BLACK RICE
(ARROZ NEGRO)

This gray-black rice—popular in Caribbean coastal Mexico and the Yucatán—won't win any beauty contests. But when it comes to flavor, few grain dishes can compete. The rice owes its richness to the cooking liquid: the broth left over from preparing black beans (see page 139).

PREPARATION TIME: 5 MINUTES   COOKING TIME: 25 MINUTES

1 tablespoon olive oil or vegetable oil
1 small onion, finely chopped
3 cloves garlic, minced
1 cup long-grain white rice (like Uncle Ben's)

1⅔ cups black bean cooking liquid
½ cup cooked black beans (optional)
½ teaspoon salt

1. Heat the oil in a large heavy saucepan. Add the onion and cook over medium heat for 2 minutes, stirring with a wooden spoon. Add the garlic and continue cooking until the onion is soft and translucent but not brown, 2 minutes more, stirring as needed. Add the rice and cook until the grains are shiny and aromatic, 2 minutes.

2. Stir in the bean broth, black beans (if using), and salt and bring to a boil. Reduce the heat to the lowest setting. Cover the pan and cook until the rice is tender, 18 minutes. Do not stir. Check the rice after 15 minutes: If it appears too wet, partially uncover the pot to let some of the liquid evaporate.

3. Remove the rice from the heat and uncover. Drape a dishcloth over the pot and re-cover the rice. Let stand for 2 minutes. Fluff the rice with a fork and serve at once.   *Serves 4*

232 CALORIES PER SERVING; 4 G PROTEIN; 4 G FAT; 1 G SATURATED FAT;
45 G CARBOHYDRATE; 306 MG SODIUM; 0 MG CHOLESTEROL

RICE WITH SHRIMP
(ARROZ CON CAMARONES)

Part pilaf and part stew, this simple rice dish turns up throughout coastal Mexico. When it comes to making a quick, colorful, satisfying supper, few dishes can top it. The rice gets a double blast of flavor, first from the fish stock, which is simmered with the shrimp shells for extra richness, then from the roasted tomato salsa. For extra color, you could add 16 to 20 mussels.

PREPARATION TIME: 10 MINUTES   COOKING TIME: 40 MINUTES

1 pound large shrimp, peeled and deveined (save the shells)
2 cups fish stock (see page 179) or bottled clam broth
2 ripe red tomatoes
½ medium white onion, cut in half
2 to 4 jalapeño chilies

3 cloves garlic
½ cup chopped fresh cilantro
1 teaspoon salt, or to taste
Freshly ground black pepper
1 tablespoon extra-virgin olive oil
1½ cups long-grain white rice
½ teaspoon ground cumin

1. Wash the shrimp and blot dry. Place the fish stock and shrimp shells in a saucepan and gently simmer, covered, for 10 minutes.

2. Roast the tomatoes, onion, chilies, and garlic in a comal or frying pan over medium heat until nicely browned on all sides: 8 to 10 minutes for the tomatoes and onions, 4 to 6 minutes for the chilies and garlic; or roast under the broiler or on a barbecue grill. Transfer to a plate to cool. Seed the chilies. (For a spicier rice dish, leave the seeds in the chilies.) Place the roasted vegetables in a blender with two thirds of the cilantro and the salt and pepper and purée to a smooth paste.

3. Heat the oil in a large, nonstick frying pan or deep sauté pan. Add the rice and cumin and fry over medium-high heat until the rice grains are shiny, about 2 minutes. Add the tomato mixture and bring to a rolling boil. Strain in the fish stock and bring to a boil. Stir in the shrimp and bring to a boil.

4. Reduce the heat to its lowest setting and cover the pan. Cook until the rice is tender and the shrimp is done, 18 to 20 minutes. Remove the pan from the heat and uncover. Drape a dishcloth over the pot and the rice again. Let stand for 2 minutes. Add the remaining cilantro and salt and pepper to taste, stirring them into the rice and fluffing it with a fork. Serve at once. *Serves 4*

440 CALORIES PER SERVING; 29 G PROTEIN; 6 G FAT; 1 G SATURATED FAT;
65 G CARBOHYDRATE; 719 MG SODIUM; 172 MG CHOLESTEROL

BEAN DISHES

STEWED PINTO BEANS WITH EPAZOTE
(FRIJOLES DE OLLA)

An olla is an earthenware pot—the kind traditionally used to cook beans in Mexico, where it would be nestled in the coals of a wood fire. Even if you use a more modern metal pot and a gas or electric burner, the combination of flavors—earthy beans, smoky lard, aromatic onion, and pungent epazote—will raise these simple stewed beans to something on the level of art. Epazote is one of the most distinctive seasonings in the Mexican pantry—a ragged-edged, green-leafed herb with a piny, pleasantly bitter, antiseptic taste. (See Mail-Order Sources, page 187.) Besides the virtue of its unique flavor, it's said to reduce the tendency of beans to cause flatulence. Will your frijoles de olla be terrible without epazote? Of course not. But to achieve the authentic flavor, do make an effort to find this distinctive herb.

PREPARATION TIME: 5 MINUTES   COOKING TIME: 1½ TO 2 HOURS, PLUS 4 HOURS FOR SOAKING THE BEANS

2 cups dried pinto beans (about 12 ounces)
1 bay leaf
½ small onion
1 clove
1 tablespoon lard (see Note below) or 1 slice
    (1 ounce) Canadian bacon, minced

1 clove garlic, peeled
7 to 8 cups water
2 sprigs fresh epazote
1 to 2 whole serrano chilies (optional)
Salt and freshly ground black pepper
Fresh tortillas

1. Spread the beans on a baking sheet and pick through them, removing any twigs or pebbles. Transfer the beans to a colander and rinse well with cold water.

2. Place the beans in a bowl with enough cold water to cover by 2 inches. Soak the beans in the refrigerator at least 4 hours or as long as overnight. Discard any beans that float on the surface. Drain the beans in the colander and rinse well.

3. Pin the bay leaf to the onion with the clove. Place the soaked beans in a large heavy pot with the lard, onion, garlic, and 7 cups of water. Gradually bring the beans to a boil, reduce the heat, loosely cover the pot, and simmer the beans for 1 hour. Add

fresh water as needed, to keep the beans covered by 1 inch of liquid.

4. Add the epazote and the optional serrano chilies and continue simmering until the beans are very tender. (You should be able to squish one easily between your thumb and forefinger.) Uncover the pot for the last 15 minutes, to let some of the cooking liquid evaporate. (The beans should be covered by at least ½ inch of broth.) Using a slotted spoon, remove and discard the onion, garlic, and epazote. Season the beans with salt and pepper to taste.

5. Serve the beans with their broth in earthenware bowls, with fresh tortillas for dipping in the broth.

Stewed Pinto Beans with Epazote

Note: For the best results, use soupy, freshly rendered lard—the kind you'd get at a neighborhood *carniceria*. Alternatively, a slice of Canadian bacon will give you a similar smoky pork flavor with less fat.

Makes 5 to 6 cups,
enough to serve 6

245 CALORIES PER SERVING; 14 G PROTEIN; 3 G FAT; 1 G SATURATED FAT;
42 G CARBOHYDRATE; 16 MG SODIUM; 2 MG CHOLESTEROL

COWBOY-STYLE PINTO BEANS (CHARROS)

Charros—cowboy-style pinto beans—are Mexico's answer to baked beans, a popular accompaniment to the grilled beef so popular in northern Mexico. The traditional recipe owes its smoky campfire flavor to a generous dose of bacon and bacon fat. My low-fat version uses Canadian bacon, which has all of the smoke flavor of conventional bacon and virtually a fraction of the fat. For speed and convenience I call for canned pinto beans, but you can certainly cook the beans from scratch, following the frijoles de olla recipe on page 135.

PREPARATION TIME: 5 MINUTES   COOKING TIME: 15 TO 20 MINUTES

4 cups cooked pinto beans (two 15-ounce cans)
1 tablespoon lard or olive oil
1 medium onion, minced
2 cloves garlic, minced
2 ounces (2 slices) Canadian bacon, finely chopped
1 large ripe tomato, seeded and finely chopped (for extra richness, roast the tomato in a comal before chopping)

1 cup beer
1 cup chicken stock or bean cooking liquid
1 to 2 tablespoons chopped pickled jalapeño chilies, or to taste
½ cup chopped fresh cilantro
Salt and freshly ground black pepper

1. Drain the beans, rinse well, and drain again. Heat the lard in a large heavy saucepan. Add the onion, garlic, and bacon and cook over medium heat until the onion is nicely browned, about 5 minutes. Increase the heat to high and add the tomato. Cook until the tomato juices are evaporated.

2. Stir in the beans, beer, stock, jalapeño, and half the cilantro. Briskly simmer the beans until they are richly flavored and most of the cooking liquid has been absorbed, 10 to 15 minutes. Stir in the remaining cilantro and correct the seasoning, adding salt and pepper to taste.   *Serves 4 to 6*

345 CALORIES PER SERVING (BASED ON 4 SERVINGS); 19 G PROTEIN; 6 G FAT; 2 G SATURATED FAT; 53 G CARBOHYDRATE; 266 MG SODIUM; 11 MG CHOLESTEROL

REFRIED BEANS
(FRIJOLES REFRITOS)

What can compare to Mexican refried beans? Properly prepared, they're soft and satisfying, rib-sticking, fluffy, and creamy. Redolent with onion and garlic, meaty with the richness of pork fat, they never lose the earthy goodness of beans. The Mexican cook achieves these seemingly contrary virtues by frying the beans in a generous dose of lard. My low-fat refries use a little lard to provide a rich mouthfeel, bolstering the smoke flavor with lean Canadian bacon. To make the beans soft and creamy, I beat in chicken stock, which reinforces the meat flavor. Here, then, are refried beans that won't make you regret that you ate them. Note: To speed up the cooking process, I call for canned beans, but you certainly can cook the pintos from scratch, following the frijoles de olla recipe on page 135.

PREPARATION TIME: 5 MINUTES   COOKING TIME: 10 MINUTES

2 corn tortillas
1 tablespoon lard or olive oil
1 small onion, minced
2 to 3 cloves garlic, minced
1 ounce (1 slice) Canadian bacon, minced
2 (15-ounce) cans pinto beans, drained, rinsed
    under cold water, and drained again

½ to 1 cup chicken or vegetable stock
Salt and freshly ground black pepper
2 tablespoons finely grated queso añejo, queso
    fresco, feta cheese, or Parmesan cheese

1. Preheat the oven to 350°F. Cut the tortillas into strips 1 inch wide. Arrange the strips on a baking sheet and bake until lightly browned, about 10 minutes. Transfer the strips to a cake rack to cool; they'll crisp as they cool.

2. Heat the lard in a nonstick frying pan. Add the onion, garlic, and Canadian bacon and cook over medium heat until just lightly browned, about 5 minutes.

3. Stir half the beans into the onion mixture. With a bean masher or potato masher, mash the beans to a smooth paste. Add the remaining beans and mash to a smooth paste. Stir in ½ cup of the stock and fry the beans until they are thick but creamy, 8 to 10 minutes, stirring with a wooden spoon. If the beans are too thick, add more stock. (The consistency should be that of soft ice cream.) Correct the seasoning, adding salt and pepper to taste.

4. Mound the refried beans on a platter. Sprinkle the top with grated cheese. Stand the tortilla chips upright in the beans. Serve at once.

Makes about 3 cups, enough to serve 6

231 CALORIES PER SERVING; 12 G PROTEIN; 5 G FAT; 1 G SATURATED FAT;
36 G CARBOHYDRATE; 107 MG SODIUM; 9 MG CHOLESTEROL

BLACK BEANS WITH AVOCADO LEAVES

In Oaxaca and Veracruz, black beans are often simmered with fresh or dried avocado leaves. The leaves impart a smoky, faintly licoricy flavor that goes great with the earthy richness of the beans. Avocado leaves can be found at Mexican markets or purchased via mail order. Or perhaps you have an avocado tree at home. (Just be sure the leaves haven't been treated with pesticides.) You can also turn these aromatic beans into refries, following the recipe on page 138.

PREPARATION TIME: 5 MINUTES   COOKING TIME: 1½ TO 2 HOURS

2 cups dried black beans (about 12 ounces)
2 cloves
1 small onion, halved
2 cloves garlic, peeled

2 avocado leaves
2 quarts water, or as needed
Salt and freshly ground black pepper
Fresh tortillas

1. Spread the beans on a baking sheet and pick through them, removing any twigs or pebbles. Transfer the beans to a colander and rinse well under cold water.

2. Place the beans in a large pot. Stick the cloves in the onion halves and add them to the beans with the garlic, avocado leaves, and water. Gradually bring the water to a boil, reduce the heat, loosely cover the pot, and simmer the beans for 1½ to 2 hours, or until they're tender. Add fresh water as needed, to keep the beans covered by 1 inch of liquid. Uncover the beans for the last 15 minutes.

3. Using a slotted spoon, remove and discard the onion, garlic, and avocado leaves. Season the beans with salt and pepper to taste. Serve the beans, in their broth, in earthenware bowls, with fresh tortillas for dipping in the broth.

Makes 5 to 6 cups, enough to serve 6 to 8

219 CALORIES PER SERVING (BASED ON 6 SERVINGS); 12 G PROTEIN; 3 G FAT; 1 G SATURATED FAT;
37 G CARBOHYDRATE; 6 MG SODIUM; 2 MG CHOLESTEROL

Vegetable Dishes

Mushroom-Stuffed Anaheim Chilies with Sweet Corn Salsa

These mushroom-stuffed chilies make a stunning vegetarian appetizer—especially when coupled with the creamy sweet corn sauce on page 31. There are lots of options for chilies: You can use Anaheim chilies, New Mexican green chilies, even small poblanos. Don't be intimidated by the large number of ingredients; the recipe is really just a series of simple steps. The contrast in flavors—gently fiery chilies, earthy mushrooms, sweet corn—is breathtaking.

PREPARATION TIME: 20 MINUTES   COOKING TIME: 10 MINUTES

8 long, slender, fresh green chilies, such as
　　Anaheim or New Mexican

FOR THE MUSHROOM STUFFING:
12 ounces button mushrooms, trimmed
2 teaspoons fresh lime juice
1 tablespoon vegetable oil
¼ cup chopped white onion

1 clove garlic
3 tablespoons minced fresh cilantro, plus 4 sprigs
　　for garnish
Salt and freshly ground black pepper

1 batch Sweet Corn Sauce (Salsa de Maíz); see
　　page 31

1. Roast and peel the peppers, following the method outlined on page 177. Make a T-shaped cut in the side of each chili. (The long side of the T should run the length of the chili.) Pinch together the ends of the chili to open the slit. Using a grapefruit spoon or the tip of a small paring knife, remove the seeds and veins.

2. To prepare the filling, wipe the mushrooms clean with a damp paper towel. Cut any large mushrooms in quarters, medium-size ones in half. Finely chop the mushrooms by hand or in a food processor. (If using the processor, work in several batches, so as to not fill the bowl more than a third of the way. Run the machine in short bursts. Overfilling the processor bowl, or overprocessing, will turn the mushrooms to mush.) Sprinkle with lime juice.

3. Heat the oil in a nonstick skillet. Add the onion and garlic and cook over medium heat until they are soft but not brown, 3 minutes. Increase the heat to high and add the mushrooms and cilantro. Cook until all the mushroom liquid has evaporated and the mixture is thick, 5 to 8 minutes, stirring often. Correct the seasoning, adding salt and pepper to taste. Let the mixture cool to room temperature. Using a small spoon, stuff the mushroom mixture into the chilies.

Mushroom-Stuffed Anaheim Chilies with Sweet Corn Sauce

4. To serve, warm the chilies in a preheated 400-degree oven. Spoon the corn sauce over the bottom of four plates. Arrange two chilies side by side on top of the sauce, the first going one way, the second going the other way. Garnish with the sprigs of cilantro and serve at once.

Serves 4 (2 chilies per person)

257 CALORIES PER SERVING; 12 G PROTEIN; 5 G FAT; 1 G SATURATED FAT;
46 G CARBOHYDRATE; 370 MG SODIUM; 3 MG CHOLESTEROL

ROASTED POBLANO CHILIES STUFFED WITH FRUITED PICADILLO
(SERVED WITH POMEGRANATES AND WALNUT SAUCE)
(CHILES EN NOGADA)

This complex dish—created more than a century ago by the Augustine nuns of Puebla—is one of the high holies of Mexican cuisine: fire-charred poblano chilies stuffed with a spiced, fruited picadillo and cloaked in a thick, creamy sauce flavored with walnuts. It's also a patriotic dish, as the white sauce, green chilies, and ruby red pomegranate seeds echo the colors of the Mexican flag. Alas, chilies en nogada is a nutritional nightmare, as the traditional version contains fatty pork, batter-fried chilies, and a sauce whose main ingredients are heavy cream and cheese. Fortunately, it's a dish that lends itself to a high-flavor, low-fat makeover. To decrease the amount of fat in the filling, I use lean pork loin. The chilies are served in all their fire-charred glory, but without the batter and deep-frying. (As far as I'm concerned, the batter just camouflages the smoke flavor.) As for the sauce, my low-fat version is built from evaporated skim milk, no-fat sour cream, and low-fat cream cheese. Here, then, is a dish that would make a proud centerpiece for any dinner, with much less fat than found in the original. Note: Ringing in at 14 grams of fat per serving, this recipe is on the higher end of the high-flavor, low-fat spectrum. When you stop to consider that traditional chiles en nogada contain 524 calories and a whopping 36 grams of fat per serving, the makeover represents an enormous improvement.

PREPARATION TIME: 30 MINUTES   COOKING TIME: 30 MINUTES

8 large poblano chilies
1 batch Fruit and Nut Picadillo (see page 144)

FOR THE WALNUT SAUCE:
⅓ cup walnuts (2 ounces)
¾ cup evaporated skim milk
¾ cup no-fat sour cream
2 ounces low- or no-fat cream cheese
1 ounce queso fresco or feta cheese

1 clove garlic
1 tablespoon chopped onion
1 tablespoon chopped cilantro
1 tablespoon cream sherry
⅛ teaspoon ground cinnamon
Salt and freshly ground black pepper
1 fresh pomegranate, broken into seeds
4 sprigs parsley

1. Roast, peel, and seed the chilies for stuffing, as described in the previous recipe. Make the picadillo (page 144) and let cool.

2. To prepare the sauce, toast the walnuts in a 400-degree oven until they're fragrant and just beginning to brown, 3 to 5 minutes. (Toasting the nuts enhances their flavor.) Combine the nuts, evaporated milk, sour cream, cream cheese, queso fresco, garlic, onion, cilantro, sherry, and cinnamon in a blender and purée until smooth. Add salt and pepper to taste. The recipe can be prepared ahead to this stage and

then refrigerated. The sauce is traditionally served at room temperature, so 1 hour before serving, let it warm to room temperature.

3. Just before serving, preheat the oven to 400°F. Using a spoon, stuff the filling through the slits on the sides of the chilies. Place the chilies in an oven-proof serving dish and bake until they're thoroughly heated, 10 to 15 minutes. Spoon the sauce over the chilies and sprinkle with the pomegranate seeds and sprigs of parsley.   *Serves 4*

387 CALORIES PER SERVING; 31 G PROTEIN; 14 G FAT; 2 G SATURATED FAT;
38 G CARBOHYDRATE; 266 MG SODIUM; 38 MG CHOLESTEROL

FRUIT AND NUT PICADILLO

This fragrant picadillo (meat hash) is the traditional filling for chiles en nogada (page 143). I so like the contrast of flavors—
the acidic sweetness of pears and peaches, the nutty crunch of toasted almonds, the meatiness of the pork—
that I often use it as a stuffing for tortilla dishes (see the flautas on page 155) and even as a dish by itself.

PREPARATION TIME: 10 MINUTES   COOKING TIME: 20 MINUTES

8 ounces lean pork or veal loin, trimmed of all fat
1 large red ripe tomato
1 (2-inch) piece cinnamon stick
3 cloves
2 allspice berries
¼ white onion, finely chopped
2 cloves garlic, minced
2 tablespoons lightly toasted slivered almonds
2 tablespoons raisins

2 tablespoons chopped citron (optional)
2 tablespoons chopped flat-leaf parsley, plus 12 whole leaves for garnish
½ teaspoon dried oregano
½ pear or apple, coarsely grated or finely chopped
½ peach, coarsely grated or finely chopped (or more apple or pear)
½ cup water
Salt and freshly ground black pepper

1. Finely chop the pork by hand or in a food processor. Place it in a large saucepan. Cut the tomato in half widthwise and squeeze out the water and seeds. Grate the tomato, skin side out, on the coarse side of a grater. (This grates the tomato flesh, leaving the skin behind.) Add the tomato to the pork.

2. Tie the cinnamon stick, cloves, and allspice berries in a piece of cheesecloth (or wrap them in foil and perforate it with a fork) and add them to the pork. Add the onion, garlic, almonds, raisins, citron if using, and the chopped parsley, oregano, pear, peach, and water.

3. Bring the mixture to a boil, reduce the heat, and simmer until the pork is cooked and the excess liquid has evaporated (the filling should be moist but not soupy), about 20 minutes. Remove and discard the spice bundle. Correct the seasoning, adding salt and pepper to taste; the filling should be highly seasoned.

Serves 2 as an appetizer or 4 as a filling

161 CALORIES PER SERVING; 15 G PROTEIN; 6 G FAT; 1 G SATURATED FAT;
14 G CARBOHYDRATE; 47 MG SODIUM; 30 MG CHOLESTEROL

CHIPOTLE-MARINATED PORTOBELLO MUSHROOM FAJITAS

Fajitas are one of Mexico's most successful culinary crossovers, enjoyed at Tex-Mex food emporiums and casual-restaurant chains throughout the United States. Fajitas take their name from the cut of meat traditionally used as a filling: the skirt steak, known in Spanish as faja, meaning "girdle." Today, fajitas are just as likely to be made with chicken or shrimp as with beef. Some years back, I created these portobello mushroom fajitas for my vegetarian wife and daughter. For the best results, cook the ingredients on a barbecue grill over presoaked chips or chunks of mesquite. But you can also cook the ingredients under the broiler.

PREPARATION TIME: 20 MINUTES, PLUS THE TIME IT TAKES TO MAKE THE SALSA
COOKING TIME: 10 TO 15 MINUTES

6 good-size portobello mushroom caps
6 large cloves garlic, slivered lengthwise

FOR THE MARINADE:
1 to 3 canned chipotle chilies with 1 tablespoon
   can juices
¼ large white onion
2 cloves garlic
⅓ cup fresh orange juice
¼ cup vegetable stock or water
2 tablespoons red wine vinegar
2 tablespoons olive oil
½ teaspoon ground cumin
½ teaspoon each black pepper and salt (optional)
3 tablespoons chopped fresh cilantro

1 cup mesquite chips, soaked for 1 hour
   (optional)

FOR THE GARNISH:
1 large ripe tomato, seeded and finely diced
1 medium white onion, finely diced
1 cup finely chopped fresh cilantro
2 cups no-fat sour cream
2 cups Salsa Chipotle (page 27) or Flame-Charred
   Tomato Salsa (page 24), or bottled salsa

1 red bell pepper, cut into ½-inch strips
1 green bell pepper, cut into ½-inch strips
1 large white onion, peeled and cut into 12 wedges
1 bunch scallions, trimmed
12 (7- to 8-inch) fat-free flour tortillas

1. Wipe the portobello caps clean with a damp paper towel. Using the tip of a paring knife, make 8 to 10 tiny slits in the rounded part of each cap and insert a sliver of garlic in each slit.

2. To prepare the marinade, place the chipotles, onion, garlic, orange juice, stock, vinegar, oil, cumin, pepper, salt, and cilantro in a blender and purée to a smooth paste. Brush a little of this mixture on the rounded part of the portobellos and place the mushrooms in a baking dish, gill side up. Spoon the remaining marinade over the portobellos and marinate for 1 hour.

3. Build a hot fire in your barbecue grill. If you are using mesquite chips, toss them on the coals just prior to grilling the mushrooms. If you're using the broiler, preheat it to high. Place the garnish of diced tomato, onion, cilantro, sour cream, and salsa in separate serving bowls.

4. Grill or broil the mushroom caps until cooked, 3 to 5 minutes per side, basting with marinade. Grill the pepper strips, onion, and scallions the same way. (Use a vegetable grate if you have one, to keep the vegetable strips from falling between the bars of the grate.) Thinly slice the portobellos and arrange them on a warm platter with the grilled peppers, onion, and scallions.

5. Warm the tortillas on the grill or under the broiler until they're soft and pliable, 15 seconds per side. Place them in a cloth-lined basket.

6. To serve, have each guest place grilled portobellos and vegetables on a tortilla. Spoon chopped tomato, onions, cilantro, sour cream, and salsa on top. Roll the tortilla into a tube for eating.

Note: Fajitas are often served on sizzling skillets at the table. To achieve this drama at home, preheat a cast-iron skillet in a 400-degree oven for 15 minutes. Just before serving, transfer the portobellos and vegetables to the skillet: They will immediately start sizzling. Warn your guests not to touch the skillet.

Serves 6

257 CALORIES PER SERVING; 9 G PROTEIN; 5 G FAT; 1 G SATURATED FAT;
50 G CARBOHYDRATE; 1,181 MG SODIUM; 0 MG CHOLESTEROL

GRILLED CORN IN THE STYLE OF OAXACA

I've always loved corn on the cob—especially when it's grilled over an open fire. But I've never had anything quite like the corn served by the street vendors of Oaxaca: the ears charred over charcoal braziers, slathered with mayonnaise, then sprinkled with grated cheese, chili powder, and lime juice. The combination will surely strike you as weird, but I promise that you'll grow to love it. I've pretty much left the recipe intact; however, I mix the mayonnaise with a little no-fat sour cream to reduce the overall fat.

PREPARATION TIME: 10 MINUTES   COOKING TIME: 12 TO 16 MINUTES

6 ears of corn
2 tablespoons mayonnaise
2 tablespoons no-fat sour cream
3 tablespoons finely grated queso añnejo, Parmesan cheese, or Romano cheese

1 to 2 tablespoons pure chili powder
2 limes, cut into wedges
Spray oil
Salt and freshly ground black pepper

1. Preheat your grill to high. Shuck the corn by peeling the husks back like banana skins. Leave them attached to the base of the cobs. Tie the husks together: The idea is to create a handle for holding the ear of corn as you eat it.

2. Place the mayonnaise and sour cream in a small serving bowl and stir to mix. Place the cheese, chili powder, and lime wedges in small serving bowls. Have these ingredients ready on the table, with a pastry brush or butter knife for spreading the mayonnaise mixture.

3. Lightly spray each ear of corn with oil and season with the salt and pepper. Grill the corn until it is nicely browned on all sides, 3 to 5 minutes per side, turning with tongs. (Position the corn so that the tied husks hang over the edge of the grill away from the hot coals.) Transfer the corn to a platter.

4. To serve, have each guest brush or spread the mayonnaise mixture on his corn. Sprinkle the ears with cheese and chili powder and squeeze on lime juice to taste.   *Serves 6*

178 CALORIES PER SERVING; 6 G PROTEIN; 6 G FAT; 1 G SATURATED FAT;
33 G CARBOHYDRATE; 107 MG SODIUM; 5 MG CHOLESTEROL

POTATOES WITH ROASTED PEPPERS
(PAPAS CON RAJAS)

Every country has its version of potatoes au gratin. Mexico's offers the electrifying addition of roasted poblano chilies.
To decrease the amount of fat, I've cut back on the cheese, adding nonfat sour cream and chicken stock (or vegetable stock)
for richness. I also try to use Yukon Gold potatoes, which have a naturally buttery flavor, so you don't need a lot of extra fat.

PREPARATION TIME: 30 MINUTES   COOKING TIME: 25 MINUTES

6 poblano chilies
4 to 5 Yukon Gold potatoes (about 2 pounds),
    peeled and cut into 1½-inch chunks
Salt
1½ tablespoons lard or canola oil
1 large white onion, thinly sliced

3 cloves garlic, thinly sliced
1 cup chicken or vegetable stock
½ cup nonfat sour cream
Freshly ground black pepper
¼ cup grated queso fresco or sharp white cheddar
    cheese (optional)

1. Roast the chilies over a high flame or under the broiler, as directed on page 177, until the skins are charred all over, 8 to 10 minutes. Place the chilies in a bowl and cover with plastic wrap. Let cool for 15 minutes. Scrape the burnt skin off each chili, using a paring knife. Seed and devein the chilies, cutting each into ¼-inch-wide strips.

2. Meanwhile, place the potatoes in a pot with lightly salted cold water to cover. Gradually bring to a boil, reduce the heat slightly, and briskly simmer the potatoes until they are just tender, about 10 minutes. Drain the potatoes, rinse with cold water until they're cool, and drain well again.

3. Heat the oil in a large nonstick frying pan. Start the onions over a medium flame, lowering the heat as needed to prevent them from burning. Cook until the onions are a deep golden brown, about 8 minutes, adding the garlic halfway through.

4. Add the chicken stock and sour cream and bring to a boil. Stir in the potatoes and chili strips. Boil the mixture until the sauce is thick and richly flavored, 6 to 8 minutes. Season with salt and pepper to taste. Transfer the mixture to a platter or serving bowl and sprinkle the optional cheese on top. Serve at once.   *Serves 6*

208 CALORIES PER SERVING; 5 G PROTEIN; 4 G FAT; 1 G SATURATED FAT;
41 G CARBOHYDRATE; 32 MG SODIUM; 3 MG CHOLESTEROL

MEXICAN PICKLED VEGETABLES (ESCABECHE)

These tangy pickled vegetables turn up in Mexico wherever drinks are served, whenever Mexicans sit down to the table. Given the snappy crispness and piquant tartness of these colorful vegetables, it's easy to understand why. Here's the basic formula; the vegetables and seasonings vary from cook to cook and region to region. The amarillo chili is a small, waxy yellow, cone-shaped chili that's especially popular for pickling. Serranos and jalapeños work well, too.

PREPARATION TIME: 10 MINUTES   COOKING TIME: NONE, BUT LEAVE 2 DAYS FOR THE VEGETABLES TO PICKLE

2 large carrots, cut into ¼-inch slices
2 stalks celery, cut into ¼-inch slices
1 small zucchini, cut into ¼-inch slices
1 medium white onion, cut in half lengthwise,
   then widthwise into ¼-inch slices
1 cup cauliflower florets, cut into 1-inch pieces

½ to 1 cup amarillo chilies or serranos, stemmed
   but left whole
2 cups distilled white vinegar
2 tablespoons kosher salt
2 bay leaves
½ teaspoon oregano

1. Combine the carrots, celery, zucchini, onion, cauliflower, and chilies in a large bowl and toss to mix. Transfer the vegetables to clean jars. Press sheets of plastic wrap on top to keep vegetables submerged.

2. Combine the vinegar, salt, bay leaves, and oregano in the bowl and whisk until the salt is dissolved. Pour the vinegar mixture over the vegetables and cover the jars. Let the vegetables pickle at room temperature for 48 hours, stirring once or twice. If you plan to keep the vegetables for longer, store them in the refrigerator (pickled vegetables will keep for several weeks).

3. Serve the pickled vegetables in earthenware bowls with drinks or at any Mexican meal.

Serves 10 to 12

23 CALORIES PER SERVING (BASED ON 10 SERVINGS); 1 G PROTEIN; 0 G FAT; 0 G SATURATED FAT;
1 G CARBOHYDRATE; 1,289 MG SODIUM; 0 MG CHOLESTEROL

PICKLED RED ONIONS WITH CHILIES
(ENCURTIDO DE CEBOLLA)

Pickled red onions accompany all sorts of Mexican dishes, from grilled beef in the north to grilled fish in Quintana Roo. Unlike most pickled vegetables, these can be prepared and served the same day, but start early to give the onions several hours to cure.

PREPARATION TIME: 5 MINUTES   COOKING TIME: NONE, BUT ALLOW 6 HOURS FOR PICKLING

1 cup distilled white vinegar
2 teaspoons salt
½ teaspoon sugar
½ teaspoon oregano (preferably Mexican oregano)

1 large red onion, peeled and thinly sliced
  crosswise
1 to 3 fresh jalapeño or serrano chilies, thinly
  sliced

1. Combine the vinegar, salt, and sugar in a large glass jar, cover tightly, and shake until the salt and sugar crystals are dissolved. Stir in the onions and chilies. Press a piece of plastic wrap on top to keep the onions submerged.

2. Let the onions and peppers pickle at room temperature for at least 6 hours, or as long as overnight. Refrigerate until serving.   *Serves 4 to 6*

25 CALORIES PER SERVING (BASED ON 4 SERVINGS); 1 G PROTEIN; 0 G FAT; 0 G SATURATED FAT;
7 G CARBOHYDRATE; 801 MG SODIUM; 0 MG CHOLESTEROL

MEXICAN PICKLED PEPPERS
(CHILES SERRANOS EN ESCABECHE)

When I was in college, just beginning to discover Mexican cooking, my roommates and I would hold chili-eating contests.
I'm not sure I'd go for quantity in the following recipe, but a few of these pickled chilies, eaten judiciously, make
a pleasing prelude to a Mexican meal. The carrot strips make the pickled peppers particularly colorful.

PREPARATION TIME: 5 MINUTES   COOKING TIME: NONE, BUT LEAVE 3 DAYS FOR THE PEPPERS TO PICKLE

1 cup green serrano chilies, stemmed
2 carrots, cut into strips the size of the chilies
1 small white onion, cut into 8 wedges

1 cup distilled white vinegar
1 tablespoon kosher salt
½ teaspoon oregano

1. Combine the chilies, carrots, and onion in a clean earthenware crock and toss to mix. Combine the vinegar, salt, and oregano in a jar, cover tightly, and shake until the salt is dissolved. Pour the vinegar over the chilies. Press a piece of plastic wrap on top of the chilies to keep them submerged in the vinegar.

2. Let the chilies pickle at room temperature or in the refrigerator for at least 3 days. Serve in small earthenware bowls or dishes.   *Serves 10 to 12*

21 CALORIES PER SERVING (BASED ON 10 SERVINGS); 1 G PROTEIN; 0 G FAT; 0 G SATURATED FAT;
6 G CARBOHYDRATE; 646 MG SODIUM; 0 MG CHOLESTEROL

Desserts

Cinnamon Chips with Fruit "Salsa"

Salsa and chips for dessert? The idea might seem oddball, but this colorful dessert is grounded in Mexican tradition. First, the chips—my version of a crisp, flat fritter called buñuelo. My low-fat recipe calls for flour tortillas to be brushed with a little butter, sprinkled with spiced sugar, and baked crisp in the oven. The "salsa" is actually a fruit salad.

PREPARATION TIME: 5 MINUTES (PLUS THE TIME TO MAKE THE SALSA)   COOKING TIME: 5 MINUTES

6 (8-inch) flour tortillas
1½ tablespoons melted butter (preferably unsalted)
   or canola oil
⅓ cup granulated sugar
1½ tablespoons ground cinnamon

½ teaspoon anise seeds
¼ teaspoon ground cloves
Fruit "Salsa" (page 154)
6 sprigs mint, for garnish

1. Preheat the oven to 400°F. Lightly brush the tortillas on both sides with melted butter and arrange them in a single layer on baking sheets. Combine the sugar, cinnamon, anise, and cloves in a bowl and whisk to mix. Sprinkle 1 tablespoon of the spiced sugar over each tortilla. Cut each tortilla into six wedges.

2. Bake the tortillas until they're lightly browned, about 5 minutes. Remove the tortillas from the oven and let cool; the "chips" will crisp as they cool.

3. Spoon the salsa into six ramekins, garnish each with a mint sprig, and place in the center of dessert plates. Arrange the chips around the salsa and serve at once.

Serves 6

202 CALORIES PER SERVING; 4 G PROTEIN; 6 G FAT; 2 G SATURATED FAT;
34 G CARBOHYDRATE; 288 MG SODIUM; 8 MG CHOLESTEROL

Fruit "Flutes" (page 155)

153

FRUIT "SALSA"

At first glance, this fruit salad really does look like salsa, the tomato red provided by strawberries, the onion white by peach, the cilantro green by fresh mint leaves. I even include a little chili: You'll be amazed how the heat of the jalapeños brings out the sweetness of the fruit. Note: For extra color and flavor, I like to add blueberries, but then you lose the salsalike appearance.

PREPARATION TIME: 10 MINUTES

1 pint fresh strawberries, washed and hulled

1 large ripe white peach or pear, cut into ½-inch dice

½ cup fresh mint leaves, thinly slivered, plus 6 whole sprigs for garnish

1 jalapeño chili, seeded and minced (for a spicier salsa, leave the seeds in)

3 tablespoons fresh lime juice

2 to 3 tablespoons light brown sugar

1. Cut the strawberries into ½-inch dice and place them in a bowl. Add the peach, mint leaves, chili, lime juice, and brown sugar and gently toss to mix. Correct the seasoning, adding lime juice or sugar to taste; the "salsa" should be a little sweet and a little sour. **Note:** You can prepare the ingredients ahead of time, but the salsa tastes best served within 10 minutes of mixing. *Serves 4 to 6*

65 CALORIES PER SERVING (BASED ON 4 SERVINGS); 1 G PROTEIN; 0 G FAT; 0 G SATURATED FAT; 16 G CARBOHYDRATE; 5 MG SODIUM; 0 MG CHOLESTEROL

FRUIT "FLUTES"
(FLAUTAS DE FRUTA)

Here's a dish that's probably never been served in Mexico, yet it's so thoroughly Mexican in spirit—tubes of crisp tortilla, cinnamon-scented fruit salad, drizzles of honey and walnuts—that you'd swear it's been a south-of-the-border specialty for centuries. Flautas (flutes) are a popular Mexican snack consisting of crisp, fried corn tortilla tubes stuffed with meat or seafood, slathered with salsa and guacamole. (For savory flautas, see page 65.) To crisp the flour tortilla tubes without deep-frying, I roll and tie them around cannoli tubes (or French cornet molds) and bake them in the oven.

PREPARATION TIME: 15 MINUTES   COOKING TIME: 20 MINUTES, PLUS TIME FOR THE TORTILLAS TO COOL

2 (8-inch) flour tortillas, cut in half
1 tablespoon melted butter
¼ cup sugar
1 tablespoon ground cinnamon
¼ teaspoon ground cloves
Spray oil
1½ cups diced fruits, including starfruit, mango, bananas, and/or oranges

1½ cups berries, including blueberries, raspberries, and diced strawberries
2 tablespoons honey
2 tablespoons chopped toasted walnuts
4 sprigs fresh mint

1. Preheat the oven to 350°F. Warm the tortillas on a nonstick baking sheet until they're soft and pliable, 1 to 3 minutes. Brush each tortilla on both sides with melted butter. Combine the sugar, cinnamon, and cloves in a bowl and stir to mix. Sprinkle one side of the tortillas with half the cinnamon-sugar mixture. Oil the cannoli tubes with spray oil. Roll half a tortilla around each cannoli tube (starting with the cut side of the tortilla, which should be positioned parallel to the tube) and tie it in place with a piece of string. For ease in unmolding the tortillas, have one end of the cannoli mold extend ½ inch beyond the edge of the tortilla. Sprinkle the outside of the tortilla tubes with the remaining sugar.

2. Arrange the tubes on the baking sheet and bake until the tortillas are lightly browned, 15 to 20 minutes. Transfer the resulting flutes to a cake rack. Remove the cannoli molds by gently twisting and pulling. Let the flutes cool to room temperature

(they'll crisp as they cool), then cut and remove the strings. The recipe can be prepared several hours ahead to this stage. (Store the flutes in an airtight container to keep them crisp.)

3. Combine the diced fruits and berries in a mixing bowl and gently toss. Stir in 1 to 2 tablespoons of the cinnamon-sugar mixture, or to taste.

4. To serve, stuff some of the fruit salad into the tortilla flutes, using a tiny spoon. Arrange the flutes on four plates or on a platter and spoon the remaining fruit salad over them. Drizzle the fruit and flutes with the honey and sprinkle with the walnuts. Garnish each with a sprig of fresh mint and serve at once.

Note: For a particularly showy presentation, place a little sweetened condensed skim milk, Mexican chocolate sauce (mole poblano, page 107), and/or cajeta (page 156) in separate plastic squirt bottles. Squirt zigzags of these sauces over the fruit salad and tortilla flutes.   *Serves 4*

237 CALORIES PER SERVING; 3 G PROTEIN; 7 G FAT; 2 G SATURATED FAT;
44 G CARBOHYDRATE; 118 MG SODIUM; 8 MG CHOLESTEROL

QUICK MILK CARAMEL (CAJETA)

Yes, I know I'm going to take some heat for this one. Cajeta is one of the glories of Mexican confectionery, a tangy, rib-stickingly rich caramel made by boiling down milk (traditionally goat's milk) to a thick, sweet, fudgy paste. This presents two problems for the low-fat cook: First, you must use whole milk. (Skim milk will burn when you try to reduce it.) Second, the preparation of cajeta requires a major commitment of time and effort. (It takes about 40 minutes of simmering and stirring to cook the milk to the proper consistency.) These difficulties set me thinking about a similar preparation I've enjoyed elsewhere in Latin America: dulce de leche (meaning "milk sweet"). This, too, requires lengthy boiling in its traditional version, but cooks from San Juan to Santiago have come up with a tasty shortcut: They boil a can of sweetened condensed milk (fat-free condensed milk, in this case) until the contents are caramel colored and as thick as fudge.

Here, then, is a quick cajeta that's delicious in crêpes (page 58), ladled over frozen yogurt or fruit, or simply eaten right off a spoon. Note: To approximate the sourish flavor achieved by making cajeta with goat's milk, whisk a little soft goat cheese, like a Montrachet, into the finished caramel.

PREPARATION TIME: 2 MINUTES   COOKING TIME: 2 HOURS, PLUS TIME FOR COOLING

1 (14-ounce) can fat-free sweetened condensed skim milk, unopened
1 teaspoon vanilla extract

½ teaspoon ground cinnamon
2 ounces soft goat cheese, like Montrachet, at room temperature (optional)

1. Place the unopened can of condensed milk in a large saucepan with water to cover by 6 inches. Bring to a boil. Reduce the heat to medium and briskly simmer the condensed milk, covered, for 2 hours, adding water as needed to keep the can immersed. It's essential to keep the can covered with 6 inches of water at all times. Alternatively, cook the unopened can of condensed milk in a pressure cooker for 20 minutes. (The can, too, should be fully submerged in water.)

2. Transfer the can to the sink with tongs and let cool to room temperature. Open it with a can opener and scrape the dark, thick, sweet caramel into a mixing bowl.

3. Stir in the vanilla extract, cinnamon, and goat cheese, if using. Store the cajeta, covered, in the refrigerator. It will keep for several days (for several weeks, if you omit the goat cheese). Let it warm to room temperature before serving.   *Serves 6*

215 CALORIES PER SERVING; 7 G PROTEIN; 2 G FAT; 1 G SATURATED FAT;
41 G CARBOHYDRATE; 103 MG SODIUM; 11 MG CHOLESTEROL

MEXICAN CARAMEL CRÊPES WITH BANANAS
(CREPAS DE CAJETA Y PLÁTANOS)

These dulcet crêpes are one of Mexico's most popular desserts. Given the filling—ripe bananas and a thick, fudgy milk caramel called cajeta—it's easy to understand their popularity. For a particularly festive presentation of the crêpes, I call for an optional flambéing with rum. Note: My low-fat crêpes contain one non-Mexican ingredient, buttermilk. This gives the crêpes a velvety softness normally acquired by loading the batter with egg yolks and melted butter.

PREPARATION TIME: 20 MINUTES   COOKING TIME: 15 MINUTES

FOR THE CRÊPES
1 egg
2 egg whites
½ cup low-fat buttermilk
¾ cup water
½ teaspoon sugar
½ teaspoon salt, or to taste
½ teaspoon ground cinnamon
¼ teaspoon ground cloves
1 teaspoon canola oil

1 cup unbleached white all-purpose flour
Spray oil

TO FINISH THE CRÊPES:
1 batch of cajeta (page 156)
2 ripe bananas
1 tablespoon unsalted butter, melted
⅓ cup dark rum (optional)
1 or more (7-inch) crêpe or omelet pans

1. To prepare the crêpes, place the whole egg and the whites in a mixing bowl and whisk to combine. Whisk in the buttermilk, water, sugar, salt, cinnamon, cloves, and oil. Sift in the flour and gently whisk just to mix. (Do not overwhisk the batter, or the crêpes will be rubbery.) If the batter looks lumpy, strain it into another bowl. It should be the consistency of heavy cream. If it's too thick, thin it with a little more water.

2. Lightly spray the crêpe pan(s) with oil and heat over a medium flame. (When the pan is the proper temperature, a drop of water spattered on it will evaporate in 2 to 3 seconds.) Off the heat, pour 3 tablespoons of the crêpe batter into the pan all at once. Gently tilt and rotate the pan to coat the bottom with a thin layer of batter. (Pour back any excess—the crêpe should be as thin as possible.)

3. Cook each crêpe until it is lightly browned on both sides, 30 to 60 seconds per side, turning with a spatula. As the crêpes are done, stack them on a plate. For the best results, spray the pans with oil between crêpes.

4. To finish the dish, lay a crêpe, dark side down, on a plate. Spread it with 2 tablespoons of the cajeta and arrange a few banana slices on top. Roll up the crêpe like a cigar and arrange it on a heatproof platter. Finish the remaining crêpes the same way. The recipe can be prepared several hours ahead to this stage and stored, covered, in the refrigerator.

5. Preheat the oven to 400°F. Brush the tops of the crêpes with melted butter. Bake the crêpes until they're heated through, 8 to 10 minutes. Warm the rum in a small saucepan but do not let it boil. (It shouldn't get hotter than body temperature.) At tableside—tying back your hair and sleeves, and taking care to avert your face and hair—touch a match to the hot rum: It will burst into flames. Pour the flaming rum over the crêpes. When the rum stops burning, transfer the crêpes to individual dessert plates and serve at once.

Makes 12 crêpes, enough to serve 6

216 CALORIES PER SERVING; 7 G PROTEIN; 4 G FAT; 2 G SATURATED FAT; 38 G CARBOHYDRATE; 176 MG SODIUM; 33 MG CHOLESTEROL

MEXICAN CARAMEL CHEESECAKE

Here's a contemporary twist on a classic Mexican dessert: a cheesecake flavored with cajeta (milk caramel). It requires only 10 minutes of preparation time (plus the time it takes the cajeta to cook), but jaws will drop with admiration when your guests taste it. Traditional cajeta is made with goat's milk, which gives it a pleasant sourish aftertaste. To achieve that flavor here, I add a little goat cheese. Not everyone likes goat cheese, however, so I've made it optional.

PREPARATION TIME: 10 MINUTES (PLUS THE TIME IT TAKES TO COOK THE CAJETA)
COOKING TIME: 40 TO 60 MINUTES

1 pound low-fat cottage cheese (1 percent)
1 pound low-fat cream cheese, at room temperature
4 ounces soft goat cheese, like Montrachet (optional)
14 ounces (1 batch) quick cajeta (made with no-fat sweetened condensed milk; see page 156)
1 cup egg substitute, or 2 eggs plus 4 egg whites

¼ cup brown sugar or piloncillo (see Note below) (or even white sugar)
2 tablespoons fresh lime juice
1 tablespoon vanilla extract
1 teaspoon grated lemon zest
1 teaspoon grated orange zest
½ teaspoon ground cinnamon
Pinch of salt

1. Preheat the oven to 350°F. (Set the rack in the lower third of the oven.) Bring 1 quart of water to a boil. Wrap a piece of foil around the bottom and sides of a lightly oiled 8-inch springform pan to prevent water from seeping in when the pan is placed in the water bath.

2. Purée the cottage cheese in the food processor, scraping down the sides. This may take several minutes. Add the cream cheese, optional goat cheese, and the cajeta and purée until smooth. Add the eggs, egg whites, brown sugar, lime juice, vanilla, lemon and orange zest, cinnamon, and salt and purée. Strain the mixture into the prepared pan. Tap the pan a few times on the work counter to knock out any bubbles.

3. Set the springform pan in a roasting pan in the oven. Add 1 inch of boiling water to the roasting pan and bake the cheesecake until it is set, 40 to 60 minutes. To test for doneness, gently poke the side of the pan—when the top no longer jiggles, the cheesecake

is cooked. Another test: An inserted skewer will come out clean when the cheesecake is cooked. Do not overcook, or the cheesecake will become watery.

4. Transfer the cheesecake to a cake rack to cool to room temperature, then refrigerate until it's cold. To serve, run the tip of a small knife around the inside of the pan and unfasten the sides. Cut the cheesecake into wedges.

Note: Piloncillo is Mexican raw sugar; it comes in a cone and has a rich, earthy, malty flavor that's utterly unique. Look for it in Mexican grocery stores. (Dark brown sugar will work in a pinch.)

Variation: For a stunning presentation, pour ½ cup of sweetened condensed milk into a squirt bottle. Place ½ cup of your favorite chocolate sauce in another bottle. Squirt lines of the sauces across the top of the cheesecake to form a zigzag or crosshatch pattern.   *Serves 10 to 12*

277 CALORIES PER SERVING (BASED ON 10 SERVINGS); 16 G PROTEIN; 10 G FAT; 6 G SATURATED FAT; 32 G CARBOHYDRATE; 537 MG SODIUM; 24 MG CHOLESTEROL

YUCA IN SPICE-SCENTED SYRUP

Here's an offbeat twist to the fruits poached in spice-scented syrup so beloved by Mexicans for dessert. The "fruit" in question is actually a starchy root vegetable—yuca—and its mild buttery flavor and soft creamy texture work surprisingly well for dessert. Actually, the idea of serving yuca as dessert isn't as wacky as it seems: This is the plant from which tapioca is made. Fresh yuca can be found at Hispanic markets and at many supermarkets. Many stores sell it frozen. When buying fresh yuca, look for firm, heavy tubers free of blemishes, soft spots, and strong odors. If the flesh looks dried out or riddled with black veins, don't buy it.

PREPARATION TIME: 10 MINUTES   COOKING TIME: 20 MINUTES

1½ pounds fresh yuca
Pinch of salt

FOR THE SYRUP:
1½ cups water
½ cup sugar
½ cup piloncillo or dark brown sugar

1 cinnamon stick
4 cloves
2 allspice berries
½ teaspoon anise seed
2 strips lemon zest
2 strips orange zest

1. Cut the yuca crosswise into 2-inch pieces and peel with a chef's knife. (Stand the pieces on end and cut off the peel with downward strokes of the knife.) Cut any large pieces in half or quarters, so that all pieces are the same size.

2. Bring 2 quarts of water and a pinch of salt to a boil in a large pot. Add the yuca and cook for 10 minutes. Add 1 cup of cold water. Return the yuca to a boil and cook for 5 minutes. Add another cup of cold water, return to a boil, and cook for 5 minutes, or until the yuca is very soft. (The successive additions of cold water help tenderize the yuca.)

3. Meanwhile, make the syrup. Combine the water, sugar, piloncillo or brown sugar, cinnamon stick, cloves, allspice, anise seed, and lemon and orange zest in a saucepan and bring to a boil. Reduce the heat and simmer for 5 minutes. Remove the pan from the heat and strain the syrup into a heatproof bowl.

4. Drain the yuca in a colander and rinse briefly with cold water. Older yuca may have woody fibers running the length of the center: With a fork, scrape out any you find. Add the yuca to the warm syrup and let it cool to room temperature. Refrigerate until serving. To serve, spoon the yuca into individual bowls and generously douse with syrup.

Serves 4 to 6

409 CALORIES PER SERVINGS (BASED ON 4 SERVINGS); 5 G PROTEIN; 1 G FAT; 0 G SATURATED FAT; 99 G CARBOHYDRATE; 29 MG SODIUM; 0 MG CHOLESTEROL

ALEGRÍAS
(CARAMEL PUFFED AMARANTH)

If you like caramel popcorn, you'll love these crunchy, sweet, cookielike cakes—a popular Mexican street snack. Alegrías take their name, appropriately, from the Spanish word for "joy." Their main ingredient is amaranth, a tiny, nutritious grain prized for its delicate nutty flavor and its ability to puff up like popcorn. Add the earthy flavor of a caramel made with piloncillo (Mexican brown sugar) and honey and you've got an irresistible fat-free treat. You can find puffed amaranth at natural foods stores, or order by mail from Nu-World Amaranth (P.O. Box 2202, Naperville, IL 60567). Or you can pop it at home, working in small batches in a large covered saucepan over medium-high heat. Unlike popcorn, you don't need oil when popping amaranth. But shake the pan as you cook it to keep the grain from scorching. Note: The grated orange zest and cinnamon aren't traditional, but I like the flavor they add.

PREPARATION TIME: 10 MINUTES   COOKING TIME: 10 MINUTES

4 ounces piloncillo or ⅔ cup dark brown sugar
¼ cup honey
1 teaspoon lime juice
½ teaspoon ground cinnamon
½ teaspoon grated orange zest
3 cups popped amaranth
Spray oil

1. In a large saucepan combine the piloncillo (or brown sugar), honey, lime juice, cinnamon, and orange zest. Cover the pan and cook the mixture over high heat for 2 minutes. Uncover the pan and continue cooking until the mixture reaches the hard-ball stage (245°F on a candy thermometer), about 5 minutes. Do not stir.

2. Remove the pan from the heat and stir in the amaranth, using a wooden spoon. Let cool slightly.

Lightly oil your hands. Using a spoon or your fingers, take 1-inch balls of amaranth mixture and press them onto a nonstick baking sheet, flattening them into 2-inch circles. When they have cooled completely, the alegrías are ready to eat. If you wish to keep them for a few days, arrange them in a cookie tin, placing waxed or parchment paper between the layers.

Makes 2 dozen

37 CALORIES PER PIECE; 0 G PROTEIN; 0 G FAT; 0 G SATURATED FAT;
10 G CARBOHYDRATE; 6 MG SODIUM; 0 MG CHOLESTEROL

TWO FLANS

Like many desserts, flan was brought to Mexico by the Spanish, but Mexican cooks have given it a distinctive personality, adding local spices and seasonings. My low-fat rendition takes advantage of the richness of sweetened condensed milk to compensate for the loss of most of the egg yolks. Below are two versions: an orange anise flan bursting with Arabic flavors and a Oaxacan chocolate flan guaranteed to satisfy the most diehard chocoholic.

ORANGE ANISE FLAN

This recipe has Spanish roots, but the flavorings are Middle Eastern. This isn't as odd as it sounds, given the fact that Spain was occupied by the Moors for several centuries and that Mexico welcomed thousands of Lebanese immigrants in the early 1900s. Orange flower water has a haunting perfumed flavor and can be found at Middle Eastern and Indian markets and in some gourmet shops. You can substitute an orange liqueur, but the flavor won't be quite the same.

PREPARATION TIME: 10 MINUTES   COOKING TIME: 1 HOUR

1 teaspoon anise seed
1½ cups sugar
1 (14-ounce) can fat-free sweetened condensed milk
1 cup skim milk

2 eggs plus 6 whites or 1¼ cups egg substitute
1 tablespoon orange flower water
2 teaspoons grated fresh orange zest
Pinch of salt
6 (6-ounce) ramekins or custard cups

1. Preheat the oven to 350°F. Grind the anise seed to a fine powder in a spice mill or coffee mill.

2. Place the sugar in a heavy saucepan with ¼ cup of water. Cover the pan and cook over high heat for 2 minutes. Uncover the pan, reduce the heat slightly, and cook the sugar, without stirring, until it is caramelized (it will turn a dark golden brown), about 5 minutes. Pour the caramel into the ramekins, rotating each to coat the bottom and sides. Be careful: Caramel gives a terrible burn. (You may want to wear oven mitts to protect your hands and arms.) Let the caramel cool completely. Bring 1 quart of water to a boil.

3. Combine the condensed milk and the skim milk, the eggs, whites, orange flower water, orange zest, salt, and ground anise in a mixing bowl and whisk to blend. Ladle this mixture into the ramekins. Set the ramekins in a roasting pan and pour ½ inch of boiling water around them. Place the roasting pan in the oven. Bake until the flans are set, 40 to 50 minutes. (To test for doneness, gently poke the side of one of the ramekins: The filling should jiggle.) Transfer the flans to a rack to cool, then refrigerate for at least 6 hours, preferably overnight.

4. To unmold, run the tip of a paring knife around the inside edge of each ramekin. Place a plate over the ramekin, invert, and shake until the flan slips loose. Spoon any caramel left in the ramekin around the flan and serve at once.   *Serves 6*

440 CALORIES PER SERVING; 13 G PROTEIN; 2 G FAT; 0 G SATURATED FAT;
93 G CARBOHYDRATE; 182 MG SODIUM; 8 MG CHOLESTEROL

OAXACAN CHOCOLATE FLAN

Cocoa beans. Almonds. Sugar. Cinnamon. Cloves. This is what Oaxacans use to prepare hot chocolate, and I've never tasted better anywhere. The combination of sweetened condensed milk and evaporated skim milk creates uncommon richness and depth of flavor.

PREPARATION TIME: 10 MINUTES   COOKING TIME: 1 HOUR

1½ cups sugar
1 cup evaporated skim milk
2 ounces Mexican chocolate or bittersweet
  chocolate, finely chopped
1 (14-ounce) can fat-free sweetened condensed
  milk
⅓ cup unsweetened cocoa powder
2 eggs plus 6 whites or 1¼ cups egg substitute

2 teaspoons vanilla extract
¼ teaspoon almond extract
½ teaspoon ground cinnamon
¼ teaspoon ground cloves
Pinch of salt
6 toasted almonds (see toasting instructions on
  page 104)
6 (6-ounce) ramekins or custard cups

1. Preheat the oven to 350°F.

2. Place the sugar in a heavy saucepan with ¼ cup of water. Cover the pan and cook over high heat for 2 minutes. Uncover the pan, reduce the heat slightly, and cook the sugar, without stirring, until it is caramelized (it will turn a dark golden brown), about 5 minutes. Pour the caramel into the ramekins, rotating each to coat the bottom and sides. Be careful: Caramel gives a terrible burn. (You may want to wear oven mitts to protect your hands and arms.) Let the caramel cool completely.

3. Place the evaporated milk in a saucepan and heat to a simmer. Whisk in the chocolate and cook until melted. Remove the pan from the heat and whisk in the condensed milk and the cocoa powder. Let cool for 5 minutes. Add the eggs, whites, vanilla and almond extracts, cinnamon, cloves, and salt and whisk well to mix.

4. Strain the flan mixture into the ramekins. Set the ramekins in a roasting pan and pour ½ inch of boiling water around them. Place the roasting pan in the oven. Bake until the flans are set, 40 to 50 minutes. (To test for doneness, gently poke the side of one of the ramekins: The filling should jiggle.) Transfer the flans to a rack to cool, then refrigerate for at least 6 hours, preferably overnight.

5. To unmold, run the tip of a paring knife around the inside edge of each ramekin. Place a plate over the ramekin, invert, and shake until the flan slips loose. Spoon any caramel left in the ramekin around the flan.   *Serves 6*

496 CALORIES PER SERVING; 14 G PROTEIN; 4 G FAT; 2 G SATURATED FAT;
103 G CARBOHYDRATE; 205 MG SODIUM; 8 MG CHOLESTEROL

MEXICAN "FRENCH" TOAST (TORREJAS)

French toast may seem like an odd dish for dessert, but throughout Mexico fried bread slices doused with dark spicy syrup are considered a great way to bring a meal to a close. To cut the amount of fat in the traditional recipe, I've eliminated most of the yolks from the egg batter, and I crisp the bread in a hot oven instead of frying it. Note: This recipe is a great way to use up stale bread—the bread is easier to work with if it's a little stale.

PREPARATION TIME: 20 MINUTES   COOKING TIME: 25 MINUTES

FOR THE TORREJAS:
1 baguette (French bread)
1 egg plus 2 whites, or ½ cup egg substitute
¾ cup evaporated skim milk
2 tablespoons cream sherry
1 teaspoon vanilla extract
¼ teaspoon almond extract
½ teaspoon ground cinnamon
Spray oil

FOR THE SYRUP:
1½ cups water
1½ cups grated piloncillo or dark brown sugar
4 strips orange zest
2 sticks cinnamon
2 cloves
2 allspice berries
½ teaspoon anise seed

1. Preheat the oven to 400°F. Cut the bread on the diagonal into eight 1-inch-thick slices and arrange them in a baking dish. Combine the egg and egg whites, milk, sherry, vanilla and almond extracts, and cinnamon in a bowl and whisk to mix. Pour this mixture over the bread slices and let soak for 15 minutes, turning the bread once or twice to ensure even soaking.

2. Lightly spray a nonstick baking sheet with oil. Arrange the soaked bread slices on top. Spray the tops of the bread with oil. Bake the bread until it is firm and golden brown, 10 to 15 minutes, turning once. Transfer the bread slices to shallow bowls or a deep platter.

3. Meanwhile, make the syrup. Combine the water, piloncillo sugar, orange zest, cinnamon, cloves, allspice, and anise seed in a saucepan and bring to a boil. Reduce the heat and briskly simmer until the syrup is richly flavored, 8 to 10 minutes. Remove the pan from the heat and let cool slightly. Strain the warm syrup over the bread and serve at once.

Note: It's customary to serve torrejas hot, but they're also quite tasty cold. *Serves 8*

262 CALORIES PER SERVING; 5 G PROTEIN; 1 G FAT; 0 G SATURATED FAT;
58 G CARBOHYDRATE; 223 MG SODIUM; 1 MG CHOLESTEROL

DRINKS

SANGRITA
(SPICED TOMATO JUICE "CHASER")

Sit down to any serious meal in Mexico and you'll be offered twin glasses of sipping tequila and sangrita. Sangrita is a spicy "chaser" based on tomato and orange or lime juice, often with a little chili powder or pickled pepper juice for punch. The presentation might be rounded out with a few radishes, scallions, or jícama slices to munch on.

PREPARATION TIME: 10 MINUTES

1 cup tomato juice
¾ cup fresh orange juice
¼ cup fresh lime juice, plus 1 or 2 lime wedges
2 tablespoons juice from pickled jalapeño peppers, or to taste

2 tablespoons finely grated onion with juices (optional)
¼ cup pure chili powder

1. In a pitcher, mix together the tomato, orange, and lime juices, the jalapeño pepper juice, and onion (if using). Add lime juice or pepper juice to taste; the sangrita should be highly seasoned.

2. Moisten the rims of eight straight-sided shot glasses or cordial glasses with the lime wedges. Spread the chili powder in a shallow bowl. Invert the glasses and dip them in the chili powder to coat the rims. Pour the sangrita into the glasses and serve at once.

Serves 8

31 CALORIES PER SERVING; 1 G PROTEIN; 1 G FAT; 0 G SATURATED FAT;
7 G CARBOHYDRATE; 177 MG SODIUM; 0 MG CHOLESTEROL

"Cocktails" Mexican style

THE REAL MARGARITA

Who really invented the margarita? There are lots of candidates, including bartenders in Tijuana, Acapulco, and even San Antonio, Texas. One thing's for sure, though: No Mexican meal would be complete without this tangy, sweet-salty tequila and fresh lime thirst quencher. Like most cocktails that are too successful for their own good, the margarita has inspired a great deal of nonsense in recent years: frozen margaritas, banana margaritas, margaritas prepared with bottled mixes. Here's an authentic margarita that will get you back to the basics of good drinking and eating. One tequila I particularly like for margaritas is Herradura Gold. Note: The sugar, orange, and lime zest aren't traditional, but I like the way they round out the flavor.

PREPARATION TIME: 10 MINUTES

2 tablespoons sugar
2 strips lime zest
2 strips orange zest
6 ounces (¾ cup) good tequila
⅓ cup Cointreau or other bitter orange liqueur

½ cup fresh lime juice
2 tablespoons water
5 fresh lime wedges
Kosher salt or coarse sea salt (optional)
4 cups ice

1. Place the sugar, lime zest, and orange zest in a mortar and pound with a pestle. The idea is to bruise the zests, extracting the fragrant oils. (If you don't have a mortar, pound the zests with the end of a wooden spoon in a bowl.)

2. Transfer the sugar and zests to a pitcher and stir in the tequila, Cointreau, lime juice, and water. If you have the time, let the mixture sit for a couple of hours in the refrigerator to allow the flavors to meld.

3. Rub the rims of four martini glasses with one of the lime wedges. Spread the salt, if using, in a shallow bowl. Dip each glass, rim side down, in the salt to coat the rim. Shake off the excess salt and right the glasses. **Note:** If you're watching your sodium intake, omit the salt.

4. Just before serving, add the ice to the margarita and stir or shake well, 2 minutes. Strain the margarita into the prepared glasses. Festoon each with a wedge of lime and serve at once.   *Serves 4*

200 CALORIES PER SERVING; 1 G PROTEIN; 0 G FAT; 0 G SATURATED FAT;
20 G CARBOHYDRATE; 2 MG SODIUM; 0 MG CHOLESTEROL

MIXED-FRUIT MARGARITA

Necessity, goes the saying, is the mother of invention. A margarita made without tequila may seem like a contradiction in terms, but if you have a Mexican restaurant without a liquor license, this is precisely what you may find yourself serving. Mexico City–born Los Angeles restaurateur Frank Romero has risen to the challenge, concocting a margarita from a soothing blend of vermouth and tropical fruit juices. You've probably never had the likes of this margarita, but I wager that you'll find yourself wanting seconds.

PREPARATION TIME: 5 MINUTES

1 or 2 wedges fresh lime
Kosher salt or coarse sea salt (optional)
1 cup fresh or canned diced pineapple
1 cup diced honeydew melon
1 cup guava nectar

⅓ cup fresh lime juice, or to taste
⅔ cup dry white vermouth
1½ tablespoons sugar, or to taste
2 cups ice cubes

1. Rub the rims of six martini glasses with the cut lime. Spread the salt, if using, in a shallow bowl. Dip each glass, rim side down, in the salt to coat the rim. Shake off the excess salt and right the glasses.

2. Combine the pineapple, melon, guava nectar, lime juice, vermouth, sugar, and ice in a blender and purée until smooth. Correct the tartness and sweetness, adding lime juice or sugar to taste. Pour the margarita mixture into the glasses without disturbing the salt and serve at once.   *Serves 6*

91 CALORIES PER SERVING; 0 G PROTEIN; 0 G FAT; 0 G SATURATED FAT;
17 G CARBOHYDRATE; 10 MG SODIUM; 0 MG CHOLESTEROL

TAMARIND NECTAR
(AGUA DE TAMARINDO)

Mexicans love fruit drinks. Visit almost any casual restaurant or market stall and you'll see a rainbow-colored assortment of beverages lined up on the bar in handsome glass jars. This brown drink may not look as pretty as the others, but when it comes to quenching a thirst, nothing can beat the smoky, sweet-sour tang of tamarind. This tan, curved, tropical seedpod harbors an orangish brown pulp that tastes uncannily like prunes soaked in lime juice. If you live in a city with a large Hispanic community, you may be able to find whole tamarind pods. (Choose ripe pods—the ones with cracked tan skins.) More commonly, the tamarind pulp is sold peeled but with the seeds in plastic bags. This is what I call for below (see Note).

PREPARATION TIME: 10 MINUTES

4 ounces peeled tamarind pulp, or 6 to 8 peeled pods
1 cup hot water

4 cups cold water
4 to 6 tablespoons sugar (or to taste)

1. Place the tamarind pulp in the bowl of a blender or food processor with the hot water and let stand for 5 minutes. Blend the mixture in short bursts at low speed until the seeds are free of pulp, 30 to 60 seconds.

2. Pour the tamarind mixture through a strainer into a pitcher, pressing hard with a wooden spoon to extract the juices and scraping the bottom of the strainer with a rubber spatula.

3. Return the seeds and pulp that remain in the strainer to the blender and mix with the 4 cups of cold water and the sugar. Strain this mixture into the pitcher and stir. Chill well.

4. Just before serving, check the tamarind nectar for sweetness, adding sugar as needed. Stir well and serve at once in tumblers filled with ice.

Note: Hispanic grocery stores often sell packages of frozen tamarind purée (pulpa de tamarindo). If you can find this, place 12 ounces in the pitcher. Stir in the cold water and sugar to taste, omitting the blending in steps 1 and 3.

Serves 4

56 CALORIES PER SERVING; 0 G PROTEIN; 0 G FAT; 0 G SATURATED FAT;

14 G CARBOHYDRATE; 9 MG SODIUM; 0 MG CHOLESTEROL

MANGO NECTAR
(AGUA DE MANGO)

This golden drink is one of the delights of a Mexican juice bar, a perfumed nectar made with nature's perfect fruit. But to get the full effect, you must use ripe mangoes—the kind you can smell from the kitchen the moment you walk into the house. Smell alone will tell you a mango's ripeness, as some varieties remain green even when they're ready to eat. To ripen mangoes, place them in a loosely sealed paper bag at room temperature. Note: If you have sensitive skin, wear gloves when working with mangoes. Some people have a violent allergic reaction to mango sap.

PREPARATION TIME: 10 MINUTES

1 large or 2 small ripe mangoes (about 1½ pounds)
2 to 4 tablespoons sugar, or to taste

2 tablespoons fresh lime juice, or to taste
4 cups water

1. Peel the mango and cut the flesh off the seed. Place the flesh in a blender with the sugar, lime juice, and water. Purée until smooth. Taste for sweetness and tartness, adding sugar or lime juice as needed.

2. Strain the mango nectar into a pitcher and refrigerate until you're ready to serve. If it's too thick, add a little more water. Serve over ice in a tall glass. Stir well just before serving.

Serves 4

137 CALORIES PER SERVING; 1 G PROTEIN; 1 G FAT; 0 G SATURATED FAT;
36 G CARBOHYDRATE; 11 MG SODIUM; 0 MG CHOLESTEROL

HOMINY "MILKSHAKE"
(BEBIDA DE POSOLE)

This creamy, pearl-colored drink belongs to a large family of grain-based beverages popular throughout Mexico. Think of it as a dairy-free milkshake, made with posole (hulled, poached white corn) instead of ice cream. For convenience, I call for canned posole here, but you can certainly cook the hominy from scratch. The recipe was inspired by a drink seller at the central food market in Mérida.

PREPARATION TIME: 5 MINUTES

½ cup cooked posole (hominy)
2 tablespoons sweetened condensed skim milk
1½- by 2-inch strip lemon zest (the yellow, oil-rich outer rind)
¼ teaspoon ground cinnamon

½ teaspoon vanilla extract
1 drop (⅛ teaspoon) almond extract
6 ice cubes
¾ cup water

1. Place the hominy in a strainer, rinse well with cold water, and drain again. Several rinsings will be required to remove the excess salt.

2. In a blender, combine the hominy with the milk, lemon zest, cinnamon, vanilla and almond extracts, ice cubes, and water and mix until smooth and creamy.

Serves 1, and can be multiplied as desired

82 CALORIES PER SERVING; 1 G PROTEIN; 0 G FAT; 0 G SATURATED FAT;
19 G CARBOHYDRATE; 84 MG SODIUM; 0 MG CHOLESTEROL

WALNUT RICE PUNCH WITH MELON (HORCHATA)

Milky white, nutty and sweet, horchata is one of the most offbeat beverages sold at a Mexican juice bar or lunch counter. Its origins lie a continent and a millennium away: The Moors brought rice to Spain when they invaded in the 8th century A.D. Rice and walnuts may seem like odd flavorings for a beverage, but the combination is amazingly refreshing. Horchata-type drinks can be found throughout the former Spanish empire; the melon is a strictly Mexican touch.

PREPARATION TIME: 5 MINUTES   COOKING TIME: NONE, BUT ALLOW 6 HOURS
FOR STEEPING AND CHILLING THE HORCHATA

2 cinnamon sticks
4 cloves
4 allspice berries
½ teaspoon anise seed
2 strips orange zest
5 cups water

½ cup uncooked white rice
¼ cup chopped walnuts
⅓ cup sugar, or to taste
½ teaspoon almond extract
2 cups diced honeydew melon

1. Tie the cinnamon, cloves, allspice, anise seed, and orange zest in a piece of cheesecloth. Combine the water, rice, walnuts, sugar, almond extract, and spice bundle in a pitcher and let steep for 6 to 8 hours, preferably overnight.

2. Remove and discard the spice bundle. Place the rice mixture and half the melon in a blender and blend until smooth. Taste for sweetness, adding sugar as needed.

3. Strain the horchata through a fine-mesh strainer into a pitcher. Stir in the remaining melon. Serve chilled.   *Serves 4*

221 CALORIES PER SERVING; 3 G PROTEIN; 3 G FAT; 0 G SATURATED FAT;
46 G CARBOHYDRATE; 20 MG SODIUM; 0 MG CHOLESTEROL

OAXACAN HOT CHOCOLATE

To say that the people of Oaxaca love hot chocolate would be an understatement. Visit the central food market in this handsome colonial city and you'll be treated to steaming bowls of the thickest, frothiest, most spice-scented hot chocolate you've ever tasted. Prowl the back streets behind the market and you'll find out just why Oaxacan hot chocolate is so good: There are shops that specialize in grinding the ingredients—freshly roasted cocoa beans, whole almonds, cloves, cinnamon sticks, and sugar—to order, according to the proportions preferred by each patron. To decrease the amount of fat in this delicious but fat-laden drink, I use a combination of chocolate and cocoa powder, replacing some of the almonds with almond extract and some of the whole milk with evaporated skim milk. The one thing I haven't sacrificed is taste.

PREPARATION TIME: 5 MINUTES   COOKING TIME: 5 MINUTES

5 tablespoons unsweetened cocoa powder
5 tablespoons sugar
2 tablespoons slivered or ground almonds, toasted
1 teaspoon ground cinnamon
¼ teaspoon ground cloves
2 ounces semisweet chocolate (preferably Mexican), finely chopped

2½ cups skim milk
1 can (12 ounces) evaporated skim milk
1 teaspoon vanilla extract
¼ teaspoon almond extract
Pinch of salt

1. Place the cocoa powder, sugar, almonds, cinnamon, and cloves in a food processor or spice mill and grind to a fine powder. Add the chocolate and grind it in as well.

2. Transfer the chocolate mixture to a heavy saucepan and whisk in 1 cup of the skim milk (enough to make a paste). Turn the heat on high and gradually add the remaining skim milk, evaporated milk, vanilla and almond extracts, and salt, whisking well. Heat the mixture to a boil, whisking steadily. Reduce the heat to medium and simmer the chocolate for 3 minutes.

3. Strain the chocolate into a pitcher and with a *molinillo* (chocolate beater) or whisk, mix until it's frothy. Pour the drink into cups and serve at once.

Serves 4

293 CALORIES PER SERVING; 17 G PROTEIN; 9 G FAT; 3 G SATURATED FAT;
39 G CARBOHYDRATE; 182 MG SODIUM; 5 MG CHOLESTEROL

SPICED COFFEE
(CAFÉ DE OLLA)

This dark, sweet, spicy coffee takes its name from the earthenware pot (olla) in which it's traditionally brewed. Cinnamon, cloves, and anise seed impart a beguiling spice flavor, while the piloncillo (Mexican brown sugar) both thickens and sweetens the brew. I can't think of a better beverage to bring a Mexican meal to a close.

PREPARATION TIME: 5 MINUTES   COOKING TIME: 10 MINUTES

5 cups water
1 cinnamon stick, plus 4 sticks for garnish
6 cloves
½ teaspoon anise seeds
2 strips orange zest

3 to 4 ounces piloncillo, chopped, or ⅓ cup brown sugar
½ cup freshly ground dark-roast coffee beans (like a French or Italian roast)

1. Combine the water, 1 stick of the cinnamon, cloves, anise seeds, orange zest, and sugar in a large pot and bring to a boil. Reduce the heat and gently simmer until the sugar is dissolved and the liquid is richly flavored, about 5 minutes.

2. Remove the pan from the heat and stir in the coffee. Let it steep for 5 minutes, then strain it into coffee mugs through a coffee filter, fine-mesh strainer, or a strainer lined with cheesecloth. Garnish each mug with a cinnamon stick and serve at once.

Serves 4

79 CALORIES PER SERVING; 0 G PROTEIN; 0 G FAT; 0 G SATURATED FAT;
21 G CARBOHYDRATE; 17 MG SODIUM; 0 MG CHOLESTEROL

BASIC RECIPES

HOW TO ROAST TOMATOES AND TOMATILLOS

One of the most distinctive techniques in Mexican cuisine is the way cooks roast tomatoes, tomatillos, onions, garlic, and other vegetables before adding them to a salsa or mole to intensify and enrich their flavor. Roasting imparts a distinctive smoke flavor (especially when it's done over a live fire) and helps caramelize the natural plant sugars. The result is a smoky sweetness that is the true secret to great Mexican cooking. Below are the four methods used by Mexicans to roast tomatoes, tomatillos, and other vegetables.

Ripe tomatoes and tomatillos (before roasting tomatillos, peel off and discard the papery husk and rinse under cold water)

TRADITIONAL METHOD (PAN-ROASTING)

Heat a comal or dry frying pan over a medium-high flame. When very hot, add the tomatoes and cook until the skins are blackened and blistered, 2 to 3 minutes per side, 8 to 12 minutes in all, turning with tongs. Transfer to a plate to cool.

BROILER METHOD

Preheat the broiler. Cut the tomatoes in half and place them, cut side down, on a nonstick baking sheet or roasting pan lined with foil. Place the tomatoes under the broiler and cook until the skins are blackened and blistered, 6 to 8 minutes. When roasting tomatillos, you can leave them whole, but turn them with tongs. Transfer to a plate to cool. Be sure to reserve the juices.

GRILL METHOD

Preheat a charcoal or gas grill to high. Place the tomatoes on the grill and roast until the skin blackens and blisters, turning with tongs. This will take 8 to 12 minutes in all. Transfer to a plate to cool.

BURNER METHOD

Place a wire rack over the burner and turn the burner on high. Arrange the tomatoes on the rack over the flame. Roast the tomatoes until the skins are blackened and blistered, 2 minutes per side, turning with tongs. Transfer to a plate to cool.

Roasting tomatoes and tomatillos

TO PEEL A TOMATO

Simply pull off the burnt skin with your fingers. Don't try to remove every last bit: A little charred skin adds extra smoke flavor.

TO SEED A TOMATO

Cut the tomato in half widthwise and squeeze each half in the palm of your hand, cut-side down, to wring out the seeds and liquid. If you like, work over a bowl and strainer. Push the pulp through the strainer with the back of a spoon. Reserve the tomato liquid that collects at the bottom of the bowl for sauces, soups, or drinking.

One large (8-ounce) peeled, seeded tomato yields ¾ to 1 cup chopped.

ROASTED PEPPER STRIPS
(RAJAS)

These smoky strips of roasted chili peppers turn up in hundreds of Mexican dishes. Roasting fresh chilies serves three purposes. First, it enables you to remove the skin, which Mexicans find unpleasant to eat. Second, it cooks the chilies, making the flesh tender and pliable. This process intensifies the peppers' natural sweetness and attenuates the heat. Finally, roasting—especially when it's done over live fire—imparts a fantastic smoke flavor that greatly enhances the taste of the chilies. Below are three methods for roasting chilies. All three are mercifully lower in fat than the deep-fry method that is traditionally used to peel peppers for making chiles rellenos.

Poblano chilies, New Mexican chilies, or jalapeños

STOVE-TOP METHOD (WORKS ESPECIALLY WELL ON A GAS STOVE, BUT CAN ALSO BE USED ON ELECTRIC)

Place a wire rack over the burner and arrange the chilies on top. (The rack keeps the chilies from falling between bars of the burner top.) Cook over a high flame until the chilies are blackened and charred on all sides, turning with tongs. This will take about 8 minutes for poblano and New Mexican chilies, somewhat less for jalapeños.

BROILER METHOD

Preheat the broiler to high. Arrange the chilies on a broiler rack and place under the broiler. Broil until the skins are blackened and charred, about 8 minutes, turning with tongs.

BARBECUE METHOD

Preheat a charcoal or gas grill to high. Place the chilies on the grate (when cooking jalapeños, it's good to use a vegetable grate). Grill until the skins are blackened and charred on all sides, 2 to 4 minutes per side, turning with tongs.

PEELING CHILIES

Whichever method you use, place the roasted chilies in a bowl and cover with plastic wrap; wrap the chilies in moist paper towels; or place in a paper bag and seal the top. Let cool for 15 minutes. As the chilies cool, the steam will loosen the charred skin.

Transfer the chilies to a cutting board and pull off the burnt skin with your fingers or scrape it off with a paring knife. Don't worry about removing every last bit of skin—a few burned pieces will add flavor. Then cut open the chilies and remove the seeds, stems, and veins. **Note:** Some people like to rinse roasted chilies under cold water to clean them, but they'll have more flavor if you don't.

BASIC CHICKEN BROTH
(CALDO DE POLLO)

Chicken broth is the very soul of Mexican cuisine. Preparing it from scratch not only will make your food taste better and more authentic, but it also will be healthier, because you can eliminate the sodium and fat found in most canned chicken broth. Plus, it will leave you with delicious cooked chicken, which is always handy to have for stuffing into tortillas or piling on tostadas.

PREPARATION TIME: 10 MINUTES   COOKING TIME: 1 HOUR

1 (3½ pound) chicken or 2 pounds chicken parts
  (backs, necks, wings)
1 bay leaf
1 medium onion, quartered
1 clove
1 large carrot, cut into 1-inch pieces

1 stalk celery, cut into 1-inch pieces
2 cloves garlic, cut in half
1 tomato, quartered
4 sprigs fresh cilantro
5 black peppercorns
10 to 12 cups cold water, or as needed

1. Remove the skin and any visible fat from the chicken and wash the bird inside and out. Pin the bay leaf to one of the onion quarters with a clove. Place the chicken, onion, carrot, celery, garlic, tomato, cilantro, and peppercorns in a large pot and add water to cover by 2 inches.

2. Bring the mixture to a boil over high heat. Skim off any fat or foam that rises to the surface. Lower the heat and gently simmer the broth until the bird is cooked, about 1 hour, adding cold water as needed to keep the chicken covered. Skim the broth often with a ladle to remove any fat or impurities that rise to the surface. (The best time to skim is after an addition of cold water—the water brings the fat to the surface.)

3. Line a strainer with paper towels and place it over a large bowl. Transfer the chicken to a plate to cool. Pour or ladle the broth through the strainer. Let the strained broth cool to room temperature, then refrigerate until cold. Skim off any congealed fat that rises to the surface. I like to freeze chicken broth in 1- or 2-cup containers, so I always have a premeasured amount on hand.

4. Meanwhile, pull the chicken meat off the bones and tear it into coarse or fine shreds. Use the bird in any recipe calling for cooked chicken.

Makes about 8 cups

16 CALORIES PER SERVING (BASED ON 8 SERVINGS); 1 G PROTEIN; 0 G FAT; 0 G SATURATED FAT;
4 G CARBOHYDRATE; 17 MG SODIUM; 0 MG CHOLESTEROL

FISH BROTH

If you've done much eating on Mexico's coasts, you've probably wondered how cooks seem to pack so much flavor into their fish soups and stews. The answer is the fish broth. The time-challenged U.S. cook often resorts to bottled clam broth (indeed, many of the recipes in this book call for it), and fine results certainly can be obtained using this time-saver. But for maximum depth of flavor, there's no substitute for a good homemade fish broth. Note: The best fish for making broth is lean and light fleshed, like snapper, pompano, halibut, hake, and mahimahi. Steer clear of oily, strong-flavored fish, like salmon and mackerel.

PREPARATION TIME: 10 MINUTES   COOKING TIME: 30 MINUTES

2 pounds fish heads and/or bones
10 black peppercorns
2 bay leaves
1 clove
1 allspice berry
1 tablespoon canola oil
1 medium onion, thinly sliced

1 carrot, thinly sliced
1 stalk celery, thinly sliced
2 cloves garlic, thinly sliced
1 tomato, finely chopped
3 sprigs flat-leaf parsley
3 sprigs fresh cilantro
2 quarts cold water

1. If you are using fish heads, remove the gills or have your fishmonger do it. If the heads are large, cut them in half with a cleaver. (Or again, have your fishmonger do it.) If you're using fish bones, cut them into 3-inch pieces. Rinse the fish pieces under cold water to remove all traces of blood. Tie the peppercorns, bay leaves, clove, and allspice berry in a piece of cheesecloth (or wrap in aluminum foil and pierce with a fork).

2. Heat the oil in a large pot. Add the onion, carrot, celery, and garlic and cook over medium heat until soft but not brown, about 4 minutes. Add the tomato and cook for 1 minute. Increase the heat to high and add the fish pieces. Cook until the fish pieces are opaque, 3 to 5 minutes.

3. Add the parsley, cilantro, spice bundle, and water and bring to a boil. Skim off any froth or foam that rises to the surface. Reduce the heat and gently simmer the stock, uncovered, until it is richly flavored, about 30 minutes.

4. Line a strainer with paper towels and place it over a large bowl. Strain the broth and let it cool to room temperature. I like to freeze fish broth in 1- or 2-cup containers, so I always have a premeasured amount on hand.   *Makes about 6 cups*

118 CALORIES PER SERVING (1 CUP); 5 G PROTEIN; 1 G FAT; 0 G SATURATED FAT;
26 G CARBOHYDRATE; 90 MG SODIUM; 0 MG CHOLESTEROL

VEGETABLE BROTH

Throughout this book, you'll find broths used as a flavoring and as a substitute for oil, lard, cream, and other fats. Vegetable broth isn't used as widely in Mexico as is chicken or fish broth. But having two vegetarians in my family, I thought it prudent to include a recipe for a meatless broth. The following recipe is a broad guideline; use whichever vegetables or vegetable trimmings you have on hand. The only vegetables that should not be used in broth are artichokes, asparagus, and beets.

PREPARATION TIME: 10 MINUTES   COOKING TIME: 1 HOUR

FOR THE SPICE BUNDLE:
5 sprigs cilantro
5 sprigs parsley
10 peppercorns
2 allspice berries
2 cloves
2 bay leaves

1 large onion, skin on, quartered
2 carrots, cut into 1-inch pieces

2 stalks celery, cut into 1-inch pieces
2 tomatoes, quartered
1 head garlic, cut in half crosswise
2 quarts coarsely chopped mixed vegetables or
   vegetable trimmings (zucchini, squash,
   pumpkin, mushrooms, eggplant, broccoli,
   cabbage, and so on)
1 to 2 tablespoons tomato paste
4 quarts water
Salt and freshly ground black pepper

1. Tie the cilantro, parsley, peppercorns, allspice, cloves, and bay leaves in a piece of cheesecloth or wrap in foil and pierce with a fork.

2. Combine the spice bundle, vegetables, tomato paste, and water in a large stockpot and bring to a boil. Reduce the heat and simmer the broth, uncovered, until it is richly flavored, about 1 hour. Add water as needed to keep the vegetables covered. Lightly season the broth with salt and pepper at the end. (Go very easy on the salt, as you may wish to reduce the broth in another recipe.)

3. Pour the stock through a strainer, pressing the vegetables with the back of a spoon to extract as much liquid as possible. Cool the broth to room temperature, then refrigerate or freeze. I like to freeze the stock in 1- and 2-cup containers, so I always have a premeasured batch on hand.

Makes about 2½ to 3 quarts

27 CALORIES PER SERVING (1 CUP); 1 G PROTEIN; 0 G FAT; 0 G SATURATED FAT;
6 G CARBOHYDRATE; 25 MG SODIUM; 0 MG CHOLESTEROL

POACHED CHICKEN/POACHED TURKEY

Many recipes in this book call for cooked chicken, so I always try to keep some on hand in my refrigerator or freezer. A Mexican would poach a whole chicken, but leaner results can be obtained with boneless, skinless breasts. Because these have a tendency to dry out, poaching is a great way to impart flavor while keeping them moist. I like to cool the chicken breasts in the broth to prevent drying out.

PREPARATION TIME: 5 MINUTES   COOKING TIME: 20 MINUTES

1½ pounds boneless, skinless chicken breasts or turkey breast

FOR THE BROTH:
6 cups water
1 tomato, quartered
1 small onion, quartered

2 cloves garlic, peeled
1 stalk celery, cut into 1-inch pieces
1 carrot, cut into 1-inch pieces
2 sprigs cilantro
1 bay leaf
6 black peppercorns
Salt

1. Wash the chicken breasts and blot them dry. Trim off any visible fat or sinews.

2. In a large shallow pan, combine the water, tomato, onion, garlic, celery, carrot, cilantro, bay leaf, and peppercorns and bring to a boil. Reduce the heat and simmer until the broth is richly flavored, 10 minutes, adding salt to taste.

3. Add the chicken or turkey breasts and poach (gently simmer) over medium heat until the meat is firm, white, and cooked thorough, 8 to 12 minutes. Remove the pan from the heat and let the chicken or turkey cool in the broth.

4. With a slotted spoon, transfer the chicken or turkey to a cutting board and tear the meat into coarse shreds with your fingers. Wrap in plastic and store for up to 3 days in the refrigerator or up to a month in the freezer. Don't forget to strain the broth and use it for soups and sauces.

Makes 4 cups, enough to serve 4 as an entrée. But for many dishes, as in tacos and panuchos, you'll be using only a few shreds of chicken per piece.

309 CALORIES PER SERVING; 54 G PROTEIN; 6 G FAT; 2 G SATURATED FAT;
6 G CARBOHYDRATE; 154 MG SODIUM; 144 MG CHOLESTEROL

A GUIDE TO CHILIES

If I had to single out one ingredient that makes Mexican cuisine Mexican, it would surely be the chili. Mexicans use an astonishing variety of chilies, both fresh and dried, to create an equally astonishing range of heat levels and flavors. True, many Mexican chilies are "hot," in the sense that they will sting your tongue and scorch your gullet. But just as many Mexican chilies have little or no heat and are prized instead for their complex earthy flavors, which are suggestive of everything from dried fruits, to chocolate, even to tobacco.

The recipes in this book call for different types of fresh and dried chilies. Many can be found at your local supermarket. Others can be purchased at a Mexican market or gourmet shop or can be ordered by mail (see Mail-Order Sources). I've tried to suggest substitutions, when appropriate. But for an authentic flavor, use the chili specifically called for.

Before we start in on the individual chilies, you'll need to know about a few chili-handling techniques. First, keep in mind that most of the heat in a chili resides in the seeds and veins, so remove these if you like a milder chili flavor. It's a good idea to wear rubber gloves when handling chilies—especially if you have sensitive skin.

A good way to mince Mexico's hottest chili, the habanero, is to hold it on the cutting board with the tines of a fork without letting it come in contact with your fingers. If you do burn your fingers with chili juices, wash them with soap and water and rub them with a little baking soda–based toothpaste to deaden the sting.

Most recipes calling for fresh chilies begin with

roasting those chilies. Roasting serves three purposes: It softens the chili so you can stuff it; it imparts an intriguing smoke flavor; and it enables you to remove the skin. On page 177, you'll find complete instructions on roasting chilies. You can blunt the heat of a jalapeño or poblano chili used for stuffing by soaking it in sugar water.

To ready dried chilies for cooking, remove the stems, tear open the chilies, and discard the seeds. Many recipes call for a chili to be toasted in a comal or under the broiler prior to seeding and soaking; this will take 20 to 40 seconds per side. Soak the chilies in warm water to cover until they're soft and pliable, about 30 minutes.

And now, here are the stars of the show.

FRESH CHILIES (CHILES FRESCOS)

CHILE VERDE (also known as ANAHEIM and CALIFORNIA GREEN): A long (6 to 8 inches), slender (1- to 1½-inches-wide), tapered, dark green chili with an herbaceous, green bell pepper flavor. The heat is mild to moderate. The size and shape make this a popular chili for stuffing. Substitute NEW MEXICAN CHILIES (see below).

HABANERO: This handsome, walnut-size, orange, yellow, or red pepper is the hottest chili in Mexico (indeed, one of the hottest in the world), a pint-size brute that packs the punch of a nuclear weapon. Yet behind the ferocious bite is a delicate fruit flavor that may remind you of apricots and smoke. Habaneros are especially popular in the Yucatán and are available at most supermarkets in the United States. Scotch bonnet chilies make an acceptable substitute. **Note:** The Petoseed company recently introduced a super-hot habanero, the Red Caribbean, with twice the firepower of a regular ha-

Mexican chilies

banero. (It rings in at nearly 450,000 Scovilles, the unit used to measure the heat of a chili. To give you an idea of just how hot this habanero is, know that a jalapeño chili measures 5,000 Scovilles.)

JALAPEÑO: No longer limited to Mexico, the jalapeño can be found in just about any supermarket. The dark green, bullet-shaped, 2- to 4-inch-long and ½- to 1-inch-wide chili has a medium to medium-hot bite. When smoked and dried, the jalapeño becomes a CHIPOTLE CHILI (see below).

POBLANO: A veritable workhorse in Mexican cooking, this dark green, sharply tapered chili is highly aromatic and moderately hot. Its large size (3 to 5 inches long and 1½ to 3 inches wide) makes it popular for stuffing. The flavor is grassy and bell pepperlike, but more earthy and aromatic. There's no exact substitute for the poblano chili. You could stuff a chile verde or New Mexican green chili the way you would a poblano, but the flavor won't be quite the same. Likewise, in a dish calling for diced poblano, you could use green bell pepper with a little minced jalapeño for heat. Fortunately, poblano chilies are available at most supermarkets.

SERRANO: This slender, tapered, dark green chili is similar in flavor and heat to a jalapeño, but smaller in size. (The two are interchangeable in cooking.) You can find serranos at most supermarkets.

DRIED CHILIES (CHILES SECOS)

ANCHO: This dried poblano chili has a brownish black, deeply wrinkled skin, a pungent aroma (which hints at dried fruits and tobacco), and a rich, meaty, pleasantly bitter flavor suggestive of wine, fruit, and chocolate. A relatively large dried chili (3 to 4 inches long and 2 to 3 inches wide), the ancho is fairly mild, but the seeds pack some serious heat. This is one of the defining flavors of mole poblano.

CASCABEL: "Sleighbell chili," a brown, cherry-size and -shaped chili, has seeds that rattle when you shake it (thus the name sleighbell). It is fruity, chocolaty, and bitter in flavor, and moderately hot. Use in salsas and marinades.

CHIPOTLE: My favorite Mexican chili, the chipotle is a smoke-dried jalapeño. The are two basic varieties: CHIPOTLES GRANDES and CHILES MORITAS. The former are longer (3 to 5 inches), with leathery, striated, tan-brown skin, and a complex, fiery smoke flavor. There's nothing better for

adding a haunting smoke flavor to a salsa or mole. Moritas tend to be smaller, sweeter, cheaper, and more one-dimensional in flavor. Chipotles are also sold in two forms: canned and dried. I prefer canned, because in addition to the smoke flavor of the chili, you get the tart vinegar-tomato tang of the packing liquid, which is called adobo. (Once you open the can, store the chilies in a ball jar with plastic wrap between the top of the jar and the lid.) Canned chipotles can be found at Mexican markets, gourmet shops, and at an increasing number of supermarkets. Look for dried chipotles at Mexican markets and via mail order.

DE ÁRBOL: Bright red and slender as a string bean, the arbol chili is the preferred dried pepper of northern Mexico. It's very hot and similar in flavor to a cayenne. You'll find these chilies at Mexican markets, gourmet shops, and via mail order.

GUAJILLO: This is the perfect dried chili for people who can't take heat. Long (4 to 6 inches) and slender (½ to 1 inch), the reddish brown, smooth-skinned guajillo has a mild, sweet, fruity, earthy flavor similar to that of paprika and of our chili powder. Guajillos are available in Mexican markets, gourmet shops, and via mail order. Paprika or chili powder can be substituted in a pinch.

MULATO: Another type of dried poblano and another important ingredient in mole poblano, the mulato is triangular in shape, 3 to 5 inches long, dark reddish brown to jet black in color, and as wrinkled as a centenarian. The aroma hints at coffee, tobacco, and wood smoke; the flavor is tart and earthy, with a pleasingly bitter finish. The chili itself is quite mild, but the seeds pack some heat.

NEW MEXICO RED: This is a long, smooth, shiny, reddish brown chili similar to a guajillo. The flavor is mild and not particularly hot. It's also called CHILE DE RISTRA (wreath chili), as it's often sold woven in wreaths. New Mexican reds are sometimes ground to make chili powder.

PASILLA: This chili is named for the raisin (*pasa* in Spanish) because of its pronounced raisin-prune flavor and wrinkled, coal black skin. Long, slender, and flat, the pasilla itself has just a hint of fire. But watch out for the seeds. The aroma is suggestive of licorice, cocoa, and raisins.

PEQÚIN: The pequín is a tiny, and I mean tiny, red chili with a sharp, fiery bite. Cayenne is a good substitute.

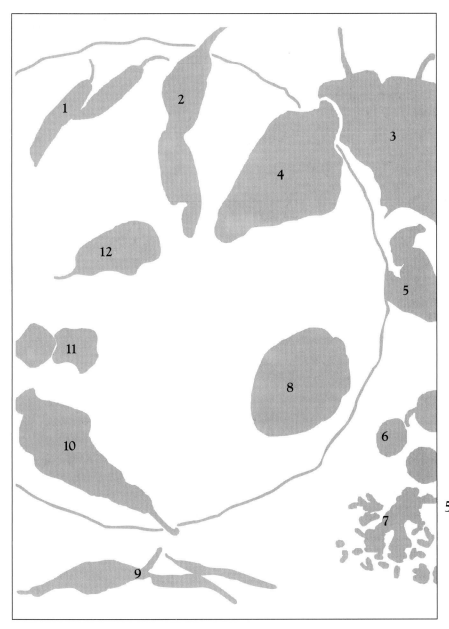

Chilies
(*photo page 182*)

1.	Chile serrano
2.	Chile guajillo
3.	Chile ancho
4.	Chile verde
5. & 10.	Chile pasilla
6.	Chile cascabel
7.	Chile pequín
8.	Chile poblano
9.	Chile de árbol
11.	Chile habanero
12.	Chile jalapeño

MAIL-ORDER SOURCES

Casa Lucas Market
2934 24th Street
San Francisco, California 94110
415-826-4334

Catalina's Market
1070 Northwestern Avenue
Santa Monica, California 90029
323-461-2535

The Chile Shop
109 E. Water Street
Santa Fe, New Mexico 87501
505-983-6080
fax: 505-984-0737

Colorado Spice
5030 Nome Street, Unit A
Denver, Colorado 80239
800-273-5082
fax: 303-373-9215
TDD (for hearing impaired) 303-373-2844

Coyote Cafe General Store
132 West Water Street
Santa Fe, New Mexico 87501
800-866-4695

Dean & DeLuca
Catalog Department
560 Broadway
New York, New York 10012
800-221-7714

The El Paso Chile Company
909 Texas Avenue
El Paso, Texas 79901
800-274-7468
915-544-3434
fax: 915-544-7552

Frieda's, Inc.
4465 Corporate Center Drive
Los Alamitos, California 90720
800-241-1771
714-826-6100
fax: 714-816-0273

Herbs of Mexico
3903 Whittier Boulevard
Los Angeles, California 90023
323-261-2521
Dried hoja santa and epazote

International Hot Foods, Inc.
905 N. California Avenue
Chicago, Illinois 60622
800-505-9999

Latin Grocer
Unlimited Latin Flavors, Inc.
6816 N.W. 77 Court
Miami, Florida 33166

Leona's de Chimayo
P.O. Box 579
Chimayo, New Mexico 87522
505-351-4660 or 800-4-LEONAS
fax: 505-351-2189

Los Chileros de Nuevo Mexico
P.O. Box 6215
Santa Fe, New Mexico 87502
505-471-6967
fax: 505-473-7306

Mo Hotta Mo Betta
P.O. Box 4136
San Luis Obispo, California 93403
800-462-3220
fax: 805-544-4051

Monterrey Foods
3939 Cesar Chavez
Los Angeles, California 90063
323-263-2143
fax: 323-263-2545

Nu-World Amaranth, Inc.
P.O. Box 2202
Naperville, Illinois 60567
800-369-6810
fax: 630-369-6819
Puffed amaranth and other amaranth products

INDEX